Organic Vegetable Gardening

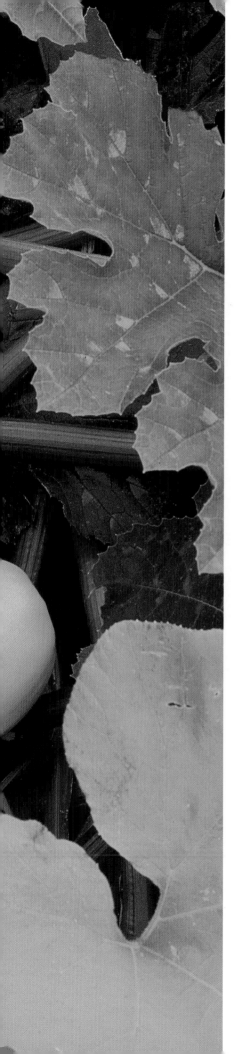

The TIME LIFE
Complete Gardener

Organic
Vegetable
Gardening

By the Editors of Time-Life Books
ALEXANDRIA, VIRGINIA

The Consultant

Shepherd Ogden is founder and president of The Cook's Garden, a mail-order seed and supply house located in Londonderry, Vermont. A member of the American Society of Journalists and Authors and a director of the Garden Writers' Association of America, Ogden has been a contributing editor for both *Organic Gardening* and *National Gardening* magazines, and his articles on gardening and environ-mental issues have been published in *New England Living, Horticulture, Country Journal, Harrowsmith, Country Living,* and the *Boston Globe.* He has written three books: *The Cook's Garden,* coauthored with his wife, Ellen, in 1989; *Step by Step Organic Vegetable Gardening* (1992); and *Step by Step Organic Flower Gardening* (1995).

In 1988 Ogden received the American Horticultural Society's GB Gunlogson Award for "extraordinary and dedicated efforts in the field of horticulture." He has also received numerous writing awards. At present he is working with Green Mountain College in Poultney, Vermont, to develop interdisciplinary programs in horticulture, business, and environmental studies.

Time-Life Books is a division of **TIME LIFE INC.**

PRESIDENT and CEO: John M. Fahey Jr.

TIME-LIFE BOOKS

Managing Editor: Roberta Conlan

Director of Design: Michael Hentges
Editorial Production Manager: Ellen Robling
Director of Operations: Eileen Bradley
Director of Photography and Research:
John Conrad Weiser
Senior Editors: Russell B. Adams Jr., Janet Cave,
Lee Hassig, Robert Somerville, Henry Woodhead
Library: Louise D. Forstall

PRESIDENT: John D. Hall

Vice President, Director of New Product Development:
Neil Kagan
Associate Director, New Product Development:
Quentin S. McAndrew
Marketing Director: James Gillespie
Vice President, Book Production: Marjann Caldwell
Production Manager: Marlene Zack
Quality Assurance Manager: Miriam Newton

THE TIME-LIFE COMPLETE GARDENER

Editorial Staff for *Organic Vegetable Gardening*

SERIES EDITOR: Janet Cave
Deputy Editors: Sarah Brash, Jane Jordan
Administrative Editor: Roxie France-Nuriddin
Art Director: Alan Pitts
Picture Editor: Jane Jordan
Text Editor: Sarah Brash
Associate Editor/Research-Writing: Katya Sharpe
Technical Assistant: Sue Pratt
Senior Copyeditor: Anne Farr
Picture Coordinator: David A. Herod
Editorial Assistant: Donna Fountain
Special Contributors: Cyndi Bemel, Jennifer Clark
(research); Vilasini Balakrishnan, Linda B. Bellamy,
Susan S. Blair, Catriona Tudor Erler (research-writing);
Bonnie Kreitler (writing); Gerry Schremp (editing);
John Drummond (art); Lina B. Burton (index).

Correspondents: Christine Hinze (London), Christina
Lieberman (New York).

Library of Congress Cataloging in Publication Data
Organic vegetable gardening / by the editors of Time-Life Books.
p.cm.—(The Time-Life complete gardener)
Includes bibliographical references (p.) and index.
ISBN 0-7835-4108-2
1. Vegetable gardening. 2. Organic gardening. I. Time-Life Books. II. Series
SB324.3.07455   1996   635'.0484—dc20   95-48919
                                                  CIP

This volume is one of a series of comprehensive gardening books that cover garden design, choosing plants for the garden, planting and propagating, and planting diagrams.

Cover: *Two rows of crinkle-leaved 'Melody' spinach, separated by a planting of frilly 'Black-Seeded Simpson' lettuce, provide an early summer crop of greens for a New Jersey organic gardener.* ***End papers:*** *'Red leaf garlic hangs in bunches beneath a walnut tree in Washington State. With good air circulation and shade, the garlic will cure in about 3 weeks and be ready for storage indoors.* ***Title page:*** *Bright gold zucchini awaits harvesting in a vegetable garden in the Northwest.*

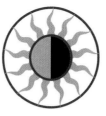

Chapter One

VEGETABLES THE ORGANIC WAY   6
Siting a Successful Vegetable Garden   8
Soil: Your Garden's Foundation   11

Chapter Two

STARTING YOUR GARDEN   22
Planting—The Key to Success   24
Planting Your Vegetable Garden   32
Caring for Your Garden throughout the Season   40

Gallery

UPDATING THE GARDEN   47
A Guide to the Gardens   56

Chapter Three

CONTROLLING PESTS AND DISEASES   61
Spotting Potential Problems   62
An Ounce of Prevention   64
Minimizing Damage in Your Garden   70

Chapter Four

REAPING THE HARVEST   77
Gathering and Storing Vegetables   78
A Garden for All Seasons   83
Putting the Garden to Bed   87

Reference

Answers to Common Questions   90
Troubleshooting Guide   94
Plant Selection Guide   100
Frost Date Maps   104
Encyclopedia of Plants   106
Acknowledgments and Picture Credits   153
Bibliography   154
Index   155

CHAPTER ONE

Vegetables the Organic Way

To vegetable gardeners, nothing tastes better than something they've grown in their own gardens. And if your vegetables are raised organically, they are as healthful as they can be, free of contamination from synthetic chemical pesticides and other possibly harmful substances.

Far from being an arcane or difficult science, organic gardening is a common-sense blend of traditional techniques and modern advances for building a fertile soil and creating a healthy garden environment. Like the owner of the Vermont garden at right, who has planted a tidy network of vegetable beds around a flowering apple tree, you'll want to tackle organic vegetable gardening methodically. Assess your site, your climate, and your needs, and then concentrate on feeding the soil that will feed your vegetables. By following the techniques presented in this book and relying exclusively on organic amendments, fertilizers, pesticides, and fungicides, you'll not only protect your health and that of the environment, you'll also enjoy a robust, productive garden.

Please refer to the key at right to identify the plants in the garden shown.

A. *Yarrow (Achillea 'The Pearl')*
B. *'Diamant' celeriac*
C. *Black salsify (Scorzonera hispanica 'Lang Jan')*
D. *'Lancer' parsnips*
E. *'Ailsa Craig' onion*
F. *'Zefa Fino' fennel*
G. *Garden peony (Paeonia lactiflora 'Red Charm')*
H. *Daffodil (Narcissus sp.)*
I. *Armenian grape hyacinth (Muscari armeniacum)*
J. *Chives (Allium schoenoprasum 'Giant Chive')*
K. *Johnny-jump-up (Viola sp.)*
L. *Welsh onion*
M. *Garlic chives (Allium tuberosum)*
N. *'Atlantic' shallot*
O. *'Walla Walla' onion*
P. *'Cortland' apple*

Siting a Successful Vegetable Garden

An orderly plot of dark, crumbly soil brimming with vigorous, carefully tended vegetables and fruits is a handsome expression of the gardener's art, as beautiful in its own way as an artfully composed perennial border. Before you begin the appetizing task of deciding which varieties to grow, however, you need to do some thoughtful planning so that the venture will be a productive one.

The first order of business is to choose the best site your property has to offer for this purpose. Although such matters as the size, convenience, and appearance of a vegetable garden are important factors to keep in mind, put topnotch growing conditions at the top of your list of concerns as you compare the possibilities your yard offers.

Soil and Microclimates

The foundation of a successful organic garden is, literally, a fertile, well-drained soil teeming with microorganisms. If yours doesn't fill the bill in its present condition, this chapter details some reliable methods organic gardeners use to turn inferior soil into a good growing medium *(pages 11-18)*. Climate, by contrast, the other variable critical to garden success, is far less amenable to manipulation and control. In this instance, your goal is to find the microclimate on your property with the sunlight, temperature range, and air circulation your vegetables need to flourish.

The Primacy of Sunlight

Of the climatic variables, sunlight is the most important. Except for a handful of shade-tolerant crops—lettuce, for one—vegetables require at least 6 hours of direct sun per day for optimal growth; if you have a spot that is in full sun for 7 or 8 hours, so much the better.

If a survey of your property turns up several places with ample sunlight, look for differences in their microclimates that can tip the balance in favor of one over the others. For gardeners in cold climates, an especially desirable location is a gentle, open slope that faces south and receives a full day of sun. Because the sunlight strikes the surface of the slope at an angle, the soil will warm up earlier in the spring and remain warm longer in the fall, making it more productive than it would

be if the ground were level. A northern exposure has a very different set of conditions—fewer hours of direct sunlight, cooler soil temperatures, and, in many parts of North America, prevailing northwesterly winds that remove heat from the soil and shorten the growing season.

High Winds and Frost Pockets

From whatever direction they come, strong winds are deleterious to the garden: They rob the soil of moisture, and they can also uproot plants and topple the supports that hold vining vegetables. As a rule, an exposed site at the top of a slope or hill is especially vulnerable to the cooling and drying effects of the wind, effects that are exacerbated in freezing weather or during a period of drought. If you have no alternative to such adverse conditions, you could plant a windbreak of

two or three staggered rows of closely spaced evergreen trees or shrubs, then site your garden on the lee side and far enough away to avoid any root competition or shading from the windbreak.

Frost pockets can be equally destructive to tender plants. The result of cold, heavy air pooling in low areas or being trapped on the uphill side of a building or a hedge running across a slope, frost pockets are colder in winter and prone to frost later in spring and earlier in fall, greatly shortening the growing season. However, you can alleviate the problem in one case: If you have a dense, solid hedge that blocks air flow, remove a section of it to allow cold air to continue its downward movement and raise the frost pocket's temperature.

Size, Looks, and Convenience

Next, you'll need to decide how much space you wish to devote to your garden plot or, if space is limited, how much you can spare for this purpose. If you are new to raising vegetables, it's prudent to keep the plot small the first year instead of possibly taking on more work than you bargained for. An area measuring no more than 10 feet square, for instance, can yield upwards of 60 pounds of vegetables a year and will give you a good idea of how much time and effort tending your garden will take. After a season's trial run, you can always expand the size the following year. The chart on page 25 provides information on how much you can expect to harvest in a season from a 10-foot row of 30 different kinds of vegetables.

When it comes to how visible a vegetable patch should be, people differ in their opinions. Some may enjoy having a burgeoning plot in full view of the terrace, while others would tuck theirs out of sight behind the garage or along one side of the house. But if you're a gardener for whom convenience outweighs aesthetics, a plot close by

AN EDIBLE LANDSCAPE
In late summer, an edging of frilly green parsley and colorful marigolds decorates a raised bed that contains a mature clump of blooming basil, onions, and rows of romaine seedlings for fall salads (below). The clipped yews in the background protect the vegetables and herbs from the cold northeast winds that buffet this New Jersey garden.

SUN AND SHELTER
A south-facing slope confers the double benefit of long hours of sunshine and shelter from chilling northerly winds on the large Wisconsin garden at left. In a sunny spot at the garden's center, a latticework trellis awaits the climbing tendrils of late-summer pole beans. Lettuce, which enjoys some protection from the sun, has been planted in the shade cast by trees at the east end of the garden.

the kitchen has many advantages. For one, you'll be more likely to be in the garden every day, checking its progress, pulling weed seedlings, and harvesting vegetables at their peak. And you won't have to carry your prized produce more than a few short steps.

The vegetable garden should also have easy access to water. From planting time to harvest, watering is one chore that can't get short shrift. You'll also find it very handy to have the compost pile—an integral part of organic gardening—close to the vegetable plot and the kitchen, since both generate waste for composting.

A Tailor-Made Design

The classic layout for a vegetable garden is a rectangular plot, often fenced to keep animals out. The plot may be divided into a series of rows, but many gardeners prefer to divide it into two or more individual beds separated by paths of hardened earth, mulch, flagstone, or turf grass.

Dividing a plot into separate beds makes it easy to group vegetables that have similar soil, moisture, and nutritional requirements. Although the surface of a bed can be level with the surrounding soil, there are great advantages to mounding the

soil so that the surface is elevated by 4 inches or more. Mounding not only ensures good drainage, it also allows the soil to warm up more quickly in the spring because more of it is exposed to the air; this lets you begin planting earlier than would otherwise be possible.

A raised bed is also the ideal space for applying intensive gardening techniques. Because the soil in the bed will be tailored to meet the nutrient requirements of the vegetables you plant there, they can be placed very close to one another without suffering the adverse effects of competition. You will reap more produce from your initial planting and also can feel confident that a subsequent crop won't be shortchanged.

A plot with multiple beds is the most efficient way to grow vegetables. If space doesn't permit this layout, however, you can disperse beds around your property, fitting them in wherever there is room and the conditions are appropriate. Planting vegetables in containers is another way to expand your growing area *(pages 29-31)*. And if you're still hungry for plants, make room among the perennials and annuals of an ornamental border for such attractive vegetable varieties as a ruffly bright chartreuse lettuce or purple broccoli. Like your vegetables, the flowering plants will thrive on an organic regimen.

A GARDEN OF CONTAINERS
A colorful array of containers filled with red and green varieties of lettuce (foreground), silvery leaved sage, a large tomato plant with ripening fruit, and rich red peppers spills down the steps of a Los Altos, California, terrace. Many favorite vegetables are now available in dwarf varieties that grow well in containers.

Soil: Your Garden's Foundation

Soil from Top to Bottom

A section of earth several feet deep reveals four distinct layers *(below)*. The surface of the soil is covered with a leafy litter, which decomposes to become part of the topsoil **(A)**. Usually measuring 4 to 8 inches in depth, topsoil owes its rich color and fertility to the organic matter it contains. Vegetable roots are largely confined to this layer. The next layer, mineral subsoil **(B)**, is as deep as 30 inches, has very little organic matter, and is inhospitable to vegetables unless it is deeply tilled and amended. The lowest soil layer **(C)** contains rock fragments broken off from the bedrock below **(D)**. Over time these fragments migrate upward and break down into particles that become part of the subsoil and, ultimately, the topsoil.

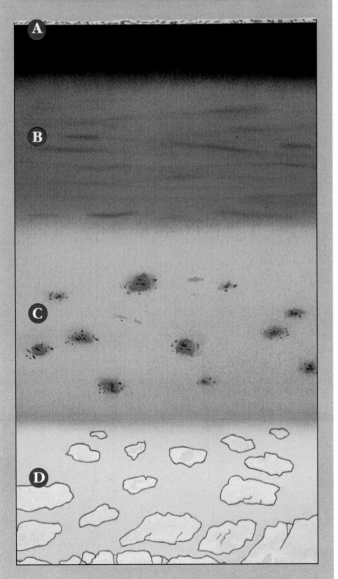

A vegetable garden imposes high demands on soil. It must nourish a succession of closely spaced plants with a variety of nutritional needs; produce a harvest within a few months; and, if the gardener wants to coax the highest yield possible from the plot, provide good growing conditions from very early spring until well after fall frosts arrive.

The raw material you have to work with may not seem promising. The typical city or suburban gardener in North America has inherited a soil that has been changed, seldom for the better, by activities such as farming, lumbering, and construction. The topsoil's natural fertility may have been depleted. Worse, the topsoil itself may have been bulldozed away, exposing the underlying, largely infertile, subsoil layer *(left)*. With the right organic techniques, however, even the most discouraging plot can be made productive.

Sand, Silt, and Clay

Many gardeners think of soil as a purely mineral substance, but in fact the mineral component of loam—the ideal soil for growing vegetables—accounts for somewhat less than 50 percent of its volume. Air and water each account for around 25 percent, and organic matter for 5 percent.

About half of the mineral component of loam is sand; the other half is clay or silt, or a mixture of the two. What distinguishes these three kinds of particles from one another is size: Sand particles, visible to the naked eye, are the largest; silt are the next largest; and clay are the smallest.

How a soil feels to the touch and how loose or dense it is will help you determine what kind of soil you have. The best time to examine it is 2 or 3 days after a heavy rain or a thorough watering; the soil should be moist but not soggy. Dig a hole several inches deep with a trowel and scoop out a handful of soil. Rub some between your thumb and fingers, then let it all fall between your fingers to the ground. If the soil feels rough and gritty and slips quickly through your fingers, it is predominantly sand. If it feels smooth and floury and adheres slightly to your fingers, it is predominantly silt. Soil that feels rather slick and tends to make a sticky lump is mostly clay. If the soil is loam, it will be loose, crumbly, and slightly moist.

Follow up with a test of how well or how poorly the soil drains. Dig a hole 10 to 12 inches deep and wide, pour in a gallon of water, and note how long it takes for all of the water to drain out of the hole. The water will disappear in about 5 minutes in a sandy soil and in 5 to 15 minutes in loam. If it takes longer than 15 minutes to disappear, you have a silty or clayey soil. Sandy, silty, and clayey soils all need improvement if vegetables are to thrive.

The Importance of Drainage

A prime virtue of a loamy soil's blend of large and small particles is that water drains neither too quickly nor too slowly, so plants aren't routinely subjected either to overdry conditions or to waterlogging. Moisture imbalances hamper plant growth in several ways. In a very sandy, fast-draining soil, plant tissues are not only parched but undernourished. This is because plants can absorb nutrients only when they are dissolved in water, so applying fertilizer to a soil that is habitually dry won't be at all effective. By the same token, as water drains through a sandy soil, dissolved nutrients are quickly carried out of the reach of plant roots.

In a heavy, waterlogged, clay soil, air is the element in short supply. Air and water alternately occupy the network of spaces running through the solid part of soil. When water is removed, whether because it drains away, is taken up by plant roots, or evaporates, air flows in to fill the empty spaces, delivering essential carbon, hydrogen, and oxygen to roots. If the soil's spaces remain filled with water, plants will suffocate.

Soil Nutrients and pH

The nutrient elements used by plants in the greatest quantities—nitrogen, phosphorus, and potassium—are supplied by the mineral and organic parts of the soil. Nitrogen is responsible for healthy leaf and stem development, phosphorus for strong root systems, and potassium for flowers and fruits. A secondary trio of elements—calcium, magnesium, and sulfur—are needed in smaller amounts. Plants need only very tiny quantities of boron, zinc, and the other trace elements, so gardeners rarely if ever need be concerned about them.

Whether the nutrients present in a particular soil are available to plants depends on the soil's pH, which is a measure of how acid or how alkaline the soil is. On a scale of 1 to 14, with 7 being the neutral point, the soil becomes progressively more acid below 7; above 7 it becomes increasingly more alkaline. Much as a refrigerator operates at an ideal temperature so that food neither spoils nor freezes, an optimal pH range enables soil to release enough nutrients to keep plants well fed. Too high or too low a pH either blocks needed nutrients from being released or delivers the nutrients at toxic levels. A pH between 6 and 7 is ideal for the majority of vegetables.

The Role of Organic Matter

Organic matter has an influence that is far out of proportion to the small amount of it found in garden soil, even in loam. In the form of partially decomposed compost, leaves, straw, and other readily available materials, organic matter can dramatically improve the structure of a deficient soil and help to bring about a good balance of air, water, and nutrients. Added to a sandy soil, it helps bind the large sand particles together, shrinks the volume of empty space in the soil, and makes the soil more water retentive. Added to clay in conjunction with sand, organic matter enlarges the soil's network of spaces, allowing water to drain more freely and air to circulate.

Still another benefit of organic matter is the nutrients it releases into the soil as it decomposes. Decaying organic matter is a food source for the array of creatures that reside in a healthy soil, including earthworms, insects, beneficial nematodes, bacteria, and fungi. This population plays a critical role in making a soil fertile and keeping it that way. One of the important contributions of these organisms is converting plant and animal tissue into a dark, crumbly material called humus, which gives good soil its rich, deep color. Humus can absorb up to 90 percent of its weight in water, so boosting the amount of humus in a poor, dry soil will help keep plants steadily supplied with moisture.

Testing Your Soil

To find out how your soil measures up in terms of pH, organic matter, and nutrients, you'll need to test it. To measure pH, you can use a hand-held electronic pH meter or litmus paper. For more detailed information on both pH and nutrient levels, analyze your soil with a ready-to-use testing kit. All of these devices are available at any large garden or home center.

To obtain a comprehensive professional analysis, submit a soil sample to your state Cooperative Extension Service or a commercial laboratory. The report you receive should state the type of soil you have and its pH level, organic matter content, and nutrient availability. It will also include

Building a Compost Pile

A well-made compost pile is an ideal habitat for microorganisms, providing the food, water, air, and warmth they need to grow and reproduce at top speed. A thriving population quickly converts ordinary wastes from kitchen and garden into an invaluable fertilizer and soil conditioner.

The microorganisms need a balanced diet of carbon and nitrogen. Fibrous materials such as dry leaves, straw, and sawdust provide plenty of carbon, while nitrogen is furnished by green materials such as grass clippings, wastes from the vegetable garden or flower bed, and kitchen scraps (vegetable or fruit only).

To start a compost pile, spread a layer of brown fibrous material several inches deep and at least 3 feet wide and 3 feet across on bare soil. Add a layer of green material

and sprinkle it with soil or a commercial compost activator to introduce microorganisms. Water until the materials are sponge damp. Continue in this fashion until the layered pile is at least 3 feet high—the size necessary to generate sufficient heat. Turn the pile once or twice a week with a garden fork to aerate it and rid the center of excess moisture. Water as needed to keep the pile slightly moist. The compost is ready to use when it is dark and crumbly.

The three-bin composter shown below can produce a large, steady supply of compost. The decomposing pile in the center bin is flanked by a newly assembled pile *(right)* and a bin containing finished compost *(left)*. Wire mesh on three sides and the gaps between the slats on the bin's front help keep the pile aerated. The slats are removable, making it easy to turn the pile. Several smaller compost bins are shown on the next page.

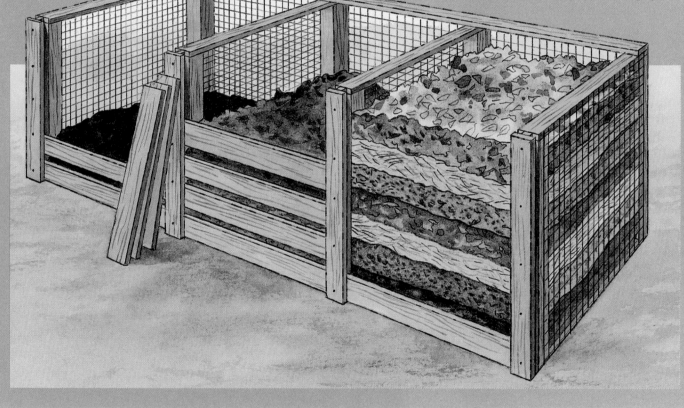

recommendations for amendments and fertilizers you can use to improve the soil, so be sure to specify that you prefer organic products.

Organic Soil Enrichment

An amendment is a material that, when added to a soil, improves its structure by changing the way mineral particles adhere to one another. Sometimes it is necessary to add two or more amendments at the same time to get the desired effect. For example, you can work shredded leaves and a

substance called greensand into a clay soil to help improve drainage. The greensand, a dark green, grainy mineral, loosens the clay particles, and the newly created open spaces allow air and water to move more freely through the soil. The shredded leaves nourish soil life and prevent the combination of clay and greensand from producing a soil so hard that roots and water can scarcely penetrate it.

Organic fertilizers supplement the soil's level of available nutrients, notably nitrogen, phosphorus, and potassium, and they also contribute to the soil's volume of organic matter. All of the fertilizers organic gardeners use are made of animal and

Decomposing waste occupies one of the two cinder-block bins at left; the other stores finished compost. The spaces between the blocks allow air to circulate. You can mortar the blocks at the back and the sides of the bins, but leave the front blocks free so you can withdraw the compost.

A Compost Bin to Suit Your Needs

Even the simplest compost bin keeps decomposing wastes tidy and compact. And as long as you have the right mix of ingredients *(page 13)* and enough of them, it will generate the heat needed to ensure speedy composting. For freestanding compost piles or those in open bins, you should start with a pile measuring 3 feet wide, deep, and high. For the ready-made bins available at garden and home centers, simply fill them according to the manufacturer's instructions.

Each of the composters shown here can be easily constructed or purchased for less than a hundred dollars. Some require manual forking and turning of the debris pile, while others need little or no attention from the gardener.

To create the bin at right, wrap a length of hardware cloth 4 feet wide and 12 feet long around two stakes hammered into the ground. Secure the ends of the hardware cloth with wires. To turn the compost pile, unfasten the cylinder, reposition the stakes adjacent to the loose pile, reassemble the cylinder, and fork in the pile.

The plastic barrel composter at left is designed to produce finished compost in a month or less. The barrel rests on rollers; turning a handle rotates the barrel and aerates the contents thoroughly. Finished compost is removed through a hinged door on the barrel; a finished batch must be removed before starting a new one.

A compact plastic compost bin like the one at left is an excellent choice where space is limited. Fresh waste material can be added continually to the top of the bin while older material is decaying to finished compost. Compost is retrieved from the pull-out drawer at the bottom of the bin. Enough air enters the pile through the large slots to supply the decay microorganisms completely, making it unnecessary to turn the pile.

plant materials such as blood, fish, and seaweed.

An organic fertilizer's nutrients are released into the soil slowly; most of them become available for use only after soil microorganisms, mainly bacteria, have broken the material down. Synthetic fertilizers, on the other hand, typically supply fast-acting shots of nutrients that stimulate rapid spurts of growth. With repeated use, synthetics eventually kill much of a soil's population of valuable organisms and can also acidify the soil. Commercial organic fertilizers are labeled to show the percentages by weight of nitrogen, phosphorus, and potassium, in that order. A labeling of 5-3-4, for example, means that the product contains 5 percent nitrogen, 3 percent phosphorus, and 4 percent potassium. See the chart on page 21 for information on organic fertilizers and amendments.

All-Purpose Compost

Of the many soil amendments and fertilizers, the single best product you can use for an organic garden is compost. Consisting mainly of partially de-

cayed plant wastes, it is an excellent source of organic matter and a reservoir for many nutrients.

As an amendment, compost can convert a sandy or clayey soil into loam. And, because it has a near neutral pH value, it helps keep soil in the range vegetables prefer. As a fertilizer, finished compost provides a good balance of 2 parts nitrogen to 1 part each of phosphorus and potassium. If it is made from a large variety of materials, compost will contain a healthy balance of trace elements as well as the major nutrients.

To make compost properly, gardeners combine two kinds of plant materials—fibrous materials such as leaves, straw, and sawdust, often referred to collectively as browns, and succulent "greens" such as grass clippings and kitchen scraps. The browns are the source of the carbon required for decomposition, while the greens furnish nitrogen. The greens and browns are assembled in a pile of alternating layers *(page 13).*

When the pile is kept about as moist as a well-squeezed sponge and its layers are turned and mixed regularly to incorporate air, the decay microorganisms are very active. The energy released

A FERTILE PLOT
The sandy soil of this Long Island vegetable garden is enriched with regular additions of compost and mulched with seaweed from nearby beaches. Before the seaweed is spread it is washed to remove the salt; as it decomposes, it will add organic matter to the soil.

Starting Your New Vegetable Garden

A sunny patch of lawn is often the best place to site a new vegetable garden, and the best time to begin the work of creating it is the season prior to planting. Clearing and tilling the plot at that point, as described in the first two steps on this page, gives the soil time to fully incorporate any amendments and fertilizers you have added; the result is a more fertile medium for seeds and seedlings when planting season arrives. Several weeks in advance of planting, till the soil lightly with a garden fork or broadfork (box, page 20) and pick up the process of bed building at the third step shown here.

Shaping the prepared soil into raised beds is well worth the effort required; better drainage and more room for root growth mean more vigorous plants and a more bountiful harvest.

1. Mark the perimeter of your vegetable plot with stakes and string. *Using a sharp square-bladed spade and working just inside the string, slice down through the sod to the depth of the spade (above); do this all the way around the plot. Next, use the spade to cut the sod into sections small enough to lift easily. Pry each one loose with the spade or a garden fork and knock the topsoil off the roots. Remove the stakes and string.*

2. Till the plot with a rotary rear-tined tiller *(above) to the depth of one tiller blade—approximately 8 to 10 inches. Work your way up and down the length of the plot, then repeat the process across the plot. After you have tilled the soil, remove any large stones, roots, weeds, or bits of sod. Incorporate amendments or fertilizers as needed to correct soil deficiencies, working them into the top 6 to 8 inches of soil with a spading fork.*

3. Using stakes and string, measure and mark off the tilled plot *into individual beds and pathways (above). Make each bed 3 to 5 feet wide, so the plants in the center will be within easy arm's reach without stepping into the bed. For convenience in moving around the beds, make them no more than 15 to 20 feet long. Pathways 2 feet or more in width allow room to maneuver tools and equipment such as a garden cart between the beds.*

4. To mound up the soil for a raised bed, first place a 1-by-4 board in the center of the bed: If you need to step into the bed, the board will distribute your weight, minimizing soil compaction. Standing on one side of the space you've staked out, use a raised-bed builder (below) or a flat rake to reach across the bed and rake tilled soil from the path area into the bed. Repeat from each side of the bed, sloping the sides a bit to minimize erosion. Then, with the back of the tool, smooth and level the surface of the bed. The bed should be 4 to 5 inches higher than the surrounding paths.

5. Mulch the paths with straw, as shown below, or another organic material to suppress weeds and conserve soil moisture. Spread straw, pine needles, and other loose, airy mulches 3 to 4 inches deep; for a denser mulch such as woodchips or ground bark, 1 to 2 inches is enough. By the end of the growing season, the mulch will have decomposed to the point where it can be dug into the soil.

during decomposition raises the mound's internal temperature to as much as 160° F, which in turn stimulates chemical processes to break the material down even further. With this method, called hot composting, the finished product will be ready in as little as a month; at the end of that time, the mass of material will have shrunk to approximately one-third of its original size.

Some gardeners prefer "cold composting," which is less work: Once the pile is assembled, it is left undisturbed. However, the materials will decay slowly, and it may be 2 years before you have finished compost. Unless you have room for several piles in different stages of decomposition, this method probably won't provide enough compost for your vegetable garden.

soil structure and to ensure a healthy population of soil organisms. In the Deep South, however, where summers are hot and humid and winters are short and mild, organic matter decomposes at a much faster rate, so gardeners need to replenish it at least three times a year.

Tilling the Garden

Tilling or cultivating the soil at least twice a year, in spring and in fall, is a task that can't be avoided. It is the time to work in any fertilizers and amendments, but the simple act of turning the soil is itself beneficial in several ways. It restores lightness to compacted soil so plant roots get the water and air

Timing Soil Improvements

Enriching the soil is an ongoing chore for the vegetable gardener. When establishing a new plot *(pages 16-17),* dig in a 2- to 3-inch layer of compost to improve soil structure; at the same time, correct any deficiencies uncovered by soil testing.

In most parts of the country, twice-yearly applications of 1 to 2 inches of organic matter, in spring and fall, are sufficient to maintain good

Double Digging for Deeper Soil

Double digging a vegetable garden is doubly heavy work, since the soil is tilled in two steps to a total depth of 2 feet instead of the more usual 8 to 12 inches. But the work is worth it, especially in heavy clay soils prone to compaction. Water, air, and nutrients move much more freely, and roots spread more widely, through the deep layer of loosened soil. If you combine double digging with intensive planting techniques, you'll be rewarded with very large harvests.

Choose a time when the soil is moist but not wet; if the weather has been dry, water it deeply. Beginning at one end of the bed, use a heavy-duty spade to dig a trench about 1 foot wide and deep; remove the topsoil to a tarp or wheelbarrow. Next, push the tines of a spading fork as far into the exposed subsoil as you can and move the fork back and forth to loosen the soil. For an extra rich soil, spread a layer of manure or compost over the subsoil. Then dig a second trench parallel to the first, moving its topsoil to the first trench and letting it slide off the spade right side up—this way the topsoil structure remains undisturbed.

Loosen the subsoil of the second trench *(far left)* and slide over topsoil dug from a third trench *(left),* being careful to keep the soil right side up. Repeat the sequence until you reach the end of the bed. Use the topsoil set aside from the first trench to fill in the last.

A Tool for Easy Tilling

A bed that has been prepared and then left to rest for weeks or months will inevitably undergo some compaction because of rain, snow, and gravity. For loosening the soil at planting time, many organic gardeners prefer to use a broadfork *(below),* a tool that alleviates the work of lifting and turning the soil required by the more commonly used garden fork. The broadfork, also called a U-bar, has long handles and five or six tines attached to a horizontal crossbar. The tines vary in length from 10 to 18 inches; the long-tined models are designed for the deeply cultivated soil of double-dug beds, the short-tined ones for single-dug beds.

To use the broadfork, hold it upright and step up and onto the crossbar, using your weight to push the tines down into the soil. Step off and pull the broadfork's handles toward you until the tips of the tines lift out of the soil. Repeat this process at 6-inch intervals across the area to be planted, moving backward to avoid stepping on soil you have already cultivated.

they need, and the increased oxygen content also stimulates the activity of soil life. And in spring, the loosened soil warms up more quickly, giving the gardener a jump on the new growing season.

There are a variety of tools for tilling, including rototillers and hand tools such as spades, spading forks, and broadforks. A rototiller makes sense for large plots, and it makes the work of preparing a new garden or turning under a cover crop *(pages 88-89)* much easier. However, rototilling the vegetable garden more than twice a year tends to compact the soil. For that reason, choose hand tools for tilling work during the growing season.

When you are ready to till, spread any amendment or fertilizer over the entire area to be cultivated *(see chart at right for application rates).* If you are using a spade or a spading fork, push the blade or the tines to their full depth into the soil, then lift the soil and turn it over. Use a broadfork as described in the box at left. If you can't avoid stepping in the area you are tilling, stand on a board to distribute your weight more evenly.

Beds versus Rows

A tilled plot is almost ready for planting. The last step is to subdivide the plot into either narrow rows or rectangular raised beds like those on page 16. Although row planting has its adherents, it has at least two major drawbacks. For one thing, an alternating pattern of rows and paths is an inefficient use of space because much less of the total area is actually devoted to crops. When you arrange your plants in beds, on the other hand, you greatly reduce the area occupied by paths. In addition, shrinking the area taken up by paths keeps the potential for soil compaction to a minimum.

Another advantage of raised beds is that their greater depth of topsoil provides better drainage and more space for the roots of vegetables to grow downward. The additional soil needed to raise the beds 4 or 5 inches is furnished by digging out the paths between the beds.

The center of each bed should be within easy arm's reach so there's no need to step into the bed when you are tending plants or harvesting vegetables. Beds with access from two sides should be no wider than 4 to 5 feet. If there is access from one side only, limit the width to 3 feet. The length of a bed is more flexible, but don't make it so long that you'll be tempted to take a shortcut across it instead of sticking to the paths surrounding it. Make the paths that run between the beds at least 2 feet wide so there will be enough room for a garden cart.

ORGANIC AMENDMENTS AND FERTILIZERS

Below is a selection of widely available organic amendments and fertilizers. In most cases, they can be worked into the soil during tilling in either fall or spring; fresh manures are best applied in the fall so they can partially decompose over the winter. Fertilizers can be applied once or twice during the growing season for crops needing a nutrient boost or for new plantings. Unless otherwise noted, amendments that change pH should be used as often as soil tests indicate.

NAME	FUNCTION	APPLICATION RATE	COMMENTS
Blood meal	Fertilizer. Provides nitrogen.	2 lbs./100 sq. ft.	Also called dried blood. When using as a side dressing, keep 2 to 3 inches away from plant stems.
Bone meal	Fertilizer. Provides phosphorus, calcium.	2 lbs./100 sq. ft.	Work into topsoil immediately after applying; otherwise the pungent odor may attract rodents.
Chicken manure, rotted	Amendment/fertilizer. Adds organic matter. Provides nitrogen, phosphorus, potassium.	1-inch layer	Work into topsoil in fall or compost before using.
Compost	Amendment/fertilizer. Loosens clay soils, binds sandy soils, increases water-holding capacity. Adds organic matter. Provides nitrogen, phosphorus, potassium.	2- to 3-inch layer	Best all-purpose amendment.
Cottonseed meal	Fertilizer. Provides nitrogen, phosphorus, potassium.	2.5 lbs./100 sq. ft.	May be contaminated by pesticides.
Cow manure, rotted	Amendment/fertilizer. Adds organic matter. Provides nitrogen, phosphorus, potassium.	1- to 2-inch layer	Work into topsoil in fall or compost before using.
Fish emulsion	Fertilizer. Provides nitrogen.	¼ oz./100 sq. ft.	Sold as concentrated liquid that is diluted for use. Can also be applied as a foliar spray.
Fish meal	Fertilizer. Provides nitrogen, phosphorus.	2 lbs./100 sq. ft.	Also called fish scrap, fish tankage. Apply just before planting or as a side dressing during the growing season.
Greensand	Amendment/fertilizer. Retards soil compaction, loosens clay soils, increases water-holding capacity. Provides potassium, trace elements.	5 lbs./100 sq. ft.	Use in conjunction with organic matter to amend clay soil.
Gypsum	Amendment. Loosens clay soils, balances pH. Provides calcium, sulfur.	2 lbs./100 sq. ft.	Also called land plaster, sulfate of lime. Pellets easier to use than powder.
Horse manure, rotted	Amendment/fertilizer. Adds organic matter. Provides nitrogen, phosphorus, potassium, trace elements.	1- to 2-inch layer	Work into topsoil in fall or compost before using.
Leaf mold	Amendment/fertilizer. Builds up soil humus content quickly. Adds organic matter. Provides nitrogen, phosphorus, potassium.	2-inch layer	Also called woods-soil when sold commercially. Can also be used as a mulch; apply a 2- to 3-inch layer.
Limestone	Amendment. Raises pH. Provides calcium, magnesium.	6 lbs./100 sq. ft. for clay 4 lbs./100 sq. ft. for loam 2 lbs./100 sq. ft. for sandy	Also called ground limestone, dolomitic limestone. Avoid hydrated lime or quicklime—they dissolve too quickly in the soil and can burn plant roots and kill soil life.
Peat moss	Amendment. Loosens clay soils, lowers pH, increases water-holding capacity. Adds organic matter.	1- to 2-inch layer	Also called sphagnum peat moss. Work into topsoil.
Rock phosphate	Amendment/fertilizer. Raises pH. Provides phosphorus, trace elements.	2.5 lbs./100 sq. ft.	Most effective if applied to acid soils.
Sawdust	Amendment. Adds organic matter. Provides nitrogen, potassium.	1-inch layer	Apply only well-rotted sawdust to soil. Best if added to the compost pile.
Seaweed meal	Fertilizer. Provides nitrogen, potassium, trace elements.	1 to 2 lbs./100 sq. ft.	Also called kelp meal. Apply in early spring and work into topsoil.
Straw	Amendment. Adds organic matter. Provides nitrogen, phosphorus, potassium.	2- to 3-inch layer	Buy straw labeled weed free. Can also by applied as a mulch, then turned under when it decays.
Sulfur	Amendment. Loosens clay soils, improves water-holding capacity, lowers pH.	Up to 1 lb./100 sq. ft. applied every 8 weeks	Also called soil sulfur. After working into topsoil, water thoroughly.
Wood ashes (leached)	Amendment/fertilizer. Raises pH. Provides potassium, calcium.	2 lbs./100 sq. ft.	Keep stored wood ashes dry to prevent nutrients from leaching out. When using as a side dressing, keep 2 to 3 inches away from plant stems.

CHAPTER TWO

Starting Your Garden

There is no rule book or single set of instructions for putting in an organic vegetable garden. At first, the task can seem a bit daunting: You must decide not only what crops to grow but also how to combine them to use your space most efficiently. In the end, your garden will be unlike any other, reflecting your choices, your experiences, your land. The garden at right, for example, represents one gardener's approach to growing tomatoes. The plants are staked upright, both to save space and to keep the fruit from rotting on the ground. Straw strewn along the path keeps down weeds and mud, and a row of glass cold-frame lids set on end protects the heat-loving tomatoes from cold Maine winds.

To build your own base of knowledge year after year, consider keeping a journal of your observations, challenges, and solutions. Along with the sheer delight of watching tiny seeds grow into food for your family's table, learning to work in partnership with nature will give you some of the greatest rewards under the sun.

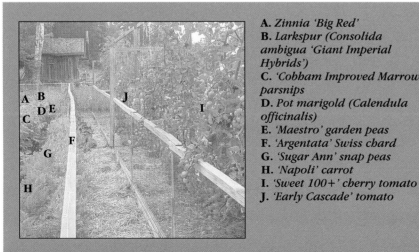

A. *Zinnia 'Big Red'*
B. *Larkspur (Consolida ambigua 'Giant Imperial Hybrids')*
C. *'Cobham Improved Marrow' parsnips*
D. *Pot marigold (Calendula officinalis)*
E. *'Maestro' garden peas*
F. *'Argentata' Swiss chard*
G. *'Sugar Ann' snap peas*
H. *'Napoli' carrot*
I. *'Sweet 100+' cherry tomato*
J. *'Early Cascade' tomato*

Please refer to the key at right to identify the plants in the garden shown.

Planning—The Key to Success

At its simplest, planning your garden means deciding what vegetables you'd like to grow, how many plants you'll need, and where and when to put them in the ground. A well-thought-out garden plan can mean the difference between an enjoyable and rewarding pastime and a season of hard work with very little to show for it.

Planning is particularly important for the organic gardener. Providing the best environment for healthy and productive plants without using synthetic fertilizers requires preparation and forethought. Laying out your garden on paper, for example, allows you to use all of your available space to its best advantage. Other techniques help you increase yield and improve the quality of your produce. Succession planting and interplanting, for instance, allow you to harvest two or more crops from the same space in one growing season, and crop rotation minimizes pests and diseases and slows the depletion of soil nutrients.

Choosing What to Plant

To decide what crops to grow in your garden, begin with a list of the vegetables that you and your family most like to eat. You also may want the list to include vegetables that are picked by commercial growers before they reach maturity, such as tomatoes, or those that don't travel well so have lost some flavor by the time you purchase them in the grocery store. Or you may want to treat yourself to unusual vegetable varieties such as golden tomatoes, watermelon with bright yellow flesh, blue potatoes, and other exotic produce that is not widely available. Another addition to the list may be heirloom vegetables that were grown by our forebears and have been rescued from extinction by groups working to save and distribute the seed.

Go over your list and make sure your selections are ones that will grow well in your area. If some are questionable, check with other gardeners or your local Cooperative Extension Service. Keep in mind that by making minor adjustments in planting times, you can often expand the number of crops that will thrive in your garden. If you live in a very hot climate, for example, you can still grow crops such as lettuce and cabbage, which prefer cooler temperatures and a mix of sun and shade. You'll just need to plant them in spring and autumn, not in the middle of summer.

If you live in the part of the North where the growing season is no more than 90 days long,

COMBINING PLANTS TO SAVE SPACE
Low-growing, rambling pumpkin plants make excellent intercropping partners with tall-growing corn, which has been planted at 2-week intervals to extend the harvest season. Both vegetables are heavy feeders, however, so the soil should be amended with generous amounts of organic material.

COMPATIBLE PARTNERS FOR PLANTING
The pairing of 'Salad Bowl' and 'Red Sails' lettuces with onions in this garden not only makes a striking visual combination, it makes good sense as well. The dense growth of the lettuces keeps weeds at bay, and their shallow roots do not compete with the young onions for space. By the time the onions need more room, the lettuces will be finished.

HOW MUCH TO EXPECT FROM YOUR GARDEN

VEGETABLE	LENGTH OF HARVEST	AVERAGE YIELD PER 10' ROW	AVERAGE HARVEST PER WEEK
Asparagus	4-6 weeks	3 lbs.	0.6 lbs.
Bean, green (bush)	2 weeks	3 lbs.	1.5 lbs.
Bean, lima (bush)	3 weeks	2 lbs. with pod	0.7 lbs.
Bean, lima (pole)	4 weeks	4 lbs. with pod	1 lb.
Bean, pole	6 weeks	10 lbs.	1.7 lb.
Beet	4 weeks	2.4 dozen	7 beets
Broccoli	4 weeks	4 lbs.	1 lb.
Cabbage	3-4 weeks	4 heads	1 head
Cantaloupe	3 weeks	9 melons	3 melons
Carrot	4 weeks	4 dozen	1 dozen
Chard	8 weeks	5 lbs.	0.6 lbs.
Corn, sweet	10 days	10 ears	1 ear/day
Cucumber	4 weeks	8 lbs.	2 lbs.
Kale	4-20 weeks	5 lbs.	0.5 lbs.
Lettuce, head	4 weeks	10 heads	2.5 heads
Lettuce, leaf	6 weeks	9 lbs.	1.5 lbs.
Okra	6 weeks	9 lbs.	1.5 lbs.
Onion	4-24 weeks	10 lbs.	0.8 lbs.
Parsnip	4 months	8 lbs.	2 lbs.
Pea, green	2 weeks	7 lbs. with pod	3.5 lbs.
Pepper, sweet	8 weeks	40 peppers	5 peppers
Potato	4 months	12 lbs.	0.8 lbs.
Potato, sweet	6 weeks	10 lbs.	1.7 lbs.
Pumpkin	1 month	10 lbs.	2.5 lbs.
Radish	2 weeks	7 dozen	3.5 dozen
Rhubarb	4-6 weeks	6 lbs.	1.2 lbs.
Spinach	4 weeks	5 lbs.	1.25 lbs.
Squash, summer	4 weeks	20 lbs.	5 lbs.
Tomato	8 weeks	30 lbs.	3.75 lbs.
Watermelon	3 weeks	4 melons	1.3 melons

choose varieties that mature quickly so that you can harvest a ripe crop before cold weather arrives. In regions where a specific pest or disease is a problem, look for named varieties that are resistant to that particular affliction *(box, page 65).* For example, the cucumber 'Fanfare' is resistant to powdery and downy mildews, angular leaf spot, anthracnose, scab, and cucumber mosaic virus, making it an ideal vegetable for places with humid summers where fungal diseases are prevalent.

Deciding How Much of Each Crop to Plant

Given the delightfully varied selection of vegetables, it's easy to overbuy seeds and plants. Before you make any purchases, it pays to find out what you can expect to harvest from one mature plant. Although the yield will depend in part on your growing conditions, certain vegetables and specific varieties are known to be strong producers. For example, one plant of the spaghetti squash 'Tivoli' is expected to produce three to five squashes during the growing season, each weighing between 3 and 5 pounds. By contrast, one plant of the yellow scalloped squash 'Sunburst' can produce 35 squashes *each month* during the peak of the growing season. In either case, a family of four—

depending on their taste for squash—could be satisfactorily fed by just one plant. To find out more about expected crop yields for particular plants, refer to the chart on the previous page.

If you plan to freeze, can, dry, or pickle some of your vegetables so that your family can enjoy the garden's bounty all year, you'll need to plant extra. Some varieties are better suited to preservation than others. The green bean 'Derby' is known to freeze well, as is the sweet corn 'Honey 'n' Pearl'. Cucumbers are divided into slicing and pickling types; choose varieties from both groups if you plan to preserve some of your crop.

If you have only a small plot for your vegetable garden, you may have to winnow your list to a number of plants that will fit comfortably. A number of techniques will help you get the most out of a small plot *(box, page 30),* but overcrowding a bed is not one of them. Cramped plants will yield less produce than those given ample room to grow, and are more susceptible to disease and infestation by insects.

Laying Out the Garden in Advance

Drawing a plan of your garden will give you the opportunity to think through important factors such as space requirements and nutrient needs before you put seeds or plants into the soil. Advance planning will also boost the results of using special techniques such as crop rotation, succession planting, and interplanting. You probably will need to work and rework the plan until you get it right, but it is much easier to erase a pencil line than to move a row of growing plants.

Artistic skills are not required for this task. Simply draw the outline of the vegetable plot to scale (using graph paper makes this easier), mark which direction is north, and then indicate plants and planting rows with circles and lines.

To begin, arrange tall plants either to the north of the bed so they don't shade shorter plants, or use them to provide screening for crops that need the shade. Vining vegetables that like to sprawl across the ground, such as pumpkins, do well along the edges of a bed where they can creep without encroaching on other plants. Group early-maturing plants together; once harvested, they will create a space for another crop. Arrange perennial vegetables—those that come back year after year, such as asparagus and rhubarb—so that they aren't disturbed when the time comes for you to till the soil for the annual plantings. Cluster plants that demand especially

A Three-Season Garden Plan

Spring

Summer

Fall

large amounts of water so that you can water them all at once. And keep vegetable families (cabbage and its relatives, legumes, squashes and melons, onions, and the tomato and its relatives) together to simplify crop rotation.

SUMMER SUCCESSION PLANTING
A recent planting of cucumbers (center) has replaced a bed of harvested spring vegetables in this New Jersey garden. After the cucumbers are finished, a fall crop of turnips could follow in the same bed. Young fennel plants and red-ribbed Swiss chard flourish in the foreground.

Rotating Crops for Garden Health

Crop rotation has two enormous advantages for the organic gardener: It puts nutrients back into the soil, and it helps prevent attacks by pests and diseases. At its simplest, crop rotation means planting each crop in a different place in the garden each time you plant. (This technique applies only to annual vegetables; perennials should not be disturbed.)

Rotation is fairly easy to implement for crops that occupy the same bed for an entire growing season; simply move each crop over by one bed every time you plant it. Rotating vegetables that finish midseason and are succeeded by a different crop requires a little forethought. When laying out

your garden, bear in mind whether plants are heavy or light feeders or are soil builders *(chart, page 28),* then arrange the crops according to their nutrient demands. For example, in one bed, first plant spring peas, which are light feeders that release nitrogen into the soil; after harvesting the peas, follow with summer squash, a heavy feeder that uses lots of nitrogen. Conversely, follow a heavy feeder such as summer squash or corn with a legume that releases nitrogen or with a cover crop that will be turned back into the soil to nourish it. Alfalfa, clover, and soybeans are examples of soil-building cover crops.

Varying where you plant your crops each season also minimizes the problems caused by diseases that attack particular plants *(box, page*

'Winterbor' Kale

66). These diseases settle into the bed where the plant is growing and overwinter in the soil, surviving to do their damage later on. Rotation of crops also discourages insect pests, even though they are of course more mobile than most diseases.

The Technique of Succession Planting

Succession planting, or planting one crop after another during the same season, maximizes your garden space and extends your harvest of certain crops. Instead of planting all your lettuce seeds at once, for example, and being faced with salad for a crowd, plant some of the seed, then wait 2 or 3 weeks and plant again. The different sections of the bed can then be harvested over a longer period of time. This technique works best with vegetables that do not produce continuously throughout the season, such as corn, carrots, radishes, bush green beans, cabbage, beets, spinach, and onions.

To use limited garden space most efficiently, practice what is called mixed crop succession. With this technique, you follow one season's harvest with a different crop in the same space. For example, in regions that have a long growing sea-

WHAT VEGETABLES NEED TO GROW

COOL SEASON			
VEGETABLE	SOIL TEMP. TO GERMINATE	FEEDING REQUIREMENTS	PRIMARY NUTRIENT NEEDS
Beet	45 - 85	Heavy	Phosphorus (P)
			Potassium (K)
Broccoli	45 - 85	Heavy	Nitrogen (N)
Brussels sprouts	45 - 85	Heavy	Nitrogen (N)
Cabbage	45 - 95	Heavy	Nitrogen (N)
Carrot	45 - 95	Light	Potassium (K)
Cauliflower	45 - 85	Heavy	Nitrogen (N)
Celery	45 - 75	Heavy	Nitrogen (N)
			Potassium (K)
Endive	45 - 75	Heavy	Nitrogen (N)
Kale	40 - 90	Heavy	Potassium (K)
Leek	50 - 95	Light	Potassium (K)
Lettuce	40 - 75	Heavy	Nitrogen (N)
Onion	50 - 95	Light	Potassium (K)
Parsnip	45 - 85	Light	Potassium (K)
Pea (soil builder)	45 - 85	Light	Potassium (K)
Radish	45 - 95	Heavy	Potassium (K)
Spinach	45 - 75	Heavy	Nitrogen (N)
Swiss chard	45 - 95	Light	Nitrogen (N)
Turnip	45 - 95	Light	Potassium (K)
WARM SEASON			
VEGETABLE	SOIL TEMP. TO GERMINATE	FEEDING REQUIREMENTS	PRIMARY NUTRIENT NEEDS
Bean (soil builder)	60 - 90	Light	Potassium (K)
Corn	55 - 105	Heavy	Nitrogen (N)
Cucumber	60 - 105	Heavy	Nitrogen (N)
			Phosphorus (P)
Eggplant	75 - 90	Heavy	Phosphorus (P)
Melon	65 - 105	Heavy	Nitrogen (N)
			Potassium (K)
Pepper	65 - 95	Light	Phosphorus (P)
Pumpkin	65 - 105	Heavy	Phosphorus (P)
Squash	65 -105	Heavy	Phosphorus (P)
Tomato	60 - 85	Heavy	Phosphorus (P)

son, you can follow a cool-season crop such as lettuce with heat-loving summer squash. When the squash are finished in autumn, plant another cool-season vegetable, such as turnips. The three-season gardening plan on pages 26-27 offers additional examples of mixed crop succession practiced throughout the growing season.

Interplanting: Making the Best Use of Space

Interplanting, or combining two plants in the same space, allows you to fit more vegetables into your allotted space. The practice, also called intercropping, can be mutually beneficial to the plants involved. A classic example of intercropping is the Native American custom of planting corn, squash, and pole beans together. This combination, called the Three Sisters of the Cornfield by the Indians, is ideal for nutrient exchange. As they grow, the beans release nitrogen into the soil for the squash and corn. In addition, the three crops use a minimum of space: Vining bean plants are supported by the tall cornstalks, while the squash spreads out along the ground.

Another way to exploit a small space is to com-bine fast-maturing, early crops with larger, slow-growing vegetables. For example, plant Brussels sprouts among spinach plants. By the time the slow-growing Brussels sprouts need more room, the spinach will have been harvested. To mark a row of seeds that are slow to germinate, such as parsnips, interplant radishes, the fast-sprouting wonder of the vegetable world. As an added bonus, when you pull the radishes, you till the soil for the nearby plants.

The practice of interplanting can also extend the growing season of spring vegetables if you combine them with taller warm-season plants. Sow spinach or lettuce on the east side of a row of trellised beans, a stand of sunflowers, or a bed of corn. The shade from the tall plants will protect the lettuce from going to seed or wilting in the hot afternoon sun and will keep it growing and harvestable. You can also extend your harvest by interplanting fast- and slow-maturing varieties of

A MOVABLE FEAST
Container-grown tomatoes, peppers, parsley, and basil flourish among pots of flowering alyssum, lobelia, marigolds, and periwinkle on a backyard patio.

Getting the Most from a Small Garden

Even the smallest of spaces can produce a lot of vegetables when you use intensive gardening methods. Your first consideration in a scaled-down garden must be to prepare and enrich the soil, since a large number of plants in a small area will compete for nutrients. See pages 11-18 for information on how to build healthy soil.

When planning your garden, emphasize vertical crops. Peas, pole beans, cucumbers, some melons, and some tomatoes are vining crops that actually perform better when they are kept off the ground. These can be grown on an attractive trellis, tied to stakes, or trained to follow twine that is anchored to the ground and an overhead frame.

Also, to reap as much harvest as possible from each plant, choose compact varieties or prolific producers. 'Tom Thumb' a "midget" head lettuce, requires comparatively little room, for example, and 'Jade Cross' Brussels sprouts yield an early, bountiful crop. As a rule, the smaller the fruit the more the

plants tend to produce, so make most of your selections from small varieties such as cherry tomatoes.

Avoid the temptation, though, to plant too many hugely prolific vegetables, such as zucchini. If you have extra plants, give or throw them away and save your space for other crops. When laying out the garden, make use of succession planting and intercropping to maximize your growing space.

In this intensively planted raised bed, cabbages, beans, lettuce, and carrots grow shoulder to shoulder; yarrow and daylilies nestle in the gaps; and vining tomatoes climb a simple trellis in back, using every available inch of ground.

the same vegetable at the same time. The growing season will last longer and you will have the opportunity to taste the different flavors of each vegetable type.

Vegetable Gardening in Containers

If your only space or sunny spot is on a patio or deck, containers can become your garden. Most vegetables will grow in boxes, tubs, or other planters, although they will require more attention than plants in the ground. Because the soil in containers dries out quickly, you'll need to water these plants regularly. The best watering setup is a drip-irrigation system with spaghetti lines to each pot and a timer to regulate the water flow. This system works especially well if you have lots of containers, if you plan to be away for several days at a stretch, or if you are growing vegetables that are extremely sensitive to moisture variation, such as cauliflower.

Every time you water container-grown plants, soil nutrients leach out, so plan to fertilize fre-

quently. Start the plants off in a good-quality potting mix and supplement them on a weekly basis with fish emulsion, liquid seaweed, or other organic fertilizers.

Choosing the Right Container

The volume or depth of soil needed for the roots of a plant determines the size of the container. Deep-rooted vegetables like leeks need a pot the size of a whiskey barrel to provide enough depth. You can plant a single plant type or a mixture of vegetables in one barrel; check the spacing requirements of different plants in the encyclopedia *(pages 106-152)* and plan your pots accordingly.

If you have a sunny spot on a porch, place a vining vegetable in a pot there. Tie one end of a string to the pot and the other to the roof or the eaves, and train the plant up the string. Pole beans, vining tomatoes, vining cucumbers, and cantaloupes are good choices for this treatment. 'Super Sweet 100' tomato plants, which bear bright red cherrylike fruit, and the 'Yellow Pear' variety, with its golden pear-shaped crop, are particularly decorative.

Sources for Seeds

Once your planning is done and you are ready to purchase seed, you should follow one basic rule: Do not make your choices based on price. Often, retailers mark down seed because it is old and less likely to germinate. It makes no sense to put in hours of labor preparing your soil, planning your garden, and planting it, only to produce weak plants—or no plants at all—because of faulty seed.

Check the freshness date on seed packets and only buy seed that has been packaged to be sold in the year you are buying it.

Hardware stores, garden centers, and mail-order catalogs are the primary sources of vegetable seed for home gardeners. Local shops are often cheaper and more convenient, but catalogs offer a greater selection of plant varieties. Moreover, local or regional seed-catalog companies feature seed that is particularly suited to your area.

As you read descriptions of the various vegetables, look for the qualities that are most important to you. You may want early maturers for a short growing season, compact plants for containers, or plants that are resistant to disease, heat tolerant, have exceptional flavor, an unusual appearance, or a combination of several characteristics. No doubt you will have to compromise on some features, but with the wealth of selection available, you should be able to find what you want. For good all-around performance, look for varieties listed as AAS, or All-America Selections, which have proved superior in gardens throughout the United States.

COOL-SEASON VEGETABLES FOLLOW SUMMER'S BOUNTY
As summer gives way to autumn, perennial crops such as the feathery asparagus at upper left have long since peaked. Newly planted crops such as Swiss chard and mizuna (center) take over the space vacated by harvested summer vegetables. Widely cultivated in China and Japan, mizuna's leafy tops make an excellent addition to soups or may be combined with other mild greens in salads.

Vegetables Best Started Indoors

Basil, 6

Broccoli, 6-8

Brussels sprouts, 4-8

Cabbage, 6-8

Cauliflower, 6-8

Celeriac, 6-8

Celery, 6-8

Eggplant, 8-10

Leeks, 8-12

Lettuce, 4-6

Onions, 10-12

Parsley, 8

Peppers, 8-10

Tomatoes, 6-8

(Note: The numbers after each vegetable tell you how many weeks before the date of the last frost to start seeds indoors.)

Planting Your Vegetable Garden

After all the soil tilling, catalog perusing, and garden planning, at last the time has come to plant your seeds. Depending on the climate in your area and the type of vegetables you want to grow, you may decide to start plants indoors, buy seedlings from a nursery, or sow seeds directly into the ground.

Starting Seeds Indoors

In northern climate zones where the growing season is 90 days or less, starting seeds indoors is imperative, especially for warm-season crops such as tomatoes, melons, and peppers. Gardeners farther south may start seedlings to get a jump on the season. It is possible, however, to start seeds too early, and that can foil well-intentioned plans. For example, if you start tomato seeds indoors 10 weeks before the last-frost date instead of the recommended 6 to 8 weeks, the plants will be ready to go outside too soon, and will grow leggy and unhealthy while waiting for warmer weather.

You can start seeds indoors either by planting each seed in its own container, which will save you from having to repot them separately later on, or by planting many seeds together in a flat. If you're planting each seed separately, any sort of recycled container will do—waxed-cardboard milk cartons, yogurt cups, egg cartons, or cell packs saved from last year's purchases—as long as you poke drainage holes in the bottom. You can also buy peat pots and peat pellets. These containers are designed to be planted directly in the ground and work especially well for plants that do not like having their roots disturbed, such as cucumbers. One type of peat pellet is held together with net. Although the net disintegrates with time, many gardeners prefer to take it off before putting the plant in the ground to free the roots. Other pellets are held together with a built-in binder that disintegrates quickly once the container is planted.

Another excellent medium for starting seeds is a homemade soil block, created by compressing a peat-compost mixture into a cube using a blocking tool, available from mail-order catalogs. Larger vegetables, such as melons, cauliflower, broccoli, cabbage, eggplant, squash, peppers, and tomatoes, benefit from being started in peat pots, pellets, or soil blocks because the seedlings have plenty of room to develop their root systems and can be transplanted directly into the ground.

If you prefer to plant your seeds in a flat or are planting many seeds of smaller vegetables, splurge on plastic seed-starting trays. These handy trays have three components: a planting tray with holes for drainage, a liner to catch water that drains off, and a domed, clear plastic lid to maintain moisture while the seeds germinate.

Seed-Starting Soil

The ideal medium for starting seeds is fine grained and loosely packed so that a seedling can push through it without difficulty. It should

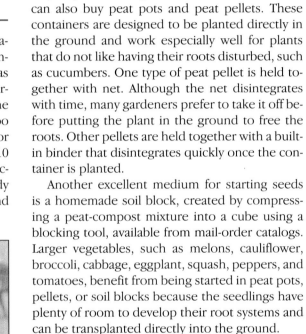

A BRIGHT WINDOW NURSERY
Seedlings and seeds that have yet to sprout share a warm, sunny, south-facing window with pots of marigolds. Once the seeds have sprouted, turn the plants daily to give them even exposure to the light.

Making a Seed-Starting Mix

Many gardeners swear by a favorite seed-starting medium, each a little different although the basic ingredients remain the same. Experiment to find the mix that works best for you.

RECIPE 1

1 part sterilized compost

1 part sand, vermiculite, or perlite

1 part peat moss

RECIPE 2

4 quarts shredded sphagnum
  peat moss

4 quarts vermiculite

1 tablespoon superphosphate

2 tablespoons ground limestone

RECIPE 3

1 quart sphagnum peat moss

1 quart vermiculite

1 quart perlite

also be as free as possible of weeds, harmful insects, and disease-causing contaminants such as fungi and other pathogens.

Seed-starting mixes usually consist of vermiculite and perlite for aeration and drainage, sphagnum moss or peat moss for bulk and moisture retention, and compost. You can make your own growing medium using any of the recipes given above or purchase it ready-mixed in bags from garden centers. If you do not wish to use moss, you can put together a satisfactory mix from 50 percent vermiculite or perlite and 50 percent screened compost. If you buy your mix, be sure to get the type formulated for seeds, rather than regular potting mix.

After Growth Begins: Seedling Care

Once your seeds are planted and covered with plastic *(right)*, they'll need a warm spot in which to germinate. Most seeds sprout faster in warm conditions, and warm-season vegetables won't germinate at all until the soil reaches a temperature of 60° to 65° F. If the interior of your home

Starting and Transplanting Seeds

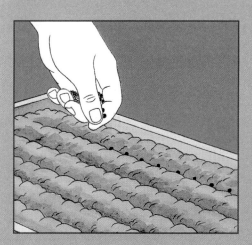

1. Fill each container to within one-half inch of the rim with moist seed-starting mix. *Gently press the soil to level it, but do not compact it. Make furrows in the soil to the appropriate depth for the seeds you are planting. Drop the seeds into the furrow, spacing them as recommended on the seed packet. Cover the seeds and gently tamp the soil along the furrow to make good contact between seed and soil.*

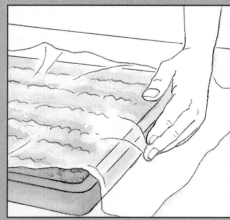

2. Mist the top layer of soil. *Cover the container to hold in moisture, using any of the following: A plastic dome from a seed-starting kit, a grocery-store produce bag, or plastic wrap. Do not water once covered. Keep the seeds in a warm spot until they sprout. When the first sprouts surface, remove the cover and place the seedlings in a spot where they will get 12 hours of light a day.*

3. Repot crowded seedlings by scooping them out with a spoon. *Immediately replant the tiny seedlings into a large container filled with lightweight potting soil. Water carefully to make good contact between the roots and the soil, but avoid swamping the plants. Place the seedlings in a spot where they will get 12 hours of light a day.*

4. To remove a young plant from a cell pack or plastic container, *grasp the stem between your index and middle fingers and tip the container. Ease the plant out; do not pull on the stem. If the plant does not slide out easily, try tapping the bottom of the container gently on the ground or squeezing the sides of the container.*

Vegetable Seeds Best Sown Directly into the Ground

Beans, bush

Beans, pole

Beets

Carrots

Collards

Corn

Cucumbers (except where season lasts less than 90-100 days)

Endive

Kale

Kohlrabi

Mustard greens

Parsnips

Peas

Potatoes

Radishes

Spinach

Swiss chard

Squash, summer (except where season lasts less than 90-100 days)

Squash, winter (except where season lasts less than 90-100 days)

Turnips

Sheltering Plants from the Cold

Plant protectors such as cold frames, portable greenhouses, and cloches provide a sheltered setting for starting plants early, hardening off seedlings, and extending the growing season of autumn vegetables. They work by transmitting light and retaining heat.

A cold frame can be as simple as a bottomless box covered with clear glass or plastic, or as sophisticated as an elaborate high-tech creation with temperature sensors that automatically open and close the lid as needed. A cloche can be small enough to protect just one plant or large enough to cover an entire row of vegetables, and can be devised from overturned bushel baskets or 1-gallon plastic milk containers with the bottoms cut out.

The large portable greenhouse at right is made from clear plastic sheeting stretched over arched wire fencing. Versatile and inexpensive, the greenhouse protects young vegetables, like these lettuces, from cold weather.

in early spring tends to be cooler than this at night, you must provide additional heat. A waterproof heating pad designed to go under pots and containers works well for this purpose. For a less costly option, place pots on top of a refrigerator or a clothes dryer.

When the seeds have sprouted, remove the plastic covering to allow air to circulate; otherwise, you may lose the seedlings to a complex of fungi known as damping-off. At this point, seedlings also need a lot of light—at least 12 hours a day. Lack of light creates thin and leggy plants, and will affect a plant's vigor and productivity for the rest of the season.

For best results, place the plants in front of a south-facing window that gets direct sun most of the day. Be sure to rotate the containers every day so that the plants receive even exposure. If you must use artificial light instead, opt for fluorescent or "grow" lights rather than incandescent ones, which do not generate the ultraviolet light required by plants. Position fluorescent lights about 2 to 4 inches from the top of the plants. Hang the lights from chains for easy height adjustment as the plants grow.

To keep the soil moist without damaging fragile seedlings, mist plants daily or set the containers on top of several layers of wet newspaper. The water in the newspaper will be drawn up and absorbed through the drainage holes in the bottoms of the pots. Feed the seedlings with a weak mixture of liquid fertilizer every 2 weeks. Experienced gardeners regulate seedlings' rate of growth by the amount of food they provide. If the seedlings are coming along quickly and cold weather is lingering longer than expected, the plants' growth can be slowed by cutting back slightly on fertilizing. Conversely, if warm weather comes early, you can accelerate growth by feeding with a richer mixture of fertilizer.

Seedlings that have sprouted too closely together will need to be thinned. If you have more seedlings than you need, simply snip off the weaker specimens to give more growing space to the vigorous ones. If you want to use all of the seedlings, carefully lift the excess from the container and transplant them to pots filled with a seed-starting mixture. Before removing a seedling, poke a hole in the mixture with the eraser end of a pencil. Either lift the seedling out with a spoon,

Cloches of water-filled plastic tubes surround plants in this New Jersey garden. The water in the plastic cloches absorbs heat and radiates it to the plants, protecting them from killing frosts in fall and early spring, thus extending the growing season. For best results, use water cloches for single upright plants such as tomatoes, peppers, and eggplant.

as shown on page 33, or use the technique called pricking out. To do this, hold the top leaves of a seedling between your thumb and forefinger as you use the pencil or other narrow object to gently lift the seedling from the container. Ease it carefully into the planting hole and press the mixture around the plant.

Buying Healthy Plants from the Nursery

For those who don't have the time or the space to start their own seeds, buying seedlings from a nursery can be a satisfactory substitute. However, not all nursery transplants are equal. You can inquire about how the plants were handled before delivery to the retailer, but examining the plants yourself is imperative.

First, check the seedlings carefully for insects or insect eggs. Favorite insect hiding places are under leaves, where the leaves meet the stem, and at the growing tip of the plant, where the young leaves are most tender. Also look underneath the container for night-feeding pests that hide in the crevices.

Choose young and vigorous plants. Avoid those that are oversized and too well established. If plants are already in flower or bearing fruit, don't be misled into thinking they will give you an earlier or more bountiful harvest. In fact, quite the opposite is true: The stress of transplanting is likely to reduce the main crop. Likewise, tall and leggy plants often fail to fill out and produce well. Instead, look for well-proportioned seedlings; plants that are ready to be transplanted will be about as wide as they are tall.

Reject plants that have roots growing several inches out of the bottom of their container. These plants have been in their pots too long and have become root-bound. In the case of cole crops, such as kale, gently scrape away a little soil to check for swollen, distorted roots, which are an indication of the condition called clubroot. And any roots that are yellow, soft, or too woody also indicate an unhealthy plant.

Tricks for Easier Seed Sowing

- When sowing seeds outdoors, run a strip of white toilet tissue down the length of each furrow and lay the seeds on top. The whiteness of the paper will make it easier to see the seeds and to gauge their spacing and depth. The fine tissue will degrade quickly into the soil.
- To make it easier to distribute tiny seeds, such as carrot seeds, mix them with sand and sprinkle the mixture over the ground from a clean salt shaker. For easier handling, carrot seeds also are sold on seed tape and in a pelleted form about the size of buckshot.
- Plant bean seeds with the scar side facing down. Bean roots grow into the ground out of the scar point; planting them all this way means they will surface at about the same time.
- To presprout seeds, space them on a double layer of damp paper towel, roll it up, and keep it moist in an open plastic bag. In 2 or 3 days the seeds will sprout. Then plant them in pots or put them into the ground, taking care not to break the fragile roots.

Hardening Off

Before transplanting any seedlings outside, you must prepare the young plants for the transition from a protected environment to the harsher conditions of the outdoors. This process is known as hardening off. A week or two before you plan to transplant the seedlings into your garden, take them outside and place them in a protected spot for about an hour. Repeat this process daily during the transition period, increasing the time by 1 hour each session.

Putting Transplants into the Ground

If you can, plant young, started plants on a cool and misty day; cooler temperatures are less likely to cause stress to new plants. If that is not possible, transplant in the evening when the temperature begins to drop. The plants will have all night to settle in before coping with the next day's hot sun.

Three Ways of Supporting Plants

For a support of crisscrossed poles, push 6- to 8-foot poles into the ground in two parallel rows about 12 inches apart as shown, and tie pairs together about 4 inches from the top. For stability, give the end units an extra leg to create a tripod and tie a pole along the length of the support on top.

To construct a tripod plant support, *take three poles measuring 6 to 8 feet long and push them firmly into the ground to form a circle; tie them together at the top. Plant vining vegetables such as peas, pole beans, squash, and pumpkins at the base of each pole. Within the circle, grow lettuce and other crops that welcome shade.*

To create a simple trellis for vining vegetables *such as peas, squash, pumpkins, pole beans, and cucumbers, choose sturdy poles that are 6 to 8 feet long and at least 1 inch square. Space them an equal distance apart and sink them about 12 inches into the ground. Staple wire fencing or nylon netting to the poles.*

ple growing room, but organize their arrangement to use the land efficiently. For example, you might place the plants in wide beds with staggered rows. A bed that is 30 inches wide could have three lettuce plants in the first row and two lettuces in the second row positioned between the plants in the first row. The third row then would have three lettuces planted parallel to the ones in the first row, and so on. Such a pattern will accommodate a few more plants without crowding. Once the plants are in the ground, be sure to water promptly and well, especially when using plastic mulch, which acts as a barrier to rainwater. (For more on using plastic mulch, see page 41.)

While the transplants are adjusting to their new environment, they may need shelter from strong sun. If the sun is particularly intense the first few days after planting, make a temporary shade structure with cloth anchored to cinder blocks or mounted on stakes, a beach umbrella, or even an overturned basket or box that allows some light to penetrate. During hot weather, be prepared to water your transplants daily until the roots are established and you see signs of growth.

Direct Sowing Outdoors

Not all seed-grown vegetables are suited for early sowing indoors. The heading types of Chinese cabbage will go to seed from transplant stress, for instance, and carrots will die. And root disturbance to corn, peas, beans, and okra plants hinders their growth. These crops and others *(list, page 34)* are simply easier to grow outdoors.

When sowing seed outdoors, the soil temperature must be within the range required by the plant type for germination to occur. Fortunately, surface soil temperature does not fluctuate as radically as air temperature because of the thermal insulation provided by the earth. Once the soil has warmed enough in spring to nurture the seeds, it's unlikely to cool again until autumn. A soil and compost thermometer with an extended spike can help you determine when the soil is warm enough to begin planting. To use the thermometer, insert the spike into the soil to the planting depth of the crop to be sown there. Check each bed with the thermometer, as temperatures may vary significantly within a garden.

Before you plant, rake the soil's surface in one direction to make it smooth. Break up large clods and remove any stones, weeds, and grass roots. Then rake in the other direction to smooth and level the bed. To avoid compacting the soil, walk on the beds as little as possible. Mark each plant-

Once you have removed each plant from its pot or cell pack, examine the roots carefully. If they are crushed tightly against the edge of their container or curled in a circle around the bottom of the pot, gently massage the rootball in your hand to loosen the clump or gently break the rootball apart.

If your beds are bare or mulched with straw or any other loose, organic material, simply dig through the mulch and soil to create a planting hole. If the beds are covered with plastic mulch, use a penknife to cut through the sheeting. For each plant, cut an X in the plastic big enough to fit the rootball, then dig the hole and place the plant in it. To create the best possible contact between the soil and the roots, press the soil down firmly around each plant.

Space the plants far enough apart to allow am-

Helpful Hints for Planting Tomatoes

To train a vining tomato plant, *pound a sturdy 8-foot-tall stake at least 1 foot into the ground, then plant the tomato at its base. Tie the plant to the stake with string or twine. To avoid damaging the stem, first loop the string around the stake and tie it tightly, then loop it around the vine and make a loose knot (inset). Continue to tie the tomato to the stake as the plant grows.*

To keep cutworms from feasting on a tomato stem, *cut a collar measuring 3 inches square from 3 layers of newspaper. Wrap the collar around the stem next to the rootball and position the tomato in the planting hole so that half of the collar is above ground (above, left). To plant a leggy tomato transplant, remove the lower leaves and lay the plant on its side in a trench. Gently bend the top of the stem upward and cover the roots and the horizontal section of stem with soil.*

ing row with string stretched across the beds and tied at either end to stakes. Using the string as a guide, dig a shallow furrow in the earth with a trowel or hoe.

Sowing the Seeds

Sow seeds in rows according to the recommended spacing on the package; do not overcrowd them. Then cover the seed with soil. As a rule of thumb, you should bury seeds three times deeper than their width. Under certain conditions, though, you may have to adjust the planting depth slightly. Seeds require a little less covering when soil is very wet and heavy, and more when the soil is sandy or the weather is dry.

Hill planting is preferred for crops that need more warmth to germinate, such as corn, cucumbers, melons, pumpkins, and squash. To create a rich reservoir for them, dig a hole 12 inches deep and across. Fill the hole with 8 inches of well-rotted compost or manure and top with 8 inches of soil. After watering, the hill should be about 3 inches high. Plant seeds to the appropriate spacing and depth along the top and sides of the hill.

The technique called broadcasting, or scattering seed over a bed, works best for cover crops such as clover and annual rye and for large beds planted with the same crop. Prepare the bed as you would for row planting, but without furrows. On a windless day, broadcast the seed by shaking it out of your hand in a loose spray. Then rake the bed lightly with a fine rake or a spike-toothed rolling cultivator to settle the seed into the soil and cover it slightly.

Label each row, hill, or bed with the vegetable's complete name and the planting date. Do not use the paper seed packet as a label; rain will make it illegible, and besides it will be far more useful in your garden-record notebook *(page 45)*. Instead, purchase wooden tags at a garden center or nursery and write the information on them with a waterproof pen.

Once planted, seeds need to be kept continually moist in order to germinate. If you have planted rows of seeds in moist soil, it isn't necessary to water at planting time, but keep a watchful eye

A STANDOUT AMONG TOMATOES
Heavy with ripening red tomatoes, the 1984 prizewinning All-America Selections tomato, 'Celebrity', is supported by a wire cage. This bush variety grows to maturity in 70 days, producing a generous crop of firm, flavorful fruit, each weighing 7 to 8 ounces. Known for its outstanding disease resistance, the cultivar adapts to most parts of the country.

Wire cages can support bush or vining tomatoes, but the cages for vining types need to be larger, about 24 inches across and 60 inches tall. Place a cage over the tomato when you plant it and tie the cage to a tall stake so it will not topple under the weight of ripening fruit.

To encourage tomato vines to produce earlier and larger—but fewer—fruit, prune the side shoots. Once three leaves appear on the shoot, pinch off the top leaf (below), stopping the shoot's growth. Leave some foliage on the plant to protect ripening fruit from harsh sun.

on the beds and sprinkle them daily, if necessary, to keep them moistened. For seed that has been broadcasted, water immediately after planting to ensure good contact between the seed and the soil, and sprinkle daily until the seeds have sprouted. Use only a gentle spray of water; a strong spray may dislodge the seeds and wash them away completely or cause them to congregate in tight clumps.

Staking and Support Systems for More-Productive Plants

Using stakes or other support systems to grow plants vertically does more than save space. When lifted off the ground, vining and trailing plants tend to be healthier and more productive. Supported in an upright position, they receive more sunlight and increased air circulation, which prevents fungus and rot. In addition, the produce stays cleaner and is easier to monitor and harvest. Cucumbers, melons, summer and winter squash, peas, pole beans, and tomatoes are all good candidates for training upward.

If you plan to stake plants, place the stake in the ground before you sow, or when you put transplanted seedlings into the ground. Do not wait until the plant grows larger, or you run the risk of damaging the roots when you insert the stake. Choose sturdy supports and bury them deep enough to bear the weight of the growing plant and its produce.

Vegetables that have twining tendrils, such as beans, will grip onto the support, but other vining plants, such as tomatoes and squash, need to be secured. Be careful not to tie the plants too tightly to the support, however, or you may damage the stem. Instead, first tie a tight loop around the support and then a looser one around the stem of the plant, as shown in the illustration opposite. Use string, cloth strips, or other biodegradable materials to tie the plants; when the season is over, both plants and ties can be thrown onto the compost pile.

Caring for Your Vegetable Garden throughout the Season

A vegetable garden does not run on a set schedule. Although some tasks do need to be performed at certain times of the year, many maintenance chores will be in response to clues that your plants provide. Try to walk through your garden every day, preferably early in the morning or in the evening. Allow yourself time to enjoy the progress your crops are making and to be alert to any problems. Carry a trowel and clippers so that you can perform the odd weeding or transplanting job on the spot. Your observations during these daily rounds will do much to keep your garden healthy.

Heading Off Problems with On-the-Spot Fixes

Early in the season, tend to crops that need thinning, since plants that are spaced an optimum distance apart will reward you with an abundant harvest. Conversely, if you come across a little extra room in a bed, tuck in a plant for some quick intercropping. Be on the lookout for weeds poking through the soil or mulch, and dig or pull them promptly. Likewise, nip insect problems in the bud before they become too serious. (For more information on pests and diseases, see chapter 3 or, for help with a specific problem, consult the troubleshooting guide on pages 94-99.)

If the weather has been dry, check the soil to make sure you've given your plants enough moisture. Probe the soil with your fingers to discover how deep the dry surface layer is. If it is dry to the root mass of a crop, it's time to water. Remember that once plants show signs of water stress, the problem has gone too far.

Before long, your diligence in the garden will begin paying off in the form of plump, healthy produce. Take a basket or other container with you on your walks so you can collect vegetables at their peak. Keep a close eye on crops like zucchini, which can be harvested when they are only as big as your finger. These vegetables grow so fast that if you leave them an extra day or two, they'll be noticeably bigger and their taste and texture may have changed. (See chapter 4 for information on how to tell when vegetables are ripe for harvesting or, for a specific variety, check the encyclopedia that begins on page 106.)

Routine Tasks

In addition to the chores you perform on your daily inspections of the garden, your vegetable plot will require such regular maintenance as mulching, watering, fertilizing, and weeding.

Your best ally in keeping your garden healthy and productive is a layer of mulch. It insulates the ground, keeping the soil warm in cool weather and cool when temperatures turn hot. It cuts down on the need for watering because it holds moisture, and it also discourages the growth of weeds. And organic mulches such as bark, grass clippings, and newspapers (black-and-white newsprint only) break down into the soil, adding nutrients and improving soil structure.

Applying Organic Mulch

For best results, apply a layer of mulch in the spring after the soil has warmed. A good rule of thumb is to wait until seedlings are up and growing, since putting down mulch too early may pre-

Cucumber plants with woodchip mulch

Black plastic mulch warms a melon patch.

Good Organic Mulches for Vegetables

Compost

Cottonseed hulls

Grass clippings

Ground corncobs

Hay and straw

Newspapers (no colored inks)

Peanut hulls

Pine needles

Rotted manure

Shredded leaves

Winter squash 'Orangetti' on grass-clipping mulch

vent the ground from warming sufficiently for heat-loving plants. For effective weed control, apply organic mulch about 4 to 6 inches thick. Half that amount will suffice in shady areas where weeds struggle to grow. Take care not to pile the mulch against the stems of the plants, since this can promote rot. As the mulch thins and decays during the growing season, replenish it, especially if you notice weeds popping through.

When you put the garden to bed for the winter, till the organic mulch into the ground. It will continue to break down during the cold months, improving the soil's nutrient value and structure. If your soil is nitrogen poor, however, tilled-in mulch, especially one with a high carbon content like shredded bark, can further deplete the nitrogen level as it decomposes. To combat this problem, dig in nitrogen-rich cottonseed meal or blood meal in the autumn, or plant a winter cover crop such as clover or annual rye.

Inorganic Mulch

Even the most devoted organic gardeners sometimes rely on an inorganic mulch like heavy black plastic sheeting because of its superior weed control and insulating properties. Weeds cannot penetrate it, and as a bonus vegetables grown on or near the surface of the ground stay cleaner and are less prone to rot. In northern climates, cover beds with black plastic before you plant to hasten the warming of the soil. The dark color absorbs heat during the day and conducts it into the soil, then radiates warmth back to the plants at night. Obviously, this extra heat is a disadvantage in hot climates; there, the plastic should be covered with an organic mulch to keep the soil cool.

To use black plastic, lay the sheeting over a bed that has been watered, and weight the edges down with boards or large stones. The plastic will hold in the moisture, but little additional rainwater will get through. To water the beds, you'll need to install a drip-irrigation system or set up soaker hoses under the sheeting. When you're ready to plant, cut slits in the plastic and insert the seedlings. At the end of each season, if the plastic is still in good shape, remove it from the bed, wash it off, fold it when it has dried, and reuse it the following year.

Watering the Garden

You cannot always count on Mother Nature to water your vegetables. As a rule, a garden should receive 1 inch of water per week, including rainfall,

although more may be needed if you have fast-draining, sandy soil or if your area is experiencing extreme heat. To keep track of the amount of rain that falls, invest in an inexpensive rain gauge. Empty it after each rain and keep a tally of the measurements. Then supplement when necessary by hand watering, either with drip- or soaker-hose irrigation or with sprinklers. Whenever possible, water early in the morning or in the evening to reduce the loss of moisture through evaporation.

Hand watering is time-consuming, but for a small garden it may be the most practical method. Aim the water at the plants' roots, rather than at the foliage, and keep the flow of water light enough that the water soaks in deeply, rather than running off. A hand-held wand that attaches to a hose makes the job of directing the water easier; such wands come with a variety of spray nozzles, including one with a very fine mist for newly planted seeds.

Overhead sprinkling works well for germinating seeds because it keeps the surface of the ground continuously moist until the seeds sprout. Once the plants are well on their way, however, it is best to choose another method of irrigation.

Drip Irrigation/Soaker Hoses

Large vegetable gardens profit greatly from drip irrigation or soaker hoses. A drip system works best for plants that are spaced fairly far apart, like tomatoes. Soaker hoses are better for closely spaced crops like salad greens. Both systems operate with low water pressure, delivering water directly to the plants' roots at rates as slow as half a gallon per hour. The slow delivery of water to the areas that need it allows moisture to soak in deeply. As a result, plants tend to grow faster and more uniformly. And because the foliage doesn't get wet, there are fewer problems with fungal diseases, which are often spread by water.

Drip-irrigation and soaker systems can be installed by the home gardener and are easily modified throughout the season as the garden changes. Basic kits are available that include all the valves, feeder lines, and other attachments necessary to set up either type of system. In addition, new drip lines may be added, old lines removed, and holes opened or plugged as the need arises. You also may purchase a timer that turns

A VERSATILE AND EFFECTIVE WATERING SYSTEM
The feeder lines of a drip-irrigation system snake through a recently planted bed in the garden above, but in a short time they will be completely covered by the growing vegetable plants (opposite, above). Such a setup can be designed to fulfill immediate watering needs and can also be adapted to meet new requirements simply by adding new feeder lines or removing old ones.

the water on and off automatically according to a programmed schedule.

If you use drip-irrigation lines in conjunction with black plastic mulch, lay the lines down under the plastic. Mark each drip emitter with a shovelful of compost to make a visible mound under the plastic sheeting, and plant accordingly.

Weed Control: Every Gardener's Problem

One of the great ironies of gardening is that while it takes a great deal of effort to produce a beautiful and productive garden, weeds flourish with virtually no attention at all. Although their persistence might tempt the gardener to give up the battle against them, they must be destroyed because they compete with crops for growing space, soil nutrients, and water, and often harbor damaging insect pests.

Weeds can be controlled effectively through mulching, which denies them the sunlight they need to grow. A few determined weeds will make their way through mulch, but the numbers will be drastically reduced. You can add to the effective-

ness of any organic mulch by putting a thick layer of newspaper (with no colored ink) underneath it. Few weeds can penetrate that barrier, and eventually the newspaper will degrade into the soil as a helpful amendment.

Unfortunately, some mulches can increase your weed problem. Compost made from seedy plants, manure from animals grazing in seedy pastures, and hay all can contain viable seed that has the potential to sprout among your vegetables. Opt for seed-free straw, rather than hay, and be sure any compost or manure you use does not contain seedy materials.

Removing and Preventing Weeds

Early eradication is another weapon an organic gardener can use in the war against weeds. When weeds are young and their root systems are just developing, they are easier to pull or hoe, and if they are removed before they set seed, many more weeds will be prevented.

Digging with a hoe or other cultivating tool—the traditional way to weed a large vegetable garden—serves the dual purpose of uprooting weeds and aerating the soil. Be careful, though, not to disturb the roots of nearby vegetables. When hoeing around corn, squash, tomatoes, and potatoes, pile up a little extra soil around the base of the plants to protect their shallow roots.

If you do not use mulch, begin tilling the bed about 3 days after you sow your seeds. This preemptive strike will damage germinating weed seeds before they take proper root. Continue tilling or hand pulling weeds as necessary throughout the season.

Pulling weeds by hand can be a backbreaking job, but it is a necessary one if weeds grow too large to be uprooted by the hoe. Take solace in knowing that each time you pull a weed you're aerating the soil, and remember that weeding does at least get your hands in the dirt. Throw pulled weeds into the compost pile, or leave them as mulch along the beds, with their roots exposed to the sun so they will dry up.

Another way to control weeds is by planting cover crops such as clover, annual rye, vetch, barley, and alfalfa. These crops, sometimes called green manure, thickly carpet the ground, choking out weeds as they grow. To minimize the possibility of wind-borne seeds taking hold in your garden, try planting hedges along the border of your vegetable plot.

Fertilizing the Garden Midseason

Weed-free, nutrient-rich soil can sustain many crops throughout the growing season without the addition of fertilizer. But some plants that produce fruits (as opposed to edible leaves, stems, or roots), such as tomatoes, eggplant, and peppers, benefit greatly from a boost in midseason, when they are setting and maturing their fruits. And vegetables grown in containers require a steady diet of diluted nutrient supplements throughout the growing season.

If the soil is not rich enough to begin with, nutrients—especially nitrogen—can leach out with watering or can be depleted by plants that are heavy feeders. Nitrogen deficiency shows up in plants as yellowing leaves and stunted growth. Watch your plants closely; if you catch the problem early and apply a midseason fertilizer, you may save your crop. Unfortunately, the warning signs sometimes become obvious only after it is too late to save the plant. When that happens, your only option is to prepare for the next growing season by amending your vegetable beds with plenty of nutrient-rich organic material such as compost and rotted manure.

When you go looking for fertilizers, you'll find two types—synthetic and organic. Synthetic fertilizers, which are produced by industrial processes, eventually decrease the organic matter in soil and change the biological activity. In addition, they contain mineral salts that acidify the soil and repel earthworms. Organic products, by contrast, which are derived from animal or plant remains, or from mined rock minerals, actually build the soil as they feed the plants. Among the possibilities are dried blood, meat and fish meal, bone

A MIDSEASON BOOST
A side dressing of compost does double duty in this vegetable garden, providing extra nutrients to the plants at midseason and improving the structure and content of the soil when it is incorporated at season's end. A midseason feeding is particularly valuable to fruiting vegetables like tomatoes and peppers.

meal, compost, cottonseed meal, and well-rotted manure *(chart, page 21)*.

Potassium-hungry crops, such as turnips, parsnips, beets, carrots, and cabbages, all benefit from an application of wood ashes during the growing season. Nitrogen feeders, including corn and tomatoes, are stimulated by a dose of rotted manure, fish emulsion, or manure tea. You can prepare your own fertilizer from compost or a combination of other ingredients, or you can purchase organic fertilizers that will provide the nutrient concentration you need.

Applying Supplemental Fertilizer

Fertilizers appropriate for established plants are sold in either solid or liquid form. Solid materials are best applied by top- or side-dressing, that is, by spreading the fertilizer around the base or to the side of the plants. Avoid getting solid fertilizer directly on plants; it can burn tender shoots and stalks. Lightly rake or hoe the dressings into the soil and water immediately to help them penetrate the soil.

Spray diluted liquid fertilizers, such as manure tea *(recipe, below)* or fish emulsion, directly onto the plant's leaves, which will absorb the nutrients quickly. Or pour the fertilizer onto the soil so that it soaks down to the plants' roots. Drip-irrigation systems have attachments that release measured amounts of liquid fertilizer while the system is running. The irrigation systems come with safety backflow preventers that stop water in the irrigation pipes from flowing back into the house drinking water.

Manure and Compost Teas

Fill a bucket two-thirds full of water. Add manure or compost to fill the container to the top, and steep for a day or two. Leaving the solid material at the bottom, pour off the liquid into another container and dilute it with more water to the color of weak tea. (To use the tea in small amounts, dip off what you need and dilute it.) Pour about 1 pint of tea around each vegetable plant that will benefit from extra nitrogen. Do not use on root vegetables, however, since their need is for potassium.

Keeping Records of Your Garden

Keeping a complete record of your garden allows you to build on accumulated knowledge and experience so that you can repeat triumphs and avoid errors. Use a loose-leaf notebook for your garden journal; you can add pages when necessary and move them around if you choose. You'll need graph paper for garden plans, ruled paper for your notes, and heavy paper or photo-album refills for mounting photographs, invoices, and catalog descriptions. To get the most out of your record book, treat it as a combination journal and scrapbook. Collect and keep the following kinds of information:

- Your garden plan. This will help you keep track of crop rotations from year to year.
- Lists of the vegetables you planted. Save your invoices, receipts, and seed packets so you can go back to the seed vendor to reorder or seek help with problems. If you ordered from catalogs, paste in their cultivar descriptions. Over the course of the season, note the performance of each plant and how you liked it. Pictures of the vegetables, such as the eggplants above, will jog your memory.
- The number of plants you grew of each vegetable and the yield. This information will assist you in making future decisions about how many plants you want or need of any vegetable or variety.
- Temperature. A daily log of high and low temperatures will give you a good sense of the weather in your area. Also note soil temperatures during the planting season.
- Rainfall. Check your rain gauge weekly and record the results. This information, along with the temperature records, will give you a clear picture of weather trends.
- Dates, especially planting, harvest, and the last spring and first fall frost dates. Note if you seeded too early or too late.
- Pests and diseases. Record the date the problem began, what you did to solve it, and how successful you were.

Updating the Garden

Many gardeners find no reason to banish the vegetable plot to a remote corner of their property. If the garden is well designed, and especially if it has the added spice of ornamentals borrowed from the flower border, it can become an attractive feature.

An appealing garden style for traditional houses is the formal jardin potager, or kitchen garden. The four-square layout features symmetrical beds separated by paths. The garden at left is a classic example of this style. Informal vegetable gardens can be beautiful as well, as evidenced by the charming "edible landscape" shown on pages 54-55. This modern free-form planting of vegetables and ornamentals yields visual pleasure and a bountiful harvest. For a list of plants and a planting guide for each garden shown, see pages 56-59.

VARIATION ON A FORMAL THEME
Sown successively from late winter through spring, leaf lettuces form frilly, edible borders around container-grown topiaries in the Pennsylvania kitchen garden at left.

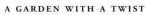

A GARDEN WITH A TWIST
Interweaving 'Ruby Red' and bright green 'Black-Seeded Simpson' lettuces adds a whimsical touch to this Virginia garden in spring. Laced among the lettuces are 'Sugar Snap' peas growing in wire cages and 'Cherry Belle' radishes.

A BACKYARD BEAUTY
A rustic arch draped with 'Scarlet Runner' beans and a wall of tomatoes trained on high stakes add vertical interest to the formal layout of this Long Island vegetable garden. The birdbath at its center echoes the wells that were often the focus of kitchen gardens of the past.

A PERIOD GARDEN IN PENNSYLVANIA

A Victorian-style fence surrounds this long rectangular plot divided into four beds by neatly manicured grass pathways. A tall, lush cone of vining 'Blue Lake' green beans thrives in the bed in the foreground along with a large patch of 'Clarimore' zucchini, three varieties of green peppers, and blue-leaved 'Premium Crop' broccoli. Across the path is a small cutting garden where white 'Mt. Fuji' phlox, thin-leaf sunflower, 'Autumn Sun' rudbeckia, and the bright orange-and-gold blossoms of 'Whirlybird Hybrids' nasturtium provide a vivid focal point. Perennial herbs occupy the bed in the far corner, and vegetables fill the fourth bed. The wrought-iron bench and the standard roses on either side of it reinforce the period look.

51

CLOSE QUARTERS
Intensively planted in fall for harvest over the mild California winter, cool-weather vegetables and annuals, some with edible flowers, make a dense, colorful patchwork. Rot-resistant redwood boards contain the double-dug raised beds, which are replenished before every planting with compost. It is the only soil amendment the owner uses.

A HILLSIDE ROCK GARDEN
Ornamental kale and billowy sweet alyssum decorate a rock retaining wall in a terraced five-level vegetable garden in Santa Barbara, California. Beyond the wall are 'Green Ice' lettuce, young filet bean plants, and 'Silver Queen' corn.

**A FRONT YARD
FEATURE**

This imaginative island garden overflowing with vegetables and flowering ornamentals is the focal point of a front yard in California. Dominated by imposing, bold-leaved 'Purple Sprouting' broccoli, the vegetables in the bed's center contribute a variety of shapes, heights, textures, and foliage colors. They also act as a foil for the alluring burst of bright purple pansies, red and yellow 'Tecolote Giants' ranunculus, and dainty white paludosum daisies in the foreground. The narrow brick path invites strollers and also provides easy access for tending the vegetables.

A Guide to the Gardens

VARIATIONS ON A FORMAL THEME

pages 46-47

A. 'Green Ripple' English ivy
B. Hen-and-chickens *(Sempervivum sp.)*
C. 'Red Salad Bowl' lettuce
D. 'Albus' white creeping thyme
E. Joseph's-coat *(Alternanthera ficoidea)*
F. 'Elegans' Siebold plantain lily
G. 'Green Joe' lettuce
H. Rosemary
I. 'Crimson Pygmy' barberry
J. Japanese painted fern
K. 'Telecurl' English ivy
L. Sweet bay tree *(Laurus nobilis)*
M. 'Argenteus' common thyme
N. 'Pagoda' parsley
O. Boxwood
P. English ivy

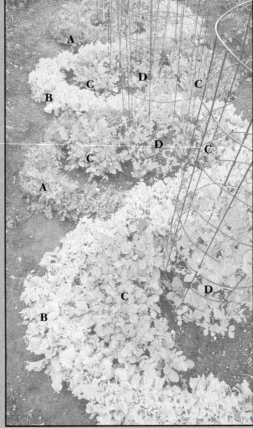

A GARDEN WITH A TWIST

page 48

A. 'Ruby Red' lettuce
B. 'Black-Seeded Simpson' lettuce
C. 'Cherry Belle' radish
D. 'Sugar Snap' peas

A BACKYARD BEAUTY

pages 48-49

A. 'Lavender Lace' Chinese wisteria
B. 'Joseph's Coat' climber rose
C. Nasturtium
D. 'Hidcote' English lavender
E. Italian flatleaf parsley
F. Sweet basil

G. Purple basil *(Ocimum basilicum cv.)*
H. Common sage
I. 'Silver Carpet' lamb's ears
J. Common thyme
K. 'Truly Yours' geranium
L. Purple sage

M. 'Early Girl,' 'Big Boy,' and cherry tomatoes
N. Wild marjoram
O. Green bell pepper
P. Cucumber
Q. Rhubarb
R. 'Scarlet Runner' beans

A PERIOD GARDEN IN PENNSYLVANIA

pages 50-51

A. Wisteria
B. Thin-leaf sunflower *(Helianthus decapetalus)*
C. 'Autumn Sun' rudbeckia
D. 'Mt. Fuji' phlox
E. 'Blue Lake' beans
F. 'Roc d'Or' yellow beans
G. 'Clarimore' zucchini
H. 'Ariane', 'Nory Charm', and 'Purple Bell' peppers

I. 'Premium Crop' broccoli
J. 'Whirlybird Hybrids' nasturtium
K. 'Tres Fin Maraichiere' endive
L. Rose
M. 'Cayenne', 'Texas Joe Parker', 'Jalapeno', and 'Sweet Banana' peppers
N. 'Rosa Bianco' and 'Agora' eggplants
O. 'Haricots Verts' filet beans

P. Sorrel
Q. Lovage
R. Lemon balm
S. 'Oakleaf' lettuce
T. 'Ruby' Swiss chard
U. 'Paros' Swiss chard
V. Arugula
W. 'Pink Mist' pincushion flower

Note: The key accompanying each garden diagram identifies the plants by letter.

CLOSE QUARTERS

page 52

A. Snapdragon
B. Johnny-jump-up
C. 'Rocambole' garlic, French shallots, 'Italian Red Bottle' and 'Walla Walla' onions
D. Pinks
E. Marigold
F. 'Buttercrunch' lettuce

G. 'Jewel Hybrids' nasturtium
H. Petunia
I. 'Rouge d'Hiver' lettuce
J. Arugula
K. Ornamental kale
L. 'Four Seasons' lettuce
M. 'Romanesco' and 'Premium Crop' broccoli

N. 'Yukon Gold' potato
O. 'Scarlet Nantes' carrot
P. 'All-America' parsnips
Q. 'Ruby' Swiss chard
R. 'Finocchio' bulbing fennel
S. 'Bounty Shelling' and 'Old Spice' peas
T. 'Scarlet Ball' turnip

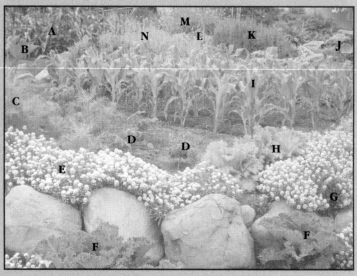

A HILLSIDE ROCK GARDEN

pages 52-53

A. 'Early Sunglow' corn
B. 'Green Comet' broccoli
C. 'Sensation Hybrids' cosmos
D. Filet beans
E. 'Carpet of Snow' sweet alyssum

F. 'Nagoya' ornamental kale
G. 'Crystal Palace' lobelia
H. 'Green Ice' lettuce
I. 'Silver Queen' corn
J. 'Richgreen' zucchini
K. Lavender

L. 'Red Ace' beet
M. Arugula
N. Dittany of Crete *(Origanum dictamnus)*

A FRONT YARD FEATURE

pages 54-55

A. 'Tecolote Giants Red' Persian buttercup
B. 'Tecolote Giants Yellow' Persian buttercup
C. Sweet alyssum (*Lobularia maritima*)
D. Paludosum daisy (*Chrysanthemum paludosum*)
E. 'Blue Princess' horned violet
F. 'Universal Antique Mix' pansy
G. Marguerite (*Chrysanthemum frutescens*)
H. 'Touchon' carrot
I. 'Green Sprouting' broccoli
J. 'Sugar Snap' peas
K. 'Slo Bolt' cilantro
L. 'Joy Choi' pak-choi
M. 'Black-Seeded Simpson' lettuce
N. Wallflower (*Erysimum 'Bowles' Mauve'*)
O. 'Chioggia' beets
P. 'Burpee's Golden' beets
Q. 'Purple Sprouting' broccoli
R. Euryops daisy (*Euryops pectinatus 'Viridis'*)
S. 'Beverly Sills' bearded iris
T. Curly parsley

Note: The key accompanying each garden diagram identifies the plants by letter.

CHAPTER THREE

Controlling Pests and Diseases

Gaining the upper hand on pests and diseases begins before they ever appear in the garden. Building and maintaining a fertile, well-drained soil as described in chapter 1 is your first line of defense, along with the tips found in chapter 2 on caring for your plants. Well-cultivated crops grown in a healthy environment will be robust and less vulnerable to devastating infestations or infections. Other, specific ways in which to prevent problems are discussed on the following pages. These include choosing plant varieties bred for disease resistance, making the garden hospitable to beneficial insects that prey on pests, and protecting plants with barriers like the chicken-wire fence that keeps rabbits and woodchucks out of the Pennsylvania garden at left.

When preventive action doesn't work, first try simple, safe techniques such as trapping the pests or using homemade sprays (pages 70-73). The organic insecticides and fungicides described on pages 74-75 should be reserved for serious, stubborn problems.

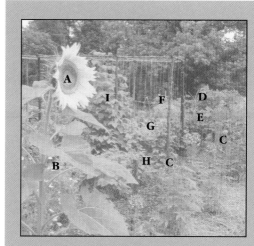

A. Common sunflower (Helianthus annuus 'Russian Mammoth')
B. Corn poppy (Papaver rhoeas 'Mother of Pearl')
C. Spider flower (Cleome spinosa)
D. 'Ruby Pearl' cherry tomato
E. 'Sunburst' pattypan squash
F. 'Carmello' tomato
G. 'White Dutch' pole beans
H. 'Astrelle Mini' filet beans
I. 'Priscilla Polish' pole beans

Please refer to the key at right to identify the plants in the garden shown.

Spotting Potential Problems

Managing pests and diseases organically depends on your ability to identify a threat to your garden so that you can take steps to prevent or eradicate it. You may already have successfully diagnosed attacks on your vegetable plants by insect or animal pests or diseases. However, it's a good idea to contact your local Cooperative Extension Service for a list of the culprits common in your area; that way you'll be forewarned of problems you haven't confronted personally. Such a list, along with the information on the following pages and in the troubleshooting guide on pages 94-99, will help you choose appropriate preventive measures.

A keen eye is crucial for heading off problems or solving them quickly. Make it a habit to examine your vegetable plants methodically every week, turning over their leaves and checking their stems—a 10-power hand lens will help you with this. If you discover chewed or yellowing leaves or other signs of trouble, describe the damage and record the date in your garden diary *(page 45)*. Along with the other items in your diary, such as the date a vegetable was planted, rotation schedules, or unusual weather, this information will help you identify the cause of a problem. Good records will also help you anticipate seasonal outbreaks.

Pests and diseases can be hard to identify, even for a seasoned gardener, so consult your local extension agent if you are stumped. A plant specimen and your diary will help the agent make the correct diagnosis.

Chewing and Sucking Insects

Insects that harm vegetables fall into two basic categories—chewing insects and sucking insects. Among the most voracious chewing pests are beetle larvae and caterpillars, which are the larvae of moths and butterflies. If chewing pests have invaded your garden, you'll see nibbles on the edges of leaves or holes chewed between leaf veins. Another telltale sign is little piles of excrement, or frass, deposited on the leaves.

In large enough numbers, chewing insects can defoliate a plant or completely devour a seedling, and they also open a plant's tissues to infection. There may be several generations of a particular pest in one season, so you have to be continuously on the alert for signs of chewing. If you find holes in foliage, look for eggs on the undersides of the

FORAGING FOR A MIDNIGHT SNACK
Clinging to a wire support for peas, a raccoon on a nighttime raid surveys a garden's bounty. In the background is a stand of corn, a favorite food of this pest.

leaves; remove any you find and drop them into a bucket of soapy water to stop them from hatching.

Sucking insects, such as aphids and leafhoppers, feed on juices in leaves, stems, or roots. Besides weakening a plant, a sucking insect can inject deadly pathogens as it feeds. Typical kinds of damage include wilting; stunted growth; yellowed, brown, or blotchy leaves; and misshapen leaves, shoots, or fruit. Aphids leave sticky trails of sugars and sap known as honeydew on the leaves.

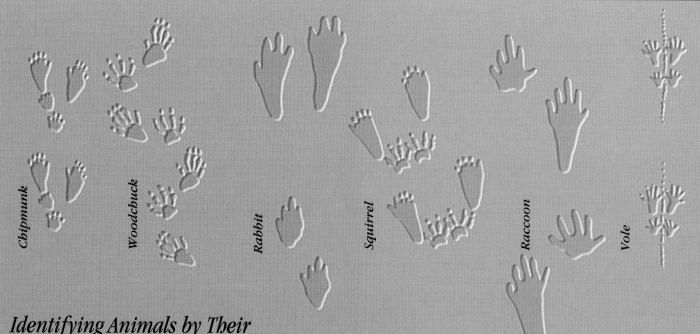

Identifying Animals by Their Footprints

Most wild animals are very shy and some are nocturnal, so you may not catch sight of a pest that has been raiding your garden. However, footprints will reveal the forager's identity and allow you to take steps to prevent repeat visits *(pages 67-69)*. To get a clear footprint, smooth the earth near the plants that are being eaten and, in the evening, lay wide bands of flour around them. The next morning, check the flour bands for footprints. Compare any you find with the drawings shown here of the prints of six common animal pests.

Chipmunk

Woodchuck

Rabbit

Squirrel

Raccoon

Vole

Diseases

Like other living creatures, plants occasionally fall victim to infectious diseases. Pathogens such as fungal spores, viruses, bacteria, and parasitic nematodes can be transported into your garden on the feet of insects or in their saliva, on infected plants bought at a nursery, or by way of wind or birds. Once in your garden, a disease organism may not manifest itself for years, remaining dormant until conditions become more favorable.

Your hands, shoes, and tools can also spread pathogens from place to place within the garden, and the simple act of accidentally nicking a stem when you are cultivating around a plant can provide an entryway for a disease organism. As a precaution, don't work in the garden when it is wet, since pathogens, especially fungal spores, are easily spread from plant to plant in drops of water.

Not all garden diseases are caused by pathogens. They also arise from environmental disorders such as mineral deficiencies or air pollution. The symptoms of noninfectious and infectious diseases can be confusingly similar, and close scrutiny is required to tell the difference. One hint for distinguishing the two is how the symptoms are distributed among your plants. If most or all of the vegetables growing in the same area have the same symptoms, an environmental cause is likely. An infectious disease, by contrast, tends to attack one plant first and then spread in a random pattern to a few plants nearby. See the troubleshooting guide for help in diagnosis.

Animal Pests

The produce of the vegetable garden is just as appealing to a number of widely distributed plant-eating animals as it is to humans. Such common animals as raccoons, rabbits, and woodchucks, for example, are capable of devastating a crop in short order. As with insects or diseases, different species call for different control measures. If you suspect that an animal pest is slipping in and out of your garden unseen, the information in the box above may help you identify the culprit.

An Ounce of Prevention

One easy way to stop garden problems before they start is to fill your vegetable plot with varieties that have been bred to resist one or more diseases without compromising flavor. Resistance is often indicated on plant labels or in catalogs by coded abbreviations of diseases. For instance, DMPM means that the plant is resistant to downy mildew and powdery mildew. In addition to the many disease-resistant cultivars, there are a smaller number that are resistant to attack by certain insects.

Not quite as trouble free but still very desirable are vegetables that are rated tolerant of a particular disease or pest. Although a tolerant variety may suffer infection or an infestation, the damage won't be bad enough to cut its production significantly.

Crops on the Move

Pests and pathogens that live in the soil will continue to multiply as long as their preferred food supply is present, so planting the same vegetables in the same bed year after year is asking for trouble. But if you shift crops from place to place every time you plant, an insect, bacterium, virus, or fungus that has established itself in your garden will be deprived of its food source and will die out.

A crop rotation scheme must be based on families of vegetables, since closely related species are likely to be attacked by the same pests and diseases. The chart on page 66 groups widely grown vegetables by family and will help you plot out a rotation scheme. Since the pathogens responsible for bean anthracnose, verticillium wilt, fusarium wilt, and other diseases can survive in the soil for up to 3 years, waiting at least that long before replanting a bed with the same family of crops will give you maximum protection.

It is also a good practice to work soil-building crops like clover and rye into your rotation plan to ensure a regular replenishment of nutrients and organic matter. The chart on page 89 provides information on when to plant six soil-building crops and what each of them does to improve the soil.

Keeping the Garden Clean

Another way to interrupt the life cycle of pests and disease organisms is to develop good gardening habits. As soon as a plant reaches the end of its productive life, pull it up and add it to the compost pile; debris left in the garden can harbor insects or pathogens from one season to the next. After clearing away crop debris, till the soil to bring eggs and larvae to the surface where birds, snakes, or other predators can find them. Turning the soil of an empty bed several times in late winter will expose insects such as corn earworms and cutworms to freezing cold. Keeping weeds under control in and around the garden is also important. Besides competing with your vegetables for water, nutrients, and light, some weeds are hosts to garden pests.

IMPROVING ON NATURE
This 'Whopper Improved' green bell pepper plant is heavy with unblemished fruit and foliage. It is resistant to the tobacco mosaic virus, a common disease that can cause yellowing of leaves, stunting, and reduced yield.

Encouraging Beneficials

All pests have natural predators. Known collectively as beneficials, these number among their ranks toads, snakes, lizards, moles, songbirds, and a number of insects, including parasitic wasps. You can buy certain insect predators, but it's also wise to make your garden attractive to native beneficials. For instance, including plants with pollen- and nectar-rich flowers, such as dill and yarrow, will draw the beneficial insects that depend on them for food. A constant water supply is also essential. A birdbath can do double duty if you make a little island of pebbles or float a piece of wood in the water for insects to alight on. See the chart on page 68 for other ways to encourage beneficials.

Barriers to Stymie Pests

A number of simple but effective barriers do a good job of keeping flying and crawling insects, slugs, raccoons, and other hungry pests away from vegetables and fruits. A sheet of black plastic or a thick layer of organic mulch will not only moderate soil temperatures and suppress weeds, it will also disrupt the life cycles of thrips, leaf miners, and other soil-borne pests. For example, 6 inches of straw mulch will deter Colorado potato beetles that have overwintered in the soil from emerging in time to feed on potato seedlings.

Plants covered by a lightweight, translucent fabric are shielded from a broad spectrum of flying and crawling insect pests such as aphids, leafhoppers, and caterpillars. While these row covers offer no protection against soil-borne eggs, larvae, or adult pests that are already in the soil, they do prevent flying and crawling adults from laying a new generation of eggs in the soil. Another good feature of row covers is the protection they give plants against bacteria and viruses transmitted by insects.

The most versatile materials for row covers are spunbonded polyester, polypropylene, and polyvinyl fabric. Because these fabrics are very lightweight, they can be draped directly on top of the vegetables—hence the name "floating row cover." They transmit to the plants about 85 percent of available sunlight, along with ample water and air. Floating row covers also slow the evaporation of soil moisture and shield plants from drying winds. In this benign environment, plants grow as well—or better—than they would if fully exposed to the elements.

Pest- and Disease-Resistant Varieties

In addition to vegetables that resist particular diseases and pests, the list below includes several tolerant varieties, which continue to grow fairly well in spite of an infestation or infection.

CABBAGE
'Danish Ballhead', 'Early Jersey Wakefield'—tolerate cabbage looper and imported cabbageworm; 'Golden Acre'—tolerates fusarium yellows; 'Red Acre'—tolerates cabbage looper and imported cabbageworm; 'Wisconsin All Seasons'—fusarium yellows

CARROT
'Napoli'—tolerates alternaria blight

CHINESE CABBAGE
'Blues'—alternaria, black speck, downy mildew, soft rot

CORN
'Lancelot'—corn rust, Stewart's bacterial wilt; 'Miracle'—corn rust; 'Silver Queen'—northern corn leaf blight, southern corn leaf blight, Stewart's bacterial wilt; 'Tuxedo'—corn rust, corn smut, Stewart's bacterial wilt

CUCUMBER
'Little Leaf'—angular leaf spot, anthracnose, cucumber mosaic, downy mildew, target leaf spot; 'Marketmore 76'—scab; tolerates cucumber mosaic, downy mildew, powdery mildew; 'Salad Bush'—cucumber mosaic, scab; 'Space Master'—cucumber mosaic, scab; 'Sweet Slice'—tolerates cucumber mosaic, powdery mildew, watermelon mosaic, zucchini yellows mosaic; 'Sweet Success'—cucumber mosaic, scab, target leaf spot

GREEN BEANS AND POLE BEANS
'Kentucky Wonder'—rusts; 'Provider'—bacterial blight, common bean mosaic, downy mildew, powdery mildew, white mold; 'Tendercrop'—bacterial blight, downy mildew, powdery mildew, white mold

LETTUCE
'Ithaca'—brown rib, lettuce mosaic, tipburn; 'Paris Island Cos'—lettuce mosaic, tipburn

ONIONS
'Early Yellow Globe'—onion smudge; 'Northern Oak'—fusarium yellows, pink root; 'Texas Grano'—pink root

PEPPERS
'Bell Boy'—tobacco mosaic; 'California Wonder'—cercospora leaf spot; 'Gypsy'—tobacco mosaic; 'Whopper Improved'—tobacco mosaic; 'Yolo Wonder'—tobacco mosaic

SQUASH
'Cocozelle'—aphids

TOMATOES
'Ace 55'—fusarium wilt, verticillium wilt; 'Beefmaster'—alternaria, fusarium wilt, gray leaf spot, nematodes, verticillium wilt; 'Better Boy'—alternaria, fusarium wilt, root knot nematodes, verticillium wilt; 'Celebrity'—alternaria stem canker, fusarium 1-2, gray leaf spot, nematodes, tobacco mosaic, verticillium wilt; 'Early Cascade'—alternaria stem canker, fusarium, gray leaf spot, verticillium wilt; 'Roma VF'—alternaria, fusarium wilt, verticillium wilt; 'Sweet Million'—fusarium wilt, nematodes, septoria leaf spot, tobacco mosaic

YELLOW BEANS
'Cherokee'—common bean mosaic, rust; 'Roc d'Or'—anthracnose, common bean mosaic

Some spunbonded row covers are designed to trap enough heat to protect plants from light frosts in spring and fall. There are also summer-weight row covers so airy that they can be left in place throughout the growing season without the risk of overheating your plants. These row covers are an especially good choice for protecting cool-weather greens like lettuce and spinach that tend to bolt when the temperature is too high.

Heavier row covers of polyethylene and polystyrene plastic are more efficient heat traps than any of the spunbonded fabrics. They are excellent for getting the garden started earlier in the year and keeping crops growing farther into fall, but can easily overheat crops in milder weather. Also, these plastics need wire hoops or some other support to keep them from crushing the plants.

Before you drape a floating row cover over a planting, weed the area thoroughly and use the techniques described on pages 70-73 to get rid of as many insects as you can. Place the fabric over the row immediately after planting; if the day is breezy, the job will be easier to do if you have a helper. Leave plenty of slack in the cover so the plants will have growing room. Weight the edges down securely with soil, rocks, or boards, making sure that there are no gaps that insects can slip through.

For cucumbers, beans, tomatoes, and other fruiting vegetables that must be pollinated to develop, remove the row covers when the crops begin to bloom. Vegetables that don't need pollination can remain covered until harvest. When you need to remove a cover for weeding and thinning, replace it as soon as you have finished the chore.

Some young vegetable plants require special protection. For example, to defend members of the cabbage family against cabbage maggots that feed on their roots, you can make a barrier that prevents adults from laying eggs in the soil at the base of the plant. Use a piece of heavy cardboard, plastic, or tarpaper measuring 6 inches square. Make a slit from one edge to the center of the square and cut out a small circle at the inner end of the slit to make room for the stem. Slip the square around the stem of the seedling at planting time. For a barrier that discourages cutworms, which chew on the stems of young vegetables at soil level, place a collar around a seedling's stem at planting time. Use a small paper cup with the bottom removed, a toilet paper roll, or a square of newspaper rolled into a tube, as shown on page 39. Bury the collar 1 to 1½ inches below ground level.

Slugs and snails are very destructive, chewing large, ragged holes in leaves and feeding on onion

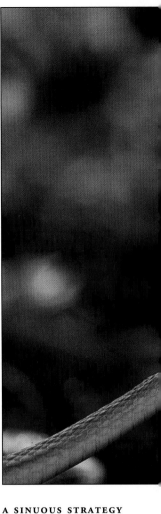

A SINUOUS STRATEGY
In search of a meal, a hungry green snake glides among beebalm blossoms ornamenting a vegetable garden. Nonpoisonous snakes like this one are a boon, hunting down insects and slugs as well as larger pests such as mice and voles.

A Family Plan for Crop Rotation

A reliable way to minimize or even eliminate soil-borne pest and disease problems is to plant a particular patch of ground with the same vegetable or its close relatives only once every 3 to 5 years. In the lean years, without their favored hosts to feed on, organisms that typically plague a certain vegetable family will decline in numbers. Use the family groups below to help you plot out a long-term rotation scheme for your garden.

BEET FAMILY—beets, chard, orach, spinach

CARROT FAMILY—carrots, celeriac, celery, fennel, parsley, parsnips

COMPOSITE FAMILY—cardoon, celtuce, chicory, endive, escarole, Jerusalem artichoke, lettuce, radicchio, salsify, sunflower

LEGUME FAMILY—beans, peas, peanuts, soybeans

MUSTARD FAMILY—arugula, broccoli, Brussels sprouts, cabbage, cauliflower, Chinese cabbage, collards, cress, kale, kohlrabi, mustard greens, radishes, rutabaga, turnips

ONION FAMILY—chives, garlic, leeks, onions, shallots

SQUASH FAMILY—chayote, cucumbers, melons, pumpkins, squash

TOMATO FAMILY—eggplant, peppers, potatoes, tomatillo, tomatoes

A FORMIDABLE FOE
Looming above its unwitting victim, a praying mantis prepares to strike a grasshopper, a pest that takes an especially heavy toll on seedlings. Though often helpful, praying mantises are indiscriminate predators, feeding on beneficial insects as well as destructive ones.

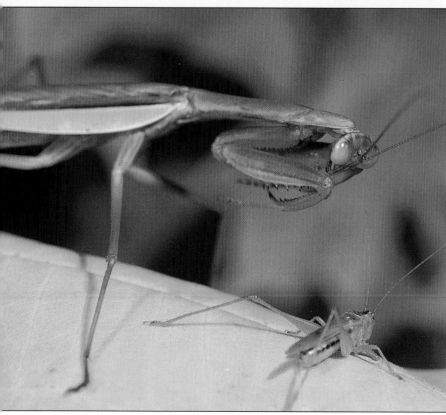

bulbs, strawberries, and tomatoes. Deter them by laying down a strip of abrasive material 2 inches wide and a quarter inch deep around a plant; when the animal crawls on the scratchy surface, its skin is damaged and it dies of dehydration. Particularly effective is diatomaceous earth, a commercial product derived from fossilized plankton. Wood ashes, talc, lime, and crushed eggshells also work well.

For a permanent barrier, surround a garden bed with a strip of copper sheet metal 4 inches wide. Bury the strip 1 to 2 inches below ground level and bend the top half-inch of the strip away from the bed. When a slug or snail touches the copper strip, a chemical reaction occurs that creates an electric current and gives the pest a shock.

Mammals: Friends and Foes

A few mammals are actually more helpful than harmful in a vegetable garden, despite their reputation. Skunks, for instance, will eat berries and ears of corn that grow close to the ground, but they also catch insects, voles, mice, and rats. Moles ignore vegetables and fruits altogether, while eating slugs, Japanese beetles, white grubs, and other pests in the soil. But some mammals, including rabbits and voles, are truly pests, and for these most organic gardeners prefer nonlethal control methods such as fences and repellent chemicals. Live traps are another option, but take care not to release an animal where it will become a headache for another gardener or be unable to survive. Before using a trap, make sure your state does not have laws against transporting and releasing wild animals. Below is a selection of mammals that can do damage and the controls that deter them:

Rabbits—A 3-foot-high fence of ¾-inch wire mesh will keep rabbits out of the garden. Dried blood meal, cow manure, or wood ashes sprinkled near plants will repel them. Replenish after a rain.

Raccoons—When corn or melons ripen, stringent measures must be taken against these intelligent animals. You can cover the individual ears or fruits with nylon stockings or net bags, but an electric fence—the only kind that works with raccoons—is easier. Two strands of electrified wire or cord around the garden are usually enough. Position the upper strand about a foot from the ground and the lower strand within 6 inches of the ground.

Woodchucks—Also called groundhogs, these eat almost anything succulent and rip up entire plants. The electric fence described above will discourage them, as will a wire-mesh fence that is at least 3 feet tall and extends 2 feet underground.

Squirrels—These animals relish tomatoes,

BENEFICIALS THAT PREY ON VEGETABLE AND FRUIT PESTS

BENEFICIAL	PESTS CONTROLLED	COMMENTS
Aphid midges	More than 60 species of aphids	Attract with pollen- and nectar-producing plants. Buy six to 10 cocoons per plant and release half in early spring and the remainder 2 weeks later.
Assassin bugs	Flies, mosquitoes, beetles, caterpillars	Provide permanent beds in or near the vegetable garden for shelter. Purchase commercial attractant.
Braconid wasps	Aphids, moth and beetle larvae, flies, codling moth, cabbageworm, hornworm, corn borer, armyworm, other caterpillars	These wasps feed on the nectar of dill, parsley, mustard, white clover, yarrow, and other small-flowered plants. Also available by mail order.
Flower flies, syrphid flies	Aphids, mealybugs, mites, thrips	These predators are attracted by daisylike flowers that produce nectar and pollen.
Lacewings	Aphids, mealybugs, mites, moth eggs, scales, small caterpillars, soft-bodied insects, thrips	Attract with nectar- and pollen-producing plants such as tansy and goldenrod. Purchase eggs and distribute throughout the garden. Purchase commercial attractant.
Ladybugs, ladybeetles	Aphids, mealybugs, soft scales, spider mites, whiteflies	Plant pollen- and nectar-producing plants. Buy adults collected in spring only. Ladybugs collected at other times of year will migrate from your garden. Buy commercial attractant.
Nematodes, beneficial, type HH	Soil-borne insects including armyworm, black vine weevil, cabbage root maggot, chafers, Colorado potato beetle, corn rootworm, cucumber beetle, cutworms, fungus gnat larvae, Japanese beetle grubs, mole cricket, root weevils, white grubs, and wireworms	Keep soil moist. Available by mail order.
Nematodes, beneficial, type NC	Soil-borne insects including armyworm, cabbage root maggot, chafers, Colorado potato beetle, cutworm, earwig, Japanese beetle grubs, onion maggot, root weevils, seed corn maggot, sowbug, white grubs, and wireworms	Keep soil moist. Available by mail order.
Pirate bugs	Aphids, insect eggs, leafhoppers, rust mites, spider mites, small caterpillars, thrips	Attract with pollen-rich plants such as goldenrod and yarrow and provide a water source such as a birdbath.
Praying mantises	Aphids, beetles, bugs, caterpillars, flies, leafhoppers, and other insects	Available by mail order, but try other controls first because praying mantises eat beneficials as well as pests.
Predatory mites	European red mites, rust mites, thrips, two-spotted spider mites	These mites prefer high humidity and rich soil and do not thrive in hot, dry areas.
Rove beetles	Aphids, fly eggs, maggots, mites, parasitic nematodes, slugs, snails, springtails	Provide organic mulch for shelter.
Soldier beetles	Aphids, beetle larvae, butterfly larvae, caterpillars, grasshopper eggs, moth larvae	Attract by growing goldenrod and other nectar- and pollen-producing plants.
Spiders	Most insects	Encourage by leaving webs intact.
Tachinid flies	Many kinds of caterpillars including cutworms, codling moths, cabbage loopers, squash bugs, and grasshoppers	Attract by growing nectar-producing plants such as dill, parsley, sweet clover, and yarrow.
Trichogramma wasps	Eggs of many moths including corn earworm, cutworm, cabbage looper, corn borer, codling moth, tomato hornworm	Several species that prey on different pests are available by mail order; be sure you buy the appropriate one. Use pheromone traps to determine when the pest is at its peak or release wasps every week for a month around the peak season.
Bats	Nocturnal flying insects	Install a bat house and provide water.
Birds	Many kinds of insects	Install birdhouses, provide water, and plant fruit-bearing shrubs and trees.
Snakes	Insects and small rodents	Provide shallow containers of water and shelter.
Toads, lizards, turtles	Slugs and most insects	Provide shallow containers of water and shelter.

UNDER WRAPS
Firmly weighted down by soil and logs, floating row covers shield young vegetables from pesky insects early in the growing season in the Maine garden above. The row covers also trap enough heat overnight to protect the plants against late, light frosts. Once all danger of insect infestation has passed, the covers can be removed.

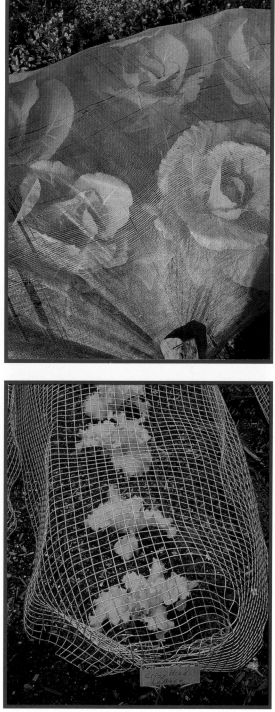

sweet corn, and sunflower seeds. Try covering corn ears and sunflowers with nylon stockings or net bags, or spray the ears with a red pepper spray (the husks will shield the kernels from the spray).

Voles—Sprinkle household ammonia on the ground around plants to repel these rodents. Also try a small-mesh wire fence, bent horizontally so that it stands at least 18 inches high with 12 inches or more lying flat on the ground, to discourage voles from burrowing into the garden.

Deer—A fence is one option, though even a 7-foot fence may not keep the best jumpers out. It is preferable for the top of the fence to slant outward at a 45° angle. First, however, experiment with net bags filled with mothballs or hair (animal or human) hung every 20 feet throughout the garden; blood meal sprinkled around the perimeter; or sweaty clothes hung on stakes. You can also try laying chicken-wire fencing on the ground around the garden in the hope that getting their feet tangled in the wire will discourage the deer.

Birds—Songbirds are generally beneficials, eating hundreds of insects in a single day. Most other kinds of birds, however, eat vegetable seedlings, lettuce, berries, and other crops. Scare tactics such as inflatable owls and balloons on which you've

BARRIERS FOR CHEMICAL-FREE PROTECTION
Rain, sunlight, and air pass easily through the diaphanous floating row cover protecting the cabbage plants at upper right. A sturdy wire cage that can be lifted for weeding and harvesting keeps the lettuce plants at right out of the reach of birds, rabbits, and other greens-loving animals.

drawn large eyes work fairly well. Place them every 30 to 40 feet around the garden and change them often to keep the birds from getting used to them. A surer method is to cover vulnerable plants. Several weeks before the fruits ripen, drape berry plants with broad-mesh plastic netting with a ½- to ¾-inch grid. For seedlings and crops like lettuce that continue to attract birds as they mature, use spunbonded floating row covers.

Minimizing Damage in Your Garden

Even a gardener's best efforts to curb pests and disease microorganisms don't always work. An outbreak occurs, and you find your vegetables rotting, wilting, or chewed to shreds. Fortunately, remedies are available to prevent a problem from getting out of hand without resorting to chemicals.

The immediate course of action is to physically remove as much of the problem as possible. If a plant is diseased, get rid of it, roots and all. Put it in a plastic bag and throw it out with your household trash. Do not compost diseased debris: Pathogens may survive the decay process and reinfest the garden when you use the finished compost.

In the case of a plant with a soil-borne disease, dig it up with a garden fork, taking care not to knock the soil from the rootball. Put the plant and the soil clinging to its roots in a plastic bag for disposal. Replant with a resistant variety or a different vegetable that is immune to the disease.

After handling a diseased plant, clean your tools and gloves with a 10 percent bleach solution to avoid spreading the disease to other plants.

Handpicking Pests

An infestation of pests usually doesn't call for total removal of the plant. If the intruders are confined to a stem or two, cut back to clean, uninfested tissue, put the plant parts in a plastic bag, and discard with the household trash. Large pests like caterpillars and snails can be picked off plants and dropped into a bucket of soapy water.

Some beetle pests, such as Japanese beetles or Colorado potato beetles, can be shaken out. Spread a sheet of plastic or a cloth on the ground under the plant to catch the beetles as they fall. Gather up the cloth and shake them off into a bucket of soapy water. This method works best in the early morning, when the beetles are sluggish.

Handpicking and shaking don't work for insects like aphids and spider mites that cling tightly to plants, but you can injure or kill many of them with a stream of water from a hose. Adjust the strength of the stream so it won't damage your plants, then spray all of the plant's leaves, top and bottom, repeating as often as necessary. Don't spray a plant that shows symptoms of a fungus, however, since the water could spread pathogens further. Also, it's better to spray in the morning or the evening if the weather is hot and sunny—water droplets can act like magnifying glasses and burn the leaves.

Trapping Insects

Another fairly easy way to rid pests from your garden is to lure them away with traps. The traps that work best are those that imitate certain sights or smells insects associate with food or potential mates. Many flying insects, particularly aphids, thrips, whiteflies, cabbage root flies, carrot rust flies, cucumber beetles, and imported cabbage-worms, are attracted to the color yellow. A simple, effective trap for these insects is a bright yellow strip or rectangle coated with a sticky glue. You can purchase such traps at garden centers or make them yourself. Paint pieces of sturdy cardboard, wood, or plastic with two coats of a paint containing a pigment known as Federal Safety Yellow No. 659. After the paint dries, use a putty knife to spread the surface with a commercial sticky glue, which will remain tacky for about 2 weeks; leave one corner uncoated so you can handle the trap without your fingers sticking to it. Fix the trap to a stake and place it beside the infested plant; the trap should be about level with the top of the plant. Set out one trap for every five to six plants and add more if the damage continues.

One disadvantage of a trap using color as a lure is that it may draw a broad spectrum of insects that includes beneficials as well as pests. To be sure that your traps attract only those species infesting your plants, consider using pheromone lures.

Pheromones are chemicals emitted by females of the species to attract mates, and flying insects can sense these chemicals from great distances. Pheromones have been identified and commercially reproduced that lure about 40 moth species, including cabbage loopers, corn earworms, and leaf rollers. The lures are placed in traps lined with a sticky substance to catch the insects. Scented traps must be used with care, for they can attract pests to your vegetable garden from miles away, making your pest problem worse. To prevent this, place the traps outside and upwind of the garden.

Controlling pests is not the only function of traps. Pheromone traps, for instance, are excellent for monitoring changes in the size of a particular pest population. They can warn the gardener of a problem as it's beginning, when there is still time to take action. Thus if your tomatoes have been troubled by hornworm caterpillars in past seasons, you can set out a pheromone trap to draw adult male hornworm moths; their arrival will signal the start of the season for mating and egg laying. Then you can take action, such as releasing trichogramma wasps, which parasitize the eggs.

You can keep tabs on flea beetles and tarnished plant bugs with white sticky traps; blue sticky traps will attract thrips. A good rule of thumb is to check a monitoring trap twice a week. It's also a good idea to continue checking it after you've started using a control measure so you can gauge its effectiveness.

Fighting Pests and Diseases with Heat

Solarization is a simple technique that uses the strong summer sun and a sheet of 3- to 4-mil clear plastic to kill soil-borne pests and diseases. This process raises the temperature of garden soil to 120° F or more—high enough to kill pests and pathogens to a depth of 3 to 5 inches. When air temperatures average 90°F, solarization takes about 4 weeks; it can take up to 8 weeks when temperatures are in the 70s. Raised beds will heat faster than level ground.

To begin, clear the bed of vegetation and debris, and add any amendments the soil needs. Rake the bed smooth, dig a trench a few inches deep around it, then soak the soil to a depth of at least 12 inches. To trap heat and moisture, cover the bed snugly with the plastic, tuck the edges into the trench, and bury them with soil.

Measure the soil temperature periodically, pulling back the plastic just far enough to insert a soil thermometer. Record the temperature at several different spots. A few days after the temperature has stabilized at 120° F or higher, remove the plastic.

To replace beneficial microorganisms killed by solarization, add microbe-rich material such as aged manure or compost to the bed. Do not cultivate it below 4 inches lest you raise surviving pathogens and reinfect the solarized soil.

Coping with Slugs and Snails

If these pests have eluded the preventive barriers you have placed around vulnerable crops, you can set traps for them. Garden centers and mail-order companies sell baited traps, but you can make your own by filling a shallow container with yeast dissolved in water or beer. Sink the trap to its rim in the soil and empty it every few days in an inconspicuous place in the garden. Then refill the container with fresh bait.

Slugs and snails are night feeders and seek a moist, cool, dark cover during the day. To take advantage of this behavior, provide them with boards or upside-down flower pots, melon rinds, or grapefruit rinds as shelter. Collect the pests that congregate under the trap and crush them or place them in the trash.

Microbial Pesticides

Like other creatures, pests are susceptible to fatal infections, and a bacterium called *Bacillus thuringiensis,* or Bt for short, is an invaluable pesticide for the organic gardener. There are some 30 different strains of this microbe, each one a magic bullet that attacks a single species of caterpillar or beetle larva; all other organisms are immune to that particular strain. Among the common pests susceptible to infection are cabbage loopers, tomato hornworms, European corn borers, and beetle larvae that feed on leaves.

Homemade Pesticides and Fungicides

If you have discharged the full arsenal of cultural, physical, and biological controls against a pest or disease without success, your remaining weapon is an organic pesticide or fungicide. The mildest and safest of these—and for that reason the ones to try first—are homemade preparations based on common, readily available ingredients. A spray made from baking soda, for instance, checks fungal diseases, especially powdery mildew, leaf blight, and leaf spot.

Recipes for baking soda fungicide and three other sprays are given below. The garlic and hot pepper sprays control insects. The soap-and-oil spray prevents fungal spores from germinating and is also an insecticide.

Before applying any of the preparations to an entire plant, spray it on a few leaves to test for sensitivity. After 2 days, examine the leaves to see whether there are any spots of discolored or dying tissue. If the leaves are damaged, dilute the spray with a little more water and test the plant again to see if it is safe to use.

When you spray a plant, be sure to cover the top and bottom of all of its leaves, as shown below. Repeat every 5 to 7 days until the pests are gone or the disease symptoms have disappeared. To prevent a repeat outbreak of a disease the following year, begin spraying in spring and continue until the fall.

Baking soda spray—Dissolve 1 tablespoon of baking soda in 1 gallon of water and add ⅛ to ¼ teaspoon of insecticidal soap to help the solution spread and adhere to the foliage.

Soap-and-oil spray—Mix 1 teaspoon of liquid

Spraying for Complete Coverage

To make sure that a plant gets a thorough application of a chemical, spray methodically from the plant's base to its top, aiming the sprayer at the underside of the leaves as shown at left. Spray until the liquid just begins to drip off the foliage. When you reach the top of the plant, reverse direction. Aim the sprayer downward to coat the upper surface of the leaves, and work your way back down to the base of the plant.

NEUTRALIZING NEMATODES WITH MARIGOLDS
A planting of African marigolds (above) can clear infested soil of root knot nematodes in one season. When the nematodes feed on the roots of these plants, they take in a chemical that keeps them from reproducing. At season's end, the marigolds can be turned under to improve the soil's texture.

Commercial Chemicals

If a homemade spray doesn't take care of a stubborn problem, you may decide that stronger measures are called for. Although the natural chemicals that organic gardeners use are derived from plants or minerals, they can have adverse effects and should be considered a last resort. Some are toxic to humans, mammals, birds, reptiles, fish, harmless insects, or soil microorganisms as well as to the pests or diseases they are directed against. Nevertheless, they are preferable to synthetic, or manufactured, chemicals because the natural substances break down quickly. In addition, they have no long-lasting detrimental effects on the environment. Synthetic chemicals, by contrast, may remain active for months or years and can be extremely harmful. The chart on pages 74-75 provides information on organic pesticides and fungicides that are safe to use on food crops. Whatever the pest or disease you are battling, always try the least toxic chemical first, apply it sparingly, and rigorously follow directions for use.

Handling Chemicals Safely

Before you use a pesticide or fungicide, read the label thoroughly and follow all of the instructions to the letter. Whenever you handle one of these chemicals, wear long pants, a long-sleeved shirt, and rubber gloves to protect your skin. Wear goggles and a dust mask or a respirator to safeguard your eyes and lungs from irritation.

Prior to tackling a job, have the right equipment on hand. For chemicals that come in the form of dust, a good choice is a duster with a rotating blower and a long, adjustable nozzle that makes it easy to thoroughly cover both sides of a plant's leaves. For spraying liquids, a hand-held pump sprayer is all most home gardeners need. However, if your garden is an ambitious one of 400 or 500 square feet or more, a pressurized backpack sprayer with a hand pump will save you time and effort.

To lessen the risk of exposing yourself to the chemical, wait for a windless time of day before applying a pesticide or fungicide. Mix only what you need for a single application so you won't have to dispose of any leftovers; you can always mix a second batch if necessary. Be careful not to spill any of the chemical on your skin or clothes or on the ground when you are filling the duster or sprayer.

Keep children and pets away until the dust settles or the spray dries. Follow the directions on the label for rinsing and disposing of containers.

dishwashing soap with ⅓ cup of corn, soybean, sunflower, safflower, or peanut oil. To apply, combine 1 to 2 teaspoons of this mixture with 1 cup of water in a hand sprayer.

Garlic spray—Combine 15 garlic cloves with 1 pint of water in a blender and purée. Alternatively, mince the garlic cloves and steep them in the water for 24 hours. Strain the liquid through cheesecloth and add a few drops of insecticidal soap.

Hot pepper spray—Purée ½ cup of hot peppers and 2 cups of water in a blender. Strain the liquid through cheesecloth. Wear gloves when handling the peppers and be careful not to get the liquid on your skin or in your eyes—it will sting and burn.

A Guide to Commercial Organic Pesticides and Fungicides

The 13 organic products included in this chart are your last line of defense against pests and diseases in the vegetable garden. When using any of them, always read the label on the container, heed all warnings, and follow all directions. Before treating an entire plant, test the product on a small portion to see if it does any damage. Apply controls in the early morning or evening, and only when the air is still. Cover a plant thoroughly, including the undersides of leaves. If you find that local merchants don't stock a control you wish to buy, all those listed here can be ordered from mail-order nurseries or garden supply companies.

	NAME	TYPE	TARGET PESTS OR DISEASES	FORM	SHELF LIFE
PESTICIDES	*Bacillus thuringiensis* (Bt)	Biological insect control; infectious bacteria	Cabbage loopers, cabbageworms, tomato hornworms, and other leaf-eating caterpillars; Colorado potato beetle larvae	Dust; wettable powder; liquid concentrate	Dry form: 2-4 years; liquid concentrate: 2-3 years
	Beneficial nematodes	Biological insect control; roundworms found naturally in soil	Soil-dwelling pests such as borers, cutworms, cucumber beetle larvae, root maggots, wireworms, white grubs	Sold in semidormant state on sponges, mixed with gel, or in granules. Products are mixed with water before applying.	Up to 2 months in refrigerator; dehydrated forms up to 6 months at room temperature, longer if refrigerated.
	Diatomaceous earth (DE)	Abrasive, desiccating pesticide; finely ground fossilized marine algae	Most soft-bodied insects and pests such as aphids, caterpillars, cabbage root flies, corn borers, leafhoppers, mites, pill bugs, slugs, snails, sowbugs, thrips	Dust; can be mixed with water to make a spray.	Lasts indefinitely if kept dry.
	Horticultural oil	Contact insecticide and miticide; ultrafine petroleum	Most pest eggs, larvae, and soft-bodied adults such as aphids, leafhoppers, leaf miners, mealybugs, mites, scale, thrips, whiteflies	Liquid concentrate	Indefinite
	Insecticidal soap	Contact insecticide	Most effective against soft-bodied and sucking insects such as aphids, mites, leafhoppers, mealybugs, scale, spider mites, thrips, whiteflies	Liquid concentrate; ready-to-use spray	Up to 5 years. Keep tightly sealed.
	Neem (azadirachtin)	Botanical broad-spectrum insecticide and repellent derived from neem tree	Aphids, beetles (cucumber, flea, Japanese, Mexican bean, potato), corn earworms, leaf miners, loopers, mealybugs, spider mites, tomato hornworms, thrips, whiteflies. Kills juveniles; repels adults.	Liquid concentrate	Minimum of 18 months
	Pyrethrum (pyrethrins)	Botanical contact insecticide containing pyrethrin compounds derived from the pyrethrum daisy	Aphids, beetles (asparagus, Colorado potato, cucumber, flea, Japanese, Mexican bean), caterpillars (cabbage loopers, corn earworms, European corn borers, fall armyworms), leafhoppers, mites, stink bugs, tarnished plant bugs, thrips, whiteflies	Dust; liquid concentrate; ready-to-use spray	Dust: up to 1 year. Liquid concentrate and spray: 1-3 years
	Repellents, garlic and hot pepper	Botanical insect and animal repellents	Aphids, cabbage loopers, leafhoppers, squash bugs, whiteflies; birds, cats, deer, dogs, rabbits	Both available as liquid concentrate	2 years
	Rotenone	Botanical broad-spectrum contact and stomach-poison insecticide; derived from South American cube plant	Aphids, beetles (asparagus, Colorado potato, cucumber, flea, Japanese, Mexican bean), cabbage loopers, corn earworms, European corn borers, leafhoppers, mites, spider mites, stink bugs, thrips, whiteflies	Dust; wettable powder; liquid concentrate, usually with pyrethrin	Dust: 2-3 years; liquid: 3 years or more
	Sabadilla	Botanical broad-spectrum contact insecticide; derived from a South American lily	Aphids, armyworms, beetles (Colorado potato, cucumber, flea, Mexican bean), cabbage loopers, caterpillars, diamondback moth larvae, European corn borers, grasshoppers, leafhoppers, squash bugs, stink bugs, thrips	Dust; wettable powder	5 years or more
FUNGICIDES	Copper	Mineral fungicide and surface protectant	Anthracnose, bacterial leaf spot, black rot, blights, downy mildews, leaf spot, powdery mildews, rusts, scabs	Dust; wettable powder; liquid concentrate	Up to 5 years
	Lime sulfur	Mineral fungicide, insecticide	Anthracnose, brown rot, leaf spot, powdery mildews, rusts, scabs	Liquid concentrate	3-5 years. Keep from freezing.
	Sulfur, elemental sulfur	Mineral fungicide, surface protectant, miticide	Black spot, botrytis molds, brown rot, leaf spot, powdery mildews, rusts, scabs	Dust; wettable powder; liquid concentrate; ready-to-use spray	Dust and powder—indefinite; concentrate and spray—3 years

TOXICITY	WHEN & HOW OFTEN TO APPLY	HOW SOON EFFECTIVE	EFFECTIVE PERIOD/ BIODEGRADABILITY	TIME NEEDED BETWEEN LAST USE & HARVEST	COMMENTS & PRECAUTIONS
Low. Harmless to mammals, fish, and nontarget insects.	Spring and summer, when pest is actively feeding. Reapply every 10-14 days if necessary and after rain.	Feeding stops within 1 hour of ingesting; pest dies in 1-3 days.	Short. Ineffective if ingested more than 48 hours after application.	No restrictions	Different strains of Bt are effective against different pests, so read label carefully. Avoid inhaling when applying because of possible allergic reaction.
Nontoxic	When soil is very moist and soil temperature is over 60°F. Single application may be effective up to 1 year.	Nematodes begin feeding on pests within 24-48 hours.	Feeding continues until food source is exhausted.	No restrictions	Follow storage and mixing directions very carefully. Spray or pour directly onto moist soil in the root zone of affected plants. Nematodes need constantly moist soil to survive.
Nontoxic to humans, mammals, birds, and earthworms; harmful to beneficial insects and bees	When plants are still wet from dew, rain, or watering; reapply after every watering, rainfall, or heavy dew.	Within 48 hours	Works as long as it remains dry.	No restrictions	Eye and lung irritant; avoid breathing dust, and wear mask and goggles. Use only natural DE, not pool-filter grade, which is much more toxic.
Very low for mammals; beneficials in larval stage may be harmed.	Use weekly in spring and summer when pests or eggs are present and temperature is between 40° and 85°F.	Kills newly hatched insects within a day; smothers eggs to prevent hatching.	Continues working until it dries.	1 month	Use only the lighter-grade horticultural oils for vegetable crops and brambles. The heavier-grade dormant oils are for use on dormant plants only and will burn vegetable crops.
Virtually nontoxic to humans, mammals, and birds; larvae of beneficials may be affected, but not adults.	Every 7-10 days when pest is present. Spray three times at 2-day intervals for severe aphid or mealybug infestation.	Immediately on contact	Breaks down quickly; effective only while still moist.	No restrictions	Works only when wet spray contacts insect. Do not apply in direct sun or when the temperature is above 85°F. To avoid damage to plants, do not use at concentrations higher than recommended. Not effective if mixed with hard water.
Active ingredient very low, but stabilizers make it harmful if swallowed. May affect beneficials in juvenile stages.	Every 7-10 days when pest larvae are present, or as needed to repel adults	Death occurs in 3-14 days.	Lasts up to 7 days; breaks down rapidly in sunlight.	No restrictions	Lung, skin, and eye irritant
Highly toxic to fish, aquatic insects, and some beneficials. Moderately toxic to mammals, birds, and bees.	When pest is present. Can be repeated at 3- to 4-day intervals.	Within 2 hours of direct contact	Broken down within 1 day by sunlight, air, moisture, and heat	No restrictions	A pest is killed only when hit directly. If it receives an inadequate dose, it may appear dead at first, then revive. Do not confuse natural pyrethrins with the synthetic compounds called pyrethroids.
Garlic oil has low toxicity; hot pepper is an extreme eye and skin irritant.	Before pests begin feeding. Apply garlic twice each season. Reapply pepper spray after rain or overhead watering.	Immediate	Both break down rapidly.	Garlic: 1 day. Hot pepper: No interval needed, since spray should never be applied to edible portion of crops.	These sprays may kill some pests, but their main effect is to repel them and deter them from feeding. Protect eyes while mixing and using hot pepper spray.
Very toxic to fish, aquatic insects, birds, beneficial insects; moderately toxic to humans, mammals	When pest populations cause unacceptable damage. Reapply in 7 days if necessary.	Pests quickly stop feeding and die within several hours to a few days.	Breaks down in 2-7 days.	5-7 days unless label recommends otherwise	Avoid using near ponds, streams, or wherever runoff may contaminate bodies of water. Avoid inhaling.
Moderately toxic to humans, mammals, bees	When pest populations are excessive or as soon as eggs hatch, at 5- to 7-day intervals and after rain or overhead watering	Pest may be killed immediately or be paralyzed for several days before dying.	Breaks down in 2 days when exposed to sunlight and air.	1 day	Sneezing is sign of overexposure to skin or lungs. Wear mask, goggles, and protective clothing. Sale and use not permitted in some states.
Moderately toxic to humans and mammals; little risk to insects	Before disease appears; apply every 7-10 days.	Regular treatments needed to prevent disease or slow spread of existing disease.	Does not degrade; can build up in soil, causing toxicity to plants.	1 day	Liquid concentrate may settle; shake well. Spray early on dry, sunny day. Copper hydroxide will burn leaves in damp weather and may leave visible residue. Wash produce well before eating.
Very high to fish. Caustic and corrosive.	Once a year in early spring while plants are dormant is usually sufficient. If needed, reapply in fall as a preventive.	Immediate; lasts several weeks.	2 or more weeks	Not applicable; used before or after growing season.	Use only in cold weather on dormant raspberries, blackberries, and other bramble fruits. May burn some varieties. Wait 2-3 weeks after using oil spray to apply lime sulfur.
Low toxicity for humans, mammals. May be harmful to bees.	Early in spring and as needed for protection; when rain is forecast to protect against waterborne disease spores.	Use as preventive or to slow spread of existing disease.	Does not break down; naturally present in soil and required by plants for normal growth.	1 day	Do not use on squash family. Repeated applications may acidify soil. Do not apply when temperature is over 85°F. Lung, eye, and skin irritant. Corrosive; wash metal sprayer after each use. Never use within a month of applying horticultural oil.

Reaping the Harvest

By late summer all your hard work has helped to transform a handful of seeds into a generous and lush cornucopia. This is the season of reward—the time to savor delicious, fresh-picked ripe vegetables. It's also the time for a new beginning, when you plant crops to harvest in the cool months ahead, like the cabbages, lettuce, beets, broccoli, and kohlrabi shown basking in the golden fall sunlight of the New Jersey garden at left.

On the following pages you will learn how to judge when various vegetables are ready to be picked and how to store them so that you can continue to enjoy homegrown produce in winter. To extend the growing season into late fall and even into winter, you'll want to plant the cold-tolerant varieties recommended here, or protect late-maturing vegetables from damaging cold by using the techniques described on pages 83-86. The chapter closes with advice on mulching, leaf composting, and planting cover crops, which will rebuild the soil and ensure a healthy growing environment for the coming year.

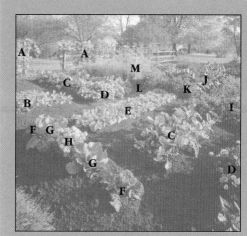

A. 'Concord' grape
B. 'Grand Duke' kohlrabi
C. 'Lutz Winter Keeper' beet
D. Marigold (Tagetes 'Yellow Sophia')
E. 'Buttercrunch' lettuce
F. 'Savoy Ace' cabbage
G. 'Early Jersey Wakefield' cabbage
H. Chrysanthemum (Chrysanthemum 'Best Regards')
I. Marigold (Tagetes 'Orange Boy O'Boy')
J. 'Green Comet' broccoli
K. Scarlet sage (Salvia splendens 'Carabiniere Scarlet')
L. 'Champion' collards
M. 'Zefa Fino' fennel

Please refer to the key at right to identify the plants in the garden shown.

Gathering and Storing Vegetables

Knowing when and how to pick vegetables helps safeguard their flavor, texture, and nutritional value. To be sure you pick at the optimal time, keep track of the expected dates of maturity for your crops and begin checking them for ripeness approximately 1 week earlier. Remember that ripening may be hastened or delayed depending upon the weather, the condition of the soil, and the effects of pests and diseases.

Determining Ripeness

Fruiting vegetables tend to deepen in color and develop a gloss or sheen as they ripen; then, as the vegetables age, their skin becomes dull. Exceptions to this rule include most eggplant cultivars, which do not change color, and the rinds of water-melons, which look dull when ripe. Root crops often protrude slightly from the soil when mature, and the foliage becomes somewhat dry and flattened. Leafy crops like lettuce can be harvested and eaten at any time, but will become bitter if they begin to bolt (produce flowers or seeds). Note also that many vegetables can be eaten before they are fully mature, with a marked difference in taste and texture. To decide what you like best, sample vegetables at different stages of growth.

Within these guidelines, a hands-on approach is the best way to determine ripeness. Gently press tomatoes to see if they are softening, feel along the shoulders of root vegetables to check their size, or pull a carrot to taste. In time, you will be able to tell when your crops are ripe and, perhaps more important, you will be able to harvest at the stage of maturity and flavor you prefer for each vegetable.

ROOT VEGETABLES FROM FALL TO SPRING
Carrots from a late planting in this garden have been pulled for fall eating. A mulch laid down later in the season will protect the remaining roots so that they can be harvested throughout the winter. Planted behind the carrots are Egyptian onions that overwinter in the ground and mature the following year.

TIPS FROM THE PROS
Crop-by-Crop Harvesting Techniques

Asparagus—Begin harvesting after one season of growth. Choose firm, tightly closed spears 4 to 8 inches high. Snap spears off or cut with a dandelion digger slightly below ground level.

Beans—Harvest every 2 to 3 days to keep plants productive. Pick shell beans when the pod is plump and full, green beans when small and tender, and dry beans when they rattle in the pod.

Carrots—If root tops are above ground, harvest before a hard freeze. Loosen soil alongside the row with a garden fork and gently pull on the leaves just above the root. For easier pulling, water beforehand to soften soil.

Corn—Pick when the ears are plump and full and the cornsilk is brown. To test for ripeness, make a small slit in the husk and press a kernel with your fingernail. The kernel will spurt milky fluid if ripe. To pick, hold the main stalk in one hand and pull down and twist the ear with the other hand.

Lettuce—Cut individual leaves of loose-leaved varieties as needed 1 inch above the ground. Cut butterhead and romaine lettuce when the heads are firm and full.

Onions—Harvest scallions when green leaves are 12 inches tall. Dig bulb onions when leaves turn brown and begin to fall over. To increase storage life, stop watering bulb onions a week before digging.

Peppers—Begin picking sweet peppers as soon as they are large enough to be usable. Cut stems 1 inch from the fruit with a sharp knife or pruning shears. Most sweet peppers become sweeter as they mature.

Potatoes—Dig new potatoes when vines begin to flower. For mature potatoes, dig when stems and leaves turn brown. Carefully loosen soil with a spading fork 2 feet from the plant's center. Work the fork toward the plant and slide it under the tubers so you can lift them without piercing them.

Squash—Harvest before the first frost. Most kinds of summer squash are ready to pick when fruits are 4 to 6 inches long and skins are still soft. Winter squash is ready when a fingernail cannot dent the rind and the stem is dry and woody. With a sharp knife or pruning shears, cut off winter squash at the juncture of stem and vine. Leave the stem attached and handle carefully.

Tomatoes—Pick when evenly colored and firm. To ripen at room temperature, pick when the color is just beginning to develop. Twist fruit off gently; pulling may damage or uproot the plant.

Timely Harvest

Most crops respond to frequent picking by producing more vegetables. As a result you get more vegetables onto the table, or into storage, while they are at their prime. As a rule of thumb, you cannot overpick a fruiting crop once it begins to bear mature vegetables. Root crops are usually once-only harvest plants, but you can enjoy a more sustained yield if you plant and thin a plot in stages. Leafing vegetables can be harvested as soon as the leaves form, but picking more than a third of a plant's leaves at one time can retard productivity.

Diligent and timely harvesting can be critical for many crops. For example, cucumbers, peas, beans, and summer squash plants will quit producing altogether if the vegetables are not picked as soon as they ripen. Some vegetables, such as winter squash, pumpkins, and root crops, must be

A Double Harvest from Cabbage and Broccoli

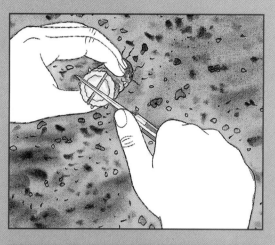

To encourage another crop from a cabbage plant that has a mature head ready for harvesting, cut off the head with a sharp knife at a point about an inch above the soil. Hold the stem firmly as you cut but do not tug on it so that the roots won't be disturbed. Then carve an X in the cut surface of the stub (left). Within a few weeks, the stub will sprout several small cabbageheads (left, below).

For a second harvest of broccoli, remove the first central head the plant produces by using a sharp knife to cut through the stem about 4 inches below the head (left); take care not to pull on the plant and disturb the roots. Several small side shoots will subsequently develop around the stub at the plant's center (left, below). Continue cutting the side shoots as they mature to encourage production.

allowed to mature fully; otherwise they will not keep well in storage.

Also, crops vary in their ability to retain flavor after ripening. Steady picking and prompt eating, drying, canning, or freezing is essential for tasty tomatoes, peas, beans, peppers, corn, cucumbers, and summer squash. Other vegetables, such as potatoes, carrots, onions, and winter squash, can be harvested in a more leisurely manner.

In general, harvesting is best done in the early morning because vegetables gathered before the sun warms them are less susceptible to spoilage and wilt. You should also try to harvest on clear, cool days when the foliage is dry. That way you can avoid inadvertently spreading disease-causing fungi and bacteria, which travel in water particles, to other plants. When bad weather is predicted, harvest tender crops that might be damaged by hard rain, wind, or hail.

Tools and Containers

A gentle hand at harvest time will contribute greatly to the quality of your produce. Tearing vegetable stems and yanking fruits from vines can damage and uproot plants, decreasing or eliminating further yield from those plants. To handpick properly, support the plant with one hand and carefully take off the vegetables with the other.

As an alternative to handpicking, certain tools can make the process of separating vegetables from plants simpler, quicker, and less traumatic for both the plant and the produce. Utility knives help prevent damage to roots when gathering vegetables that form heads, such as cabbage and broccoli. Knives or pruning shears cut cleanly through the heavy stems of tomatoes, eggplants, bell peppers, pumpkins, squash, cucumbers, and okra. Scissors are useful for harvesting leafy crops like lettuce, whereas digging tools are essential for extricating root vegetables that are embedded in the ground or growing in soil that is hard and dry.

Have on hand a variety of clean, dry containers for sorting and carrying vegetables. Place soft, fleshy vegetables that bruise easily in shallow containers with flat bottoms. Plastic buckets, crates, bushel baskets, and laundry baskets work well for firmer vegetables.

Washing the Vegetables

Cleaning the crop is important for prolonging storage life and for retaining flavor, texture, and nutritional value. And although you are unlikely to have

exposed your organic garden to dangerous chemicals, even low-toxicity organic pesticides must be thoroughly washed away before you consume the food. Cleaning not only removes dirt and other unwanted substances, in some cases it also actually helps to preserve freshness. Greens, for instance, will quickly dry out unless they are rinsed in cool water, dried, and placed in an unsealed plastic bag before refrigeration. Be sure they are thoroughly dried before storage, since water droplets may harbor fungus spores that cause rot.

Vegetables grown on trellises or covered with floating row covers do not typically require much cleaning. Similarly, vegetables whose edible parts are protected by thick skins, husks, or pods do not usually need to be washed if the exterior covering will be discarded. Vegetables to be stored, such as root crops, should simply be wiped off with a

SOAKING UP THE SUN
These winter squash and pumpkins will sit in a sunny window for a week or so to toughen their skins and reduce their moisture content. After their period of sunning, they will keep all winter if stored in a dry, airy place at 50 °F.

clean, dry cloth. Dip winter squash and pumpkins (including stems) in a solution of 1 part bleach to 10 parts water to kill surface bacteria and fungi.

Planning for Storage

Preparation for storage begins in the garden. Many of the cold-hardy plants, such as root vegetables, cabbage, onions, and winter squash, will last until spring if properly stored. When choosing varieties for your fall garden, look for traditional "good keepers" such as 'Long Season' beets, 'Yellow Globe' onions, and 'Kennebec' potatoes. To increase their storage life, do not fertilize vegetables for about a month before harvesting, since vegetables growing in soil whose nitrogen content is high late in the season tend to keep poorly. Likewise, withhold water for a month before harvesting, otherwise the vegetables' tissues will be watery and more likely to spoil quickly.

All the produce you store should be free of blemishes. Even small breaks in a vegetable's skin can open the way to the bacteria and fungi responsible for rot.

Curing enhances the storage life of these vegetables. By drying and hardening the skin, shell, or rind, you protect the inner flesh from bacteria and fungi. Pumpkins and winter squash should be cured in a sunny room for 7 to 10 days. Most root vegetables need only a few days in a well-ventilated, warm, sunny room before storing. Potatoes, however, should be dried for 2 weeks in an area protected from the sun; in direct light, a toxin that turns the skins greenish often develops.

Leeks in the Basement

Even though few homes today have root cellars, it is easy to adapt an area of your home for short-term storage. (For vegetables that prefer drier air and warmer temperatures, such as winter squash and pumpkins, an attic or spare room makes a good storage area.) Root vegetables such as beets, carrots, leeks, and turnips keep best at temperatures of 32° to 40° F and can be stored in sheds, garages, porches, barns, or window wells for up to a month after harvest. For longer storage, these vegetables need an area that mimics their underground growing environment—cool temperatures and high humidity. You can experiment with converting a corner of an unheated basement into a root cellar. Mount a humidity meter and thermometer in the area (see the chart on page 82 for the ideal temperatures and humidity levels). Place

Storing Onions and Garlic

For onions and garlic that will keep all winter, select late-maturing types with thin necks and, if you plan to braid and hang them, long, strong stems. Gently dig the vegetables and brush off any soil. If the weather is dry, place the bulbs outdoors in a lightly shaded area; otherwise, choose an airy, dry shelter such as a carport. Spread the bulbs on wire mesh set on a support so that air can circulate on all sides. When the outer skins are dry and brittle and the stems have withered, the bulbs are ready to store. Either braid the stems together for hanging or cut them off an inch above the bulbs and put the onions and garlic in mesh bags or other airy containers. For best results, store in a dry area at 36° F.

TECHNIQUES FOR A LONG STORAGE LIFE

CROP	TEMP./ HUMIDITY	STORAGE LIFE	COMMENTS
Beets	32° F; 95%	2-5 months	Clip tops to 1 inch and layer in boxes with sawdust, sand, or peat moss in a basement or other cool, humid area. Can also be left in ground and dug up as needed.
Cabbage	32° F; 90%	2-4 months	Store in separate area due to strong odor. Cut off damaged or rotten leaves. Wrap heads in paper or layer in straw and store in basement or other cool, humid area.
Carrots	32° F; 95%	4-5 months	Cut off tops and layer in boxes with moist sand or sawdust and store in a basement or other cool, humid area. In mild climates carrots can be overwintered in the garden.
Potatoes	40° F; 90%	3-8 months	Harvest before the first hard freeze. Potatoes that have been frozen will rot in storage. After curing, pack loosely in well-ventilated boxes or mesh bags and store in a dark, cool, humid area such as a basement.
Winter squash	50° F; 60%	3-8 months	Store unblemished high-quality fruits only in a warm, dry area such as an attic or unheated spare room. Check often for signs of mold or spoilage and promptly remove damaged fruits.

vegetables in well-ventilated containers such as mesh bags, baskets, or slatted wooden boxes, or hang them in braids and bunches. Open outside vents or windows periodically to let in cool air on fall nights. If your basement is dry, sprinkle water on the floor as needed. If you have trouble maintaining humidity levels, pack root vegetables in damp sand or sawdust to help them stay crisp.

Root vegetables can also be stored outdoors in a cold frame. To protect the frame from wind, place it adjacent to the foundation of your house or garage. Layer the produce in loose, clean straw or sawdust surrounded with rodentproof wire mesh. For extra protection against cold, stack hay bales around the frame and cover the top with several layers of heavy canvas and a final layer of straw.

Even though you have stored only the highest-quality produce, check regularly for signs of spoilage. Promptly remove any vegetable that has gone bad along with the hay or sawdust immediately around it. As a precaution, wipe off adjacent vegetables with a dry cloth and, if necessary, add clean sawdust or straw around the remainder.

Saving Seed

Gathering seed was a standard gardening task before the proliferation of seed companies in the 19th century. Although the seeds of premium hybrids may not reproduce or may revert to one of the parent types, collecting seed is a fairly simple process and is especially worthwhile if you are growing unusual varieties that may be difficult to obtain elsewhere.

Harvesting your own seeds also lets you develop varieties that are suited to your particular garden and tastes. When choosing plants for seed, look for specimens that are healthy and that epitomize the variety's best features. Over time, you can have a hand in improving the quality of your vegetables by collecting seed from plants that perform in your garden with exceptional yield, flavor, keeping quality, or resistance to pests and diseases.

Determining when to harvest vegetables for seed will depend upon what type of crops you are using for seed collection. In general, you will be gathering two types of seeds—wet and dry. Tomatoes, cucumbers, squash, and melons bear fleshy fruit and wet seeds. To collect seed from these plants, wait till the fruit is slightly overripe, then pick it and remove the seeds. Dry seeds are harvested from crops such as beans, peas, and corn. These should be left to mature several weeks past their prime before picking for seed collection.

The next step in seed collection is cleaning. To clean fleshy fruits, scoop the seeds into a strainer, rinse with cool water, and dry on paper towels for a week or two. Seeds in pods can be shelled and spread to dry on a wire-mesh screen in a well-ventilated room.

Once they are thoroughly dry, the seeds of most kinds of vegetables can be stored in glass jars or in cans with tightfitting plastic lids in a cool, dry area of your home. Do not use plastic bags and containers because they may be permeable to air, thus exposing the seeds to moisture and reducing their viability. Beans and peas, however, need different handling because they are susceptible to fungus if stored in airtight containers. Keep them instead in small cloth bags or paper envelopes. As a preventive measure, you can give seeds a light sprinkling of silica gel. This desiccant, sold at craft stores, hardware stores, and camera supply shops, will absorb moisture and keep the seeds dry.

A Garden for All Seasons

Extending a vegetable garden's growing season is challenging but well worth the effort. By either protecting plants to encourage their maturation early or late in the season or planting cold-tolerant vegetables for harvesting in fall and winter, you will be bringing along crops during the months when cold weather would usually kill them. Since every garden is a unique combination of soil, climate, cultivars, and growing methods, you should experiment with various techniques for lengthening your garden's period of productivity.

Protecting Your Plants

Simple cold frames, row covers, and plant caps or cloches can help maintain a consistent microclimate, protecting crops from the damage inflicted by frost, wind chill, and sudden dips in temperature. By trapping solar energy, cold frames will extend your season a month or more at each end. Cloches and row covers aren't as efficient but can still add several weeks of growing time, allowing you to harvest warm-weather crops like tomatoes, peppers, and cucumbers even after the first frost.

Expect to try several kinds of protection—what works in your garden one year may not be as effective during a season that is unusually cold (or warm). When choosing the degree of protection you want, keep in mind that the more complicated and comprehensive the method the more maintenance and upkeep it demands—and even the simplest methods will require periodic monitoring. Some protective devices you can build yourself, or you can purchase readymade equipment through specialized mail-order catalogs.

Cozy Cloches

Cloches, small caps that protect a single plant or a few closely spaced small ones, can be either made or purchased to fit different crops. The first cloches were bell-shaped glass jars used in 17th-century French market gardens. Today, you can choose from a variety of lightweight, portable cloches made of wax paper, plastic, glass, and polyethylene tubes filled with water *(page 35)*. You can also make cloches by recycling household articles such as gallon-sized plastic milk jugs with the bottoms cut out and the caps removed. To keep milk-jug cloches from blowing away, insert a slim stake

FENDING OFF FROST
Polyethylene spread on a wire frame keeps a crop of greens warm on a frosty fall morning (foreground). When the day warms up, the plastic can be folded back lengthwise along the row to admit light and prevent overheating. In the background, a floating row cover of lightweight spunbonded fabric is draped directly over the plants.

beside the growing plant and set the jug over the plant, with the stake protruding from its mouth.

Cone-shaped cloches can be constructed from sheets of fiberglass-reinforced plastic. Cut the material into a semicircle, pull the straight edges together, and staple them to form a cone. These cloches can be made in a wide range of sizes to fit your crops and will last for a number of years. The hole on top of the cone provides some ventilation, although on warmer days you may need to remove the cloche altogether.

A tomato cage can be easily adapted for use as a cloche. Set the tomato cage over the plant and wrap it with clear plastic, taping the overlap to hold it in place. On cold nights drape a second piece of plastic over the top and secure it with tape.

Plants covered with a cloche should be monitored closely to avoid overheating and moisture buildup. You can cut slits in the cloche for ventilation, and you should periodically remove it, especially on warm days.

Hardworking Row Covers

Row covers are one of the most effective and practical season extenders. When frost threatens, you can quickly and easily install row covers over a single row or an entire section of your garden.

Floating row covers made of spunbonded poly-

IMPROVISED SHELTERS
In the garden above, a cold frame made of cinder blocks and castoff windows is open on a warm day to prevent the lettuce crop from overheating. At left, corrugated fiberglass covers a row of greens, while plastic milk jugs with the bottoms removed keep single plants snug.

A DOORSTEP GREENHOUSE
A cylinder of reinforced plastic tied around the whiskey-barrel planter at left blocks the wind and creates a warm environment for leaf lettuce. The house wall and the paving on which the planter is set absorb heat during the day and continue to radiate it after the sun goes down.

ester can be placed directly over plants without a supporting structure. These fabric covers allow water, air, and sunlight to penetrate to the plants beneath while offering about 4 degrees of frost protection to around 28° F. If winds threaten, you can bury the edges of the covers in the soil or weight them down with rocks. Floating row covers come in rolls of various sizes and are sold at most garden stores or through specialty catalogs.

Another material commonly used for row covers is transparent polyethylene plastic. It is too heavy to lay directly on plants, however, and must be supported by wire, PVC pipes, or wood arches. A polyethylene row cover offers a greater degree of frost protection than a row cover of spunbonded fabric, but it needs more frequent monitoring than the fabric cover to prevent overheating and excessive humidity; on a sunny day, the temperature beneath a plastic row cover may be 20° F higher than the air outside. On warm days you'll need to fold half the polyethylene sheet back lengthwise to increase air circulation and moderate the temperature. You can also buy polyethylene that has been slitted to allow for good circulation, but it will provide less frost protection than a solid sheet.

Cold Frames, Warm Plants

With a cold frame set in your vegetable garden, you can overwinter ready-to-harvest frost-tolerant crops or seedlings that will remain dormant dur-

ing the cold months, then resume growth the following spring. You can either buy a cold frame or build it yourself out of lumber. For a makeshift cold frame, simply arrange concrete blocks or bales of hay in a rectangle around the plants and use a sheet of glass, an old window sash, or heavy clear plastic as a lid, slanting it slightly to prevent water from collecting. When cold nights threaten, cover the lid with thick canvas, old blankets, or several layers of hay.

Regulating the Cold Frame's Climate

Cold frames require daily monitoring. Early in the fall, steady sun can quickly dry out and damage plants grown under glass or plastic. Check your cold frame each day, watering as necessary to keep the soil slightly moist.

You must also be diligent about monitoring the temperature inside the cold frame. Sudden temperature changes damage plants and can cause wilting or retard growth. If daytime temperatures reach 60° F or more, raise the lid or remove it and replace it at night when the temperature falls. At an outside temperature of 40° F, the lid should be propped open only a few inches and closed again at night. The need to vent the cold frame will decrease as the season advances toward winter.

If you discover that manually opening and closing the cold frame is a chore you'd rather do with-

out, you can buy a thermostatic device that automatically opens and closes the lid as needed. Many prefabricated cold frames come equipped with such a device.

Hardy Plants for Cold Weather

With planning and care you can have a thriving cold-weather garden, one that will yield fresh vegetables long after the normal season has ended. Many crops that perform well in cool spring weather and are harvested in summer can be planted a second time for a fall harvest. In general, vegetables that grow best in cool weather are leafy greens and root crops. When choosing cultivars for harvesting in the cooler temperatures and shorter days of fall and winter, look for characteristics such as cold hardiness and a short time to maturity. Some good candidates for the late-season garden are listed on page 85.

Timing is critical in planning the autumn garden, and it may take a season or two of trial and error to determine the best time to begin your fall plantings. Keep in mind that your goal is to schedule plantings so that crops will be mature when winter arrives, a date that will vary with your particular climate. Shorter days and colder soil and air temperatures will increase the time required to reach maturity by 20 to 40 percent. You will be able to extend your harvest by continuing to plant at 1- to 2-week intervals until approximately 6 weeks before the first frost date for your region.

Some of the cultivation practices you use during other seasons will need to be modified to suit the fall garden's special conditions. The following are among the most important things to remember:

• Seedlings should be well thinned and plants should be spaced slightly farther apart than in spring and summer gardens to allow greater exposure to the sun.

• You may need to shade fall seedlings from the late-summer sun. You can buy black polyethylene-mesh shade cloth from a garden center or hardware store or improvise your own sun protection from old window screens or open snow fencing supported on cement blocks.

• Frequent irrigation of newly planted crops will be necessary if your area typically receives little rain in late summer and early fall.

And finally, try using a diluted seaweed spray on your crops for a few weeks before the first frost date. This will raise mineral levels in the leaf tissue and help prevent freezing.

Mulched Lettuce

Tips and Techniques for a Long Season

Beets—Sow outside about 10 weeks before the average first frost date. Pick mature beets before the first hard freeze. Harvest immature beets in autumn or mulch heavily to overwinter.

Broccoli—Sow seed directly by mid-July in colder climates and by August in milder ones. Protect with floating row covers. Some cultivars can withstand temperatures below freezing as long as the weather is evenly cool. Grow all winter where temperatures remain above 40° F.

Brussels sprouts—Sow in succession for harvesting from early fall to late spring. Cold-hardy cultivars survive temperatures as low as 14° F. Freezing temperatures enhance flavor.

Cabbage—Set out cold-hardy transplants no earlier than 10 to 12 weeks before the first frost.

Carrots—Mulch with 8 to 12 inches of hay before the ground freezes. Dig all winter.

Cauliflower—Plant in time for it to mature in cool weather, but before the first frost. Or, plant frost-tolerant cultivars like 'White Sails' and protect with floating row covers.

Celeriac—Mound soil around plants and mulch heavily to continue harvest into the winter. Grow as a winter crop in mild climates.

Chard—After the first frost, protect with floating row covers or mulch deeply to extend the harvest into winter. Plant as a winter crop in a cold frame.

Garlic—Plant 2 to 4 weeks before the first frost for harvest the following summer.

Leeks—Harvest cold-hardy cultivars such as 'Blue Solaise' all winter in areas where temperatures stay above 10° F. Pull the last of the leeks before seed stalks appear in the spring.

Lettuce—Sow leaf lettuce at least 7 weeks before the first frost and heading types 10 weeks before; mulch heavily to insulate soil. Cold-hardy cultivars can be overwintered in cold frames or under row covers in mild climates.

Onions—Some varieties, including Egyptian onions and 'Walla Walla', can be overwintered with a thick layer of mulch in mild climates or in a cold frame in severe climates. For an early spring crop of shallots in cold climates, plant after the first frost. If planted earlier, they may send up top growth that would be damaged by winter cold.

Spinach—Plant hardy cultivars such as 'Winter Bloomsdale' about a month before the first frost. Sow in late winter in a cold frame for an early spring crop.

Putting the Garden to Bed

As the harvest season winds down and your garden turns from green to gold, there are still a few chores to be done. Putting the garden properly to bed can yield a substantial payoff in the form of earlier, healthier spring produce. Sowing cover crops such as alfalfa and winter rye will protect your beds from erosion and compaction of the soil as well as provide nutrients when they are tilled under in the spring. A clean winter garden will be less likely to harbor pests and weeds, and soil that is cultivated, fertilized, and mulched will save you valuable time and labor when planting season comes.

Cleaning and Storing Tools and Equipment

Proper storage of garden equipment prolongs its life and can also help to protect next year's garden from disease. Tools, stakes, trellises, tags, and cages should be removed from the garden and cleaned. If any of the equipment has been used near diseased or infested plants, dip it in a disinfecting solution of 1 part bleach to 10 parts water. Wipe down the metal parts of tools with mineral oil to prevent rust, and sharpen dull blades. Drain and store hoses and irrigation systems.

Remove and store sheets of plastic mulch, or recycle them if they are damaged. Carefully check cold frames for cracks and make sure that the lids fit snugly. Even a small leak can expose plants to damaging cold.

Dealing with Garden Debris

Garden debris is a favorite winter home for many harmful insects, which attach eggs, cocoons, or larvae to the stems and leaves of dried and faded plants. By cleaning out your garden beds now, you will help eliminate pest and disease problems next season.

Before the ground freezes in the fall, clear your garden of all vegetation except cover crops and overwintering or perennial vegetables such as asparagus, rhubarb, and Jerusalem artichokes. Do not leave any vegetables to rot lest you encourage insect infestation. Weeding is especially critical at this time as well, since fall is when many perennial weeds establish deep root systems and prodigiously set seed. Be thorough in your weeding—

pull out all foliage, seed heads, stems, and roots. Weeds left in the fall garden will return with renewed vigor in the spring.

Carefully dispose of mature weed seed heads and plants that show signs of disease or insect infestation, putting the debris in a tightly sealed bag and discarding according to your local ordinances for green trash.

If you notice signs of insects or diseases on your plants as you clear the garden, consult the troubleshooting guide on pages 94-99, a reputable nursery, or your local Cooperative Extension Service office for an analysis of the problem and possible solutions.

MAKING THE BEDS
Fertilized, cultivated, and mulched in fall, these raised beds will be ready for spring planting weeks earlier than a slower-to-thaw plot at ground level would be. The two smaller beds at the rear are an ideal size for accommodating temporary cold frames that can shelter the new season's first hardy crops.

Looking Ahead to Spring

If you cultivate your beds in the fall, you can plant as soon as the soil warms up in the spring. Fall is a good time to apply fertilizers that require longer periods to break down. Ground phosphate rock, greensand, and granite dust will slowly release potassium, phosphorus, and other nutrients if lightly spaded into the soil and left over the winter. Fresh manure can be applied directly to your beds at the rate of 2 to 3 bushels per 100 square feet. It will rot by the time you plant the following spring.

Autumn's Gift to Spring

The scattered leaves of autumn can be a true windfall for a vegetable garden's soil. Decomposed leaves are rich in potassium and micronutrients; also, they increase the soil's capacity to retain moisture. Nature will compost the leaves for you if you simply pile them in an enclosure, but this method may take several years. To hasten the process, shred the leaves with a mulching mower or a leaf shredder and add them to your compost pile *(page 13)*. Or, if you have more leaves than the compost pile can handle, make a separate mound of shredded leaves. To prevent snow and rain from leaching nutrients, cover the mound with a sheet of black polyethylene weighted down with rocks or bricks. In the spring, you will have a supply of dark, crumbly leaf compost to use as mulch or as a soil amendment.

Winter Mulch and Cover Crops

Mulch applied to the fall garden is another way of adding organic matter to the soil; it also prevents soil erosion and protects your maturing cold-hardy vegetables. Even if you mulched heavily during the growing season, the parts of your garden that are not planted with a cover crop will benefit from a thick layer of mulch in the fall. Shredded leaves, alfalfa hay, peat, straw, and buckwheat hulls are all good choices. For perennial vegetables, berries, and herbs, apply several inches of loose, airy mulch such as straw or pine needles after the soil freezes. This will protect their roots from the damaging effects of alternate freezing and thawing.

In cool climates, crops like carrots, leeks, garlic, parsnips, salsify, and turnips can be left for winter harvest if they are given a protective blanket of at least 6 inches of mulch in the fall. In areas with

READY, SET, GROW
The shallots planted in this raised bed in the fall will grow until cold weather arrives. Dormant over the winter months, the plants will resume growing in the spring and produce an early harvest.

A LIVING MULCH
A cover crop of winter rye sown in the paths beside rows of cold-hardy cabbage in this New Jersey garden quickly covers the soil. Sown in early fall, the rye controls weeds, prevents erosion, and contributes nutrients to the soil when it is tilled under in the spring.

SOIL - IMPROVING COVER CROPS			
COMMON NAME	SEEDING RATE (lbs./1,000 sq. ft.)	WHEN TO SOW	COMMENTS
Austrian winter pea	2-4	Early spring or early fall	Winter-hardy, nitrogen building. Provides organic matter when tilled under in the spring.
Barley	2½	Early to midfall	Extensive root system prevents erosion. Winter-hardy, provides organic matter when tilled under in the spring.
Crimson clover	1	Early spring through early fall	Good for erosion control and nitrogen building. Winter-hardy and shade tolerant; can be sown under upright vegetables such as corn.
Hairy vetch	1	Late summer to early fall	Winter-hardy, nitrogen building. Provides large amounts of organic matter when tilled under.
Ryegrass	1	Early spring to late summer	Quick growing, cold tolerant. Extensive root system loosens compacted soil, protects against erosion. Dense growth chokes out weeds. Dies back during the winter in the North. Easy to till under.
Winter rye	2½	Fall	Winter-hardy, vigorous grower in a variety of soils. Extensive root system adds organic matter to the soil. Good source of straw for mulch.

severer winters, cover the rows with bales of straw or at least a foot of mulch just before the first hard freeze. During winter thaws you can pull up the vegetables, making sure to harvest all of them before the next planting season.

Growing a crop specifically to nourish and reinvigorate the soil can benefit even the smallest garden. Such cover crops, as they are known, prevent erosion, choke out weeds, and keep the soil aerated. And when tilled under, these plants act as green manure—a high-powered nutrient and a soil conditioner. Your choice of a cover crop will vary depending upon the result desired for your specific garden. Deep-rooted plants such as alfalfa and clover bring up nutrients from deep in the ground to the topsoil; legumes add nitrogen to your garden; and winter rye protects against erosion and keeps down weeds.

To give your cover crop time to establish itself before winter, sow seeds directly among maturing fall vegetables or fill in bare spots. Clover, vetches, and winter peas lend themselves to interplanting with end-of-season crops. Quick-growing timothy or buckwheat can fill gaps between winter squash and pumpkin vines.

You can also reap the advantages of a cover crop throughout the growing season by planting one in the paths beside your raised beds. A low-growing variety such as Dutch white clover is especially suitable for this purpose. Clover will control weeds, lower soil temperature—which encourages root growth—and help to retain soil moisture.

Updating Your Journal

Finally, update your garden journal *(page 45)*. Make notes, record observations, and reflect on how well your garden served your needs. Were the beds spaced close enough for easy cultivation and harvesting? If not, you may want to redesign your garden plot. Did you have too many vegetables of one kind and not enough of another? Note which cultivars thrived in your garden, which didn't, and why. Record cultivation techniques and interplanting combinations that worked well. Indicate periods of unusual weather. If you spent hours watering by hand, consider installing a drip-irrigation system. If weeding overwhelmed you, next year you may want to try mulching with black plastic or solarizing the soil to kill weeds *(box, page 71)*. Record any pest or disease problems you may have had, how you solved them, and what steps need to be taken in the spring to avoid those problems. Floating row covers, beneficial insects, lures, traps, botanical insecticides, and disease- and pest-resistant cultivars can all be used as part of an organic approach to disease and pest management.

Reviewing the past growing season will give you a clearer sense of your own preferences as well as the particular needs of your garden. When you make next year's choices, you will have guidelines based on conditions prevailing in *your* plot—with its unique combination of soil, climate, cultivars, growing methods, and gardening style.

Answers to Common Questions

RAISED BED GARDENING

My father planted his garden in rows with good results, and I'm inclined to do the same thing. But nowadays everyone talks about raised beds. What are the advantages of raised beds?

The main advantages are that they are more productive and take less work than conventional row gardening. Because you prepare the soil intensively with organic matter and fertilizers *(pages 13-21)*, you can plant vegetables very closely, getting more crops from far less space than row gardening requires. As the leaves of the vegetables touch, they shade the soil and slow weed growth. Paths don't take up as much space in a raised-bed garden as they do when vegetables are planted in rows, so you don't have to spend as much time weeding and maintaining them.

I'm building a deck and have pressure-treated scrap wood left over. Can I use it as an edging material for raised beds, or would the chemicals used in the pressure treatment contaminate vegetables grown in the beds?

The chemicals used to pressure-treat wood are quite toxic and might very well contaminate your crops. For raised beds, use ordinary wood scrap or cheap grades of redwood, black locust, or other rot-resistant wood for longevity. You can also make raised beds without constructing edges *(pages 16-17)*. They really aren't needed except to improve appearance, although they may cut down on grasses creeping into the beds.

COMPOSTING AND SOIL CONDITIONING

Is there anything I shouldn't put into my compost pile?

Yes. Don't use domestic pet or human waste, since they may carry dangerous diseases or parasites. Don't use meat or meat scraps, which attract vermin and cause a stench as they decay. Don't compost diseased portions of plants that you've cut away; dispose of them with the household trash or by burning, if that is permitted in your area. Don't use coal ashes, as these contain toxic wastes; wood ashes in moderation are fine. Don't add any synthetic materials or chemicals or any plants that have been treated with herbicides or pesticides. And don't compost weeds that have set seed or you'll spread them around the garden when you use the compost. Manures, vegetable and fruit kitchen wastes, and nonseedy plant wastes are all fine.

What is sheet composting?

It's a fancy name for covering the soil with the same kinds of organic matter used in a compost pile and letting them decay slowly, without turning or watering. Sheet composting has two advantages: It adds organic matter that conditions the soil as it decays, and it acts as a mulch to keep weed growth down and the soil moist. Make sure the material contains no weed or other seeds; it won't be massive enough to heat up, so seeds will remain viable. On the downside, sheet-composted material may provide a breeding ground for slugs, pill bugs, earwigs, and other unwanted insects. It may also deplete the soil of nitrogen unless high-nitrogen materials such as farmyard manure are included.

Where's the best place to build my compost pile, in the shade or in the sun? And should I cover it with black plastic?

The best place for the pile is close to the garden so the hose reaches it and you don't have to carry the finished compost very far. A shady spot is probably best because the composting organic matter won't dry out as fast as it would in sun. Covering the pile with black plastic holds in moisture and keeps the temperature in the pile higher, so it decays faster. The plastic will also prevent hard rains from dissolving and leaching nutrients from the pile.

Whenever I put my kitchen wastes into the compost pile, raccoons, opossums, dogs, and who knows what else tear the pile apart to get at them. Is there a convenient way I can compost my kitchen wastes without having this problem?

An easy solution is to house special garbage-eating worms called red wigglers in a container that marauding animals can't get into and let them turn your kitchen scraps into compost. A sturdy wood box with a lid and a hardware-cloth bottom will serve nicely, or you can buy a plastic worm bin from a mail-order garden supply company, along with red wigglers.

I've tried making compost, but it doesn't heat up, and it smells bad. What's the problem?

It probably doesn't heat up because the pile doesn't have enough nitrogen-rich material such as fresh farm-animal manure. A pile that's layered with 3 or 4 parts of plant wastes to 1 part of fresh manure and is kept moist but not sopping wet will heat up. Your compost smells bad because little or no air is getting into the pile, and anaerobic bacteria are decomposing it. Rebuild it, adding manure and layering in straw, pine needles, or other coarse materials to get air into the pile. Aerobic bacteria will continue to decompose the pile, but it will not smell bad.

My soil is very acid, and I need to raise its pH from 5 to at least 6.5. What's the organic way to do this?

Two substances that are especially good at raising a soil's pH are leached wood ashes and ground limestone. Wood ashes work faster, but ground limestone sweetens the soil over a longer period of time. Use 10 pounds of limestone or 2 pounds of wood ashes per 100 square feet, worked into the top 6 inches of soil, to raise the pH 1 point. Don't raise it more than 1 point per year. If you use 10 pounds per 100 square feet this year and 5 pounds next year, your soil pH will increase 1.5 points to reach your target level.

PROPAGATING, PLANTING, AND FERTILIZING

Is rooting hormone—the kind you use to stimulate root formation on cuttings—organic?

Yes. Rooting hormones are naturally occurring plant substances and are perfectly all right to use in an organic garden. Cuttings from sweet potato vines should be dipped in rooting hormone before planting, and you can also dip root cuttings from small bush fruits such as currants to stimulate rooting. Gardeners in areas with long growing seasons can also use the hormone to root stem cuttings of their early eggplant, tomato, and pepper crops for subsequent plantings.

Is companion planting—putting beans and onions side by side because they like each other—a valid organic technique or an old wives' tale?

Companion planting is a valid technique, but not because plants "like" each other. It works for one of several reasons: because the companions have different needs and thus don't compete with one another for nutrients; because their root zones are at different levels and their roots don't compete for space; or because one of the companions helps protect the other from predatory insects.

What is manure tea and how do I use it?

Manure tea is one of the secrets to success in an organic garden. Put 1 gallon of fresh, rotted, or dried farm-animal manure or manure-based compost in a burlap or muslin bag and close it securely (use poultry, goat, horse, or cow manure only). Put the bag in a 5-gallon bucket and fill it with water. Let the manure steep for 3 days to a week. Spray this manure tea onto growing plants every 3 to 4 days. It is especially helpful when they are growing rapidly or setting flowers or fruit. You'll be amazed at how well plants respond.

I know some organic gardeners who swear by foliar seaweed spray. Is there any value in this?

Yes. Foliar seaweed spray is an extract of seaweed containing many trace elements that are essential for vigorous growth in many plants. These nutrients can be absorbed through a plant's leaves as well as its roots, so regular application of foliar seaweed spray is certainly beneficial.

Is one kind of mulch better than another?

Organic gardeners use all sorts of materials to cover bare soil—black plastic, cardboard, leaves, shredded bark, compost, grass clippings that are free of pesticides and herbicides, farm-animal bedding, and spoiled hay are just a few of the possibilities. Even stones can serve as mulch if they cover the surface of the soil completely. For most situations it is best to use an organic mulch because it offers multiple benefits—suppressing weeds, conserving soil moisture, acting as a fertilizer, and decaying into soil-conditioning humus.

PESTS AND DISEASES

How can I attract beneficial insects into my garden?

Reserve a portion of the garden for whatever weeds volunteer there. Beneficial insects are adapted to the local flora, using it as a source of food, as hunting grounds for prey, and for shelter. Also, make sure you plant a number of umbelliferous plants in your garden—those whose flower heads look like Queen Anne's lace. Among them are fennel, carrot, and dill. These are nectar sources for several beneficials, including green lacewings. Finally, don't use pesticides. Beneficial insects are more susceptible to pesticides than pests and will be the first to be killed off.

I understand that rotenone, ryania, and sabadilla are all organically acceptable pesticides. Should I dust the garden routinely with them as a preventive?

No. Although these pesticides are derived from plants and are active for a comparatively short time, each of them kills a broad spectrum of insects and can do the same kind of ecological damage as chemical pesticides. The goal is not a garden free from pests—you simply want to keep their numbers to a manageable level. Try beneficial insects, the physical controls described in chapter 2, and other, less toxic methods of organic insect control before reaching for these pesticides. They should only be used as a last resort, and then only on a spot basis where a fierce outbreak of pests is under way.

I've heard that organic gardeners use homemade sprays containing hot chili peppers, garlic, or tobacco on their vegetables to ward off pests. Do they work?

Yes. Many insects won't go near a plant sprayed with these substances. But never use a tobacco spray on any vegetables of the nightshade family, which includes tomatoes, potatoes, and eggplant; tobacco is also a nightshade-family member and harbors a mosaic virus that can be spread to these crops by spraying.

I carefully start my plants from seed, then set them in the garden. Many times I find them snipped off just above the soil line, as if they were felled like little trees, but I haven't seen any pests chewing on their stems. What's causing this?

Your problem is almost certainly cutworms, grayish brown wormlike grubs that eat through the stems of tender seedlings. The reason you haven't seen them is that they feed at night and hide in the soil, under mulch, or in other sheltered places during the day. The answer is to put protective paper collars around your seedlings at planting time. The illustration on page 38 shows how to make these barriers, which are very effective.

I have tried growing broccoli several times, but something always eats tiny holes in the seedlings' leaves. What can I do about this?

Your problem is flea beetles—fast-moving little pests that eat shot holes in the leaves of many members of the cabbage family, including broccoli. Before setting out your seedlings, try planting early crops of radishes and mustard greens, which the flea beetles will attack. When these "trap crops" are full of beetles, pull the plants and destroy them. Next, place bright yellow commercial sticky traps or homemade traps *(pages 70-71)* every 10 feet in the space reserved for broccoli to attract and kill any remaining beetles. Then plant your seedlings.

Most years my strawberry plants get powdery mildew on their leaves. How can I prevent this organically?

Thin your plants to increase the flow of air between them, and pick off and destroy infected foliage. You can apply lime sulfur, available at garden centers, as directed on the package, or spray plants with a solution of 1 tablespoon of baking soda in a gallon of water; adding ⅛ to ¼ teaspoon of insecticidal soap will help the spray stick to the leaves. Don't increase the proportion of baking soda, as a higher concentration can damage leaves.

Here in the West, gophers are an awful problem. They burrow through the soil, eating the roots off many plants, even pulling whole plants down into their burrows. What can I do to control them?

A king snake, black snake, or gopher snake is a great boon where gophers are a problem, and some cats are avid gopher hunters. But lacking these predators, you might try mechanical gopher traps; some gardeners use them to good effect.

My beet leaves have little white trails twisting and turning on them. Eventually, the leaves turn yellow and die. What is this and how do I stop it?

The problem is leaf miners—little insect larvae that burrow through the soft tissue between the outer layers of the leaves. If there are nearby stands of lamb's-quarters, a common weed, pull them out, since they may harbor these pests. Also, cover your beets when young with a lightweight floating row cover that lets in air, water, and light. It will keep adults from laying their eggs on the beet larvae.

Troubleshooting Guide

Even the best-tended gardens can fall prey to pests and diseases. To catch such problems early on, inspect your plants regularly for warning signs. Improper pH levels and other environmental conditions can cause symptoms like those of some infectious diseases. If wilting, yellowing, or other symptoms appear on neighboring plants, the cause is probably environmental; pests and infectious diseases usually strike more randomly.

This guide will help you identify and solve 21 common problems. Good fertility, drainage, air circulation, garden sanitation, and a healthy population of soil organisms will help prevent infection. Encourage or introduce beneficial insects that prey on pests, and use row covers, handpicking, and other nonchemical methods of prevention and control. If chemical treatment becomes necessary, use an organic insecticide or fungicide sparingly. Your aim is to control problems without harming beneficials or the soil organisms essential to the organic garden.

PESTS

PROBLEM: Leaves curl, are distorted in shape, may yellow, and may be sticky and have a black, sooty appearance. A clear, sticky substance often appears on stems and leaves. Buds and flowers are deformed, new growth is stunted, and leaves and flowers may drop.

CAUSE: Aphids are pear shaped, semi-transparent, wingless sucking insects. They are about ⅛ inch long and may be green, yellow, red, pink, black, or gray. Infestations are worst in spring and early summer, when the pests cluster on new shoots, the undersides of leaves, and around flower buds. Plants grown in soil with a high nitrogen content are especially likely to attract aphids.

SOLUTION: Spray plants frequently with a steady stream of water from a garden hose to knock aphids off plants and discourage them from returning. In severe cases, prune off heavily infested parts and spray with insecticidal soap, horticultural oil, or pyrethrum. Introduce ladybugs, green lacewings, gall midges, and syrphid flies. Do not apply excessive amounts of nitrogen fertilizer.
SUSCEPTIBLE PLANTS: MOST VEGETABLES.

PROBLEM: In spring, large irregular holes appear in leaves; entire leaves and stems may also be eaten, and seedlings may disappear. Shallow gouges and round holes appear in fruits.

CAUSE: Caterpillars, including armyworms, cabbage loopers, imported cabbageworms, the larvae of diamondback moths, parsley worms, tomato hornworms, and tomato fruitworms, come in a variety of shapes and colors and may be smooth, hairy, or spiny.
These voracious pests are the larvae of moths and butterflies.

SOLUTION: Handpick. Use *Bacillus thuringiensis* (Bt) or insecticidal soap, but only after identifying the species to determine if it is vulnerable to either treatment. Introduce or encourage soldier bugs, assassin bugs, minute pirate bugs, parasitic wasps, and lacewings. Spade soil deeply in early spring to kill overwintering pests.
SUSCEPTIBLE PLANTS: MOST VEGETABLES, ESPECIALLY MEMBERS OF THE CABBAGE FAMILY.

PROBLEM: Leaves and stems have ragged holes or are skeletonized and may be covered with black droppings. Young plants may die, and older plants may be defoliated.

CAUSE: Colorado potato beetles are ⅓-inch-long oval-shaped chewing insects with yellow-and-black-striped wing covers. Emerging from the soil in spring, they feed and then lay bright orange eggs on the undersides of leaves; eggs hatch in 1 week. The plump ⅗-inch-long larvae are orange-red with black spots. They feed, enter the soil to pupate, and emerge as adults in 1 to 2 weeks. There are one to three generations a year.

SOLUTION: Handpick eggs, beetles, and larvae, and drop into soapy water. Use a thick layer of organic mulch to inhibit adults emerging from soil. Plant resistant varieties and rotate crops. Spray with Bt San Diego strain. Introduce ladybugs and spined soldier bugs. Cultivate soil in fall to kill overwintering adults. Spray with neem, pyrethrum, or rotenone.
SUSCEPTIBLE PLANTS: POTATOES, EGGPLANT, PEPPERS, TOMATOES.

PROBLEM: Holes appear in leaves, stalks, or husks and at the bottom of ears of corn, breaking the stems. Ears are disfigured and tunneled, and kernels are eaten. Tomatoes are eaten away inside.

CAUSE: Corn earworms are 1- to 2-inch-long yellow, green, or white caterpillars, and European corn borers are 1- to 2-inch-long beige caterpillars with brown spots and dark heads.

SOLUTION: Plant resistant varieties. Introduce tachinid flies and parasitic wasps. Spray with BtK, neem, or pyrethrum. Place 5 drops of mineral or vegetable oil in silk whorl just as silk starts to brown. Spade soil in fall to expose pupae. *SUSCEPTIBLE PLANTS: CORN EARWORM— CORN AND TOMATOES; EUROPEAN CORN BORER—BEANS, BEETS, CELERY, CORN, PEPPERS, POTATOES, AND TOMATOES.*

PROBLEM: Large oval holes appear in leaves and flowers, and new shoots may be eaten. Older plants are stunted and weakened and may fall over. Roots may be stunted. Plants may die.

CAUSE: Cucumber beetles are ¼ inch long and yellowish green with black spots or stripes. In spring, larvae hatch in 10 days to feed on plant roots and pupate in soil. Adults emerge to feed on leaves, flowers, and fruit. There are one to four generations a year. Adults and larvae carry cucumber mosaic and bacterial wilt, diseases that can kill plants.

SOLUTION: Handpick adults. Use row covers, but remove from plants that need insect pollination when flowering begins. Plant resistant varieties. Introduce beneficial nematodes, tachinid flies, and braconid wasps. Apply rotenone and sabadilla. *SUSCEPTIBLE PLANTS: CUCUMBERS, MELONS, PUMPKINS, SQUASH, AND OTHER MEMBERS OF THE CUCUMBER FAMILY. MAY ALSO ATTACK BEANS, CORN, EGGPLANT, PEAS, POTATOES, AND TOMATOES.*

PROBLEM: Stems of emerging seedlings are cut off near the ground, and the plants topple over and die. Seedlings may be completely eaten. Leaves of older plants show ragged edges and holes.

CAUSE: Cutworms, the larvae of various moths, are fat, hairless, and a soft gray-brown in color. These 1- to 2-inch-long night feeders do most of their damage in the late spring. In the daytime, they curl up into a C-shape and are found under debris or below the soil surface next to the plant stem.

SOLUTION: Place cutworm collars around base of plant. Force cutworms to the soil surface by flooding the area, then handpick them. Introduce parasitic braconid wasps, tachinid flies, and beneficial nematodes. Use diatomaceous earth (DE), crushed eggshells, wood ashes, and oak-leaf mulch around plants to discourage cutworms. Cultivate the soil in late summer and fall and again in spring. *SUSCEPTIBLE PLANTS: YOUNG SEEDLINGS AND TRANSPLANTS.*

PROBLEM: Numerous tiny round holes appear in leaves, making plant look as if it has been peppered with shot. Seedlings may weaken or die.

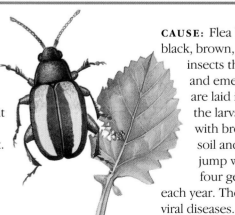

CAUSE: Flea beetles are ¹⁄₁₀-inch-long black, brown, bronze, or striped chewing insects that overwinter as adults and emerge in spring to feed. Eggs are laid in the soil near the plant; the larvae, ¾-inch-long white grubs with brown heads, pupate in the soil and emerge as adults, which jump when disturbed. Two to four generations are produced each year. These beetles spread several viral diseases.

SOLUTION: Use row covers and white or yellow sticky traps. Spread diatomaceous earth (DE) or wood ashes around plants. Cultivate soil often to expose eggs and larvae. Introduce beneficial nematodes, braconid wasps, and tachinid flies. Pyrethrum, rotenone, and sabadilla may be used. *SUSCEPTIBLE PLANTS: MEMBERS OF THE CABBAGE FAMILY, EGGPLANT, TOMATOES.*

PROBLEM: Holes are chewed in leaves, which may be reduced to skeletons with only veins remaining. Eventually, plants may be stripped of all foliage.

CAUSE: Japanese beetles have shiny metallic blue or green bodies and copper-colored wings. Voracious in the summer, they prefer feeding in sunny locations. Eggs are laid in soil in grassy or weedy areas. The fat ¾-inch-long grubs are grayish white with dark heads. They overwinter in the soil below the frostline, where they feed on the roots of grass. They pupate in late spring or early summer and emerge as adults in May, June, and July to feed and lay eggs. One generation is produced a year.

SOLUTION: Handpick small colonies, placing them in a can filled with soapy water. Use neem as a repellent. Spray with pyrethrum or rotenone. The larval stage can be controlled with milky spore disease or beneficial nematodes, both of which can be applied to the whole garden and nearby lawn areas. Introduce or encourage parasitic wasps and tachinid flies. Keep the garden well weeded. *SUSCEPTIBLE PLANTS: ASPARAGUS, BEANS, BLACKBERRIES, CORN, OKRA, POTATOES, RASPBERRIES, RHUBARB, STRAWBERRIES, TOMATOES.*

PROBLEM: Leaves are skeletonized. Pods and stems may be eaten, and plants may die.

CAUSE: Mexican bean beetles are ¼-inch-long oval-shaped yellowish brown to copper-colored insects. With 16 black dots forming three rows across the wing covers, they look very much like a lighter-colored version of the beneficial ladybug. The yellow to orange oval larvae have long black-tipped spines. Adults overwinter in debris and emerge in early summer to feed and lay yellow egg masses on the undersides of leaves. One to four generations are produced a year.

SOLUTION: Plant resistant cultivars. Handpick adults and larvae and remove leaves with orange egg masses; drop into a container of soapy water. Cover with floating row covers until well grown. Encourage or introduce spined soldier bugs and parasitic wasps. Spray undersides of leaves thoroughly with pyrethrum, neem, sabadilla, or rotenone. In fall, remove infested plants and clean garden of debris, and cultivate soil to destroy overwintering adults. *SUSCEPTIBLE PLANTS: GREEN BEANS AND LIMA BEANS ARE ESPECIALLY SUSCEPTIBLE; BLACK-EYED PEAS, KALE, SOYBEANS.*

PROBLEM: Light-colored sunken brown spots appear on the upper surfaces of leaves, or tiny holes appear in leaves and stems (these are caused by stink bugs). Foliage may wilt, discolor, and fall from plant. Shoots and flower buds may be distorted or blackened, and plant may be stunted. Vegetables may be scarred or dimpled.

CAUSE: The plant bug family of sucking insects includes the ¼-inch-long oval tarnished plant bug, mottled brown and tan with a black-tipped yellow triangle on each forewing; the ⅝-inch-long squash bug, black or brown on top and yellow, yellowish brown, or grayish underneath; and the shield-shaped ½-inch-long stink bug, which is named for its unpleasant odor and is brown, tan, green, or mottled with five segmented antennae. Adults are active from late spring to late summer. Eggs are laid on the undersides of leaves. Up to five generations are produced a year.

SOLUTION: Handpick adults and larvae, remove leaves with egg masses, and drop into soapy water. Use row covers. Trap tarnished plant bugs with white sticky traps. Introduce or encourage beneficials including tachinid flies, big-eyed bugs, parasitic wasps, and damsel bugs. Spray plants with water, dilute soap solution, or insecticidal soap. Control adults and larvae with rotenone and sabadilla. *SUSCEPTIBLE PLANTS: TARNISHED PLANT BUG—MOST VEGETABLES; SQUASH BUG—ALL MEMBERS OF THE SQUASH FAMILY, ESPECIALLY PUMPKINS AND SQUASH; STINK BUG—BEANS, CABBAGE, CORN, OKRA, PEAS, SQUASH, TOMATOES.*

PROBLEM: Plants do not develop; young plants may wilt and die; older plants may be stunted. Roots and root crops have tunnels or are hollowed out, and they later rot.

CAUSE: Root maggots are the larvae of various small flies including cabbage, onion, and carrot rust flies. The legless, wormlike ⅓-inch-long larvae are white to yellowish white and enter the plant through roots or underground stems. Active from spring to midsummer, they thrive in cool, moist, highly organic soil. Eggs are laid at the bases of stems.

SOLUTION: Use floating row covers. Place diatomaceous earth or wood ashes around plants. Rotate crops. Do not fertilize with fresh manure. Apply beneficial nematodes to soil before planting. In fall, remove debris and infected plants. Cultivate soil in spring and fall.
SUSCEPTIBLE PLANTS: CABBAGE MAGGOT— CABBAGE FAMILY; ONION MAGGOT—ONION FAMILY; CARROT RUST FLY—CARROT FAMILY.

PROBLEM: Large ragged holes appear on leaves, especially those near the ground. New leaves and entire young seedlings may disappear. Ripe fruits are destroyed. Telltale shiny silver streaks appear on leaves and garden paths.

CAUSE: Slugs and snails hide during the day and feed on low-hanging leaves and fruits at night or on overcast or rainy days. They prefer damp soil in a shady location and are most damaging in summer, especially in wet regions or during rainy years.

SOLUTION: Keep garden clean. Handpick. Trap with saucers of beer or inverted grapefruit halves. Surround beds with copper-foil barriers or barrier strips of wood ashes, coarse sand, cinders, or diatomaceous earth (DE). Encourage rove beetles. Cultivate soil in spring.
SUSCEPTIBLE PLANTS: MOST VEGETABLES, ESPECIALLY LEAFY VEGETABLES LIKE LETTUCE, AND THE FRUIT OF TOMATOES AND STRAWBERRIES.

PROBLEM: Leaves become stippled or flecked, then discolor, curl, and wither. Webbing may appear, particularly on growing tips and on undersides of leaves. Vegetables and fruits may be stunted.

CAUSE: Mites are pinhead sized, spiderlike sucking pests that can be reddish, pale green, or yellow. A major problem in hot, dry weather, several generations of mites may occur in a single season. Eggs, and the adults of some species, overwinter in sod and bark and on plants that retain foliage.

SOLUTION: Regularly spray undersides of leaves, where mites feed and lay eggs, with a strong stream of water or a diluted insecticidal soap solution. Remove and destroy heavily infested leaves, stems, or entire plant. Introduce predators such as ladybugs, predatory mites, and green lacewing larvae. Use horticultural oil, neem, or pyrethrum.
SUSCEPTIBLE PLANTS: ASPARAGUS, BEANS, CUCUMBERS, EGGPLANT, MELONS, SQUASH, STRAWBERRIES, SUGAR PEAS, TOMATOES.

PROBLEM: Leaves turn yellow and plant is stunted. When plant is shaken, a white cloud of insects rises from it.

CAUSE: Whiteflies, 1/16-inch-long sucking insects that look like tiny white moths, generally collect on the undersides of young leaves. Found year round in warmer climates but only in summer in colder climates, they like warm, still air. Whiteflies are often brought home with greenhouse plants and can carry viruses and secrete honeydew, which promotes a fungus called sooty mold.

SOLUTION: Inspect plants before buying. Keep the garden weeded. Spray affected plants with a strong stream of water from a garden hose. Spray with insecticidal soap or horticultural oil. Use yellow sticky traps. Introduce lacewings and parasitic wasps. Pyrethrum or rotenone can be applied.
SUSCEPTIBLE PLANTS: MOST VEGETABLES, ESPECIALLY MEMBERS OF THE SQUASH AND TOMATO FAMILIES, AND MELONS.

PROBLEM: Plants wilt, are stunted, or die. Roots are damaged. Crops are thin and patchy.

CAUSE: Wireworms, which bore into and feed on seeds, corms, roots, and other underground plant parts, are the gray, creamy, or dark brown larvae of various species of click beetles. The ½- to 1½-inch-long jointed, shiny, tough-skinned larvae hatch in spring and may persist in the soil for up to 6 years. They are especially a problem in newly turned sod.

SOLUTION: Before planting a new crop, bury pieces of potato or carrot to trap wireworms, then dig up. Cultivate soil to a depth of 10 inches to expose larvae. Apply beneficial nematodes to soil. *SUSCEPTIBLE PLANTS: MOST VEGETABLES, ESPECIALLY CORN, LETTUCE, POTATOES, AND TURNIPS.*

D I S E A S E S

PROBLEM: In spring, brown spots ringed with yellow form a bull's-eye pattern on mature leaves. Spots merge to cover leaves, which die and drop off. Spots and cankers may appear on stems. Tomatoes may rot at the stem end and have dark, leathery, sunken areas. Potatoes develop brown, corky, dry spots. In the fall, dark irregular spots appear on leaves, and there may be a white mold on the undersides; fruits and tubers may have dark rotting spots.

CAUSE: Early blight, which occurs in the spring, and late blight, which occurs in the fall, are fungal diseases. Drought, insect damage, or nutrient deficiencies increase vulnerability to early blight. Late blight is most common in wet weather when nights are cool.

SOLUTION: Rotate crops and plant resistant cultivars. Treat early blight with copper fungicide. Plant only seed potatoes certified disease free. Destroy infected plants and debris at the end of the season. *SUSCEPTIBLE PLANTS: ESPECIALLY TOMATOES AND POTATOES; ALSO EGGPLANT AND PEPPERS.*

PROBLEM: Overnight, young seedlings suddenly topple over. Stems are rotted through at the soil line.

CAUSE: Damping-off, a disease caused by several soil fungi, infects seeds and roots of seedlings at ground level. The problem often occurs in wet, poorly drained soil with a high nitrogen content.

SOLUTION: Add fresh compost to the planting medium to provide beneficial bacteria and fungi that will compete with the damping-off fungi. Top the medium with a thin layer of sand or perlite to keep seedlings dry at soil level. Provide well-drained soil and plenty of light, and avoid overcrowding. Plants started in containers are more susceptible than those sown outdoors. Do not overwater seed flats or seedbeds. *SUSCEPTIBLE PLANTS: ALL VEGETABLES.*

PROBLEM: Leaves become mottled with light green or yellow spots or streaks. New growth is spindly and misshapen, and plant is often stunted. Fruits and pods may be discolored or streaked.

CAUSE: Mosaic viruses, which can infect plants at any time in the growing season.

SOLUTION: Viral infections cannot be controlled. They spread by direct contact between plants and also by hands, tools, and insects. Plant resistant varieties. Remove and destroy infected plants. Introduce lacewings and ladybugs to control virus-transmitting aphids and leafhoppers. Don't plant susceptible crops where mosaic disease has occurred. *SUSCEPTIBLE PLANTS: BEANS, CUCUMBERS, PEPPERS, POTATOES, SQUASH, TOMATOES.*

PROBLEM: White or pale gray powdery growth appears on upper surface of leaf, eventually spreading to cover entire leaf; followed by distortion, yellowing, withering, and leaf drop. The powdery growth may also be seen on stems, buds, and shoots. Plants are stunted.

CAUSE: Powdery mildew, a fungal disease, is especially noticeable in late summer and early fall when cool, humid nights follow warm days. Unlike most fungal diseases, powdery mildew does not occur readily in wet conditions. More unsightly than harmful, it rarely kills the plant.

SOLUTION: Grow mildew-resistant varieties. Allow adequate room between susceptible plants. Spray plants daily with water to kill spores. Remove and destroy badly infected plant parts or entire plant. Spray plants with a solution of baking soda. Apply a horticultural oil or sulfur. *SUSCEPTIBLE PLANTS: ESPECIALLY BEANS, CUCUMBERS, MELONS, PUMPKINS, AND SQUASH; OCCASIONALLY EGGPLANT, PEPPERS, AND TOMATOES.*

PROBLEM: Plants wilt on warm days or are stunted, abnormally yellowish in color, or low in yield. Roots may be swollen and have knotty growths and swellings. Individual stems may die back. Plant may die.

CAUSE: Soil nematodes, microscopic roundworms that live in the soil and feed on roots, inhibit a plant's uptake of nitrogen. Damage is worst in warm, moist, sandy soils in sunny locations. Nematodes overwinter in infected roots or soil, and are spread by soil, transplants, and on tools.

SOLUTION: Since nematodes are microscopic, only a laboratory test will confirm their presence. Be suspicious if roots are swollen or stunted. Dispose of infected plants and the soil that surrounds them, or solarize the soil *(box, page 71).* Plant resistant species or cultivars and rotate crops. Plant a cover crop of African marigolds *(pages 72-73).* Add nitrogen fertilizer, especially crab or fish meal. Add compost to soil and use organic mulch to encourage fungi that prey on soil nematodes. *SUSCEPTIBLE PLANTS: VIRTUALLY ANY VEGETABLE OR FRUIT.*

PROBLEM: One side or entire plant suddenly droops or wilts, with symptoms usually appearing first on lower and outer plant parts. Leaves may turn yellow before wilting. Plant fails to grow and eventually dies. Seedlings are stunted, wilt, and eventually die. A cut made across the stem near the base reveals dark streaks or other discoloration on the tissue inside or releases an oozing, sticky white substance.

CAUSE: Wilts, some caused by bacteria and others by fusarium or verticillium fungus, display similar symptoms. Bacterial wilt occurs in midsummer, fusarium wilt in hot weather, and verticillium wilt in cool weather. These microorganisms penetrate roots and stems and clog the water-conducting vessels. Both fungi and bacteria are long-lived, remaining in the soil for years after the host plant has died.

SOLUTION: Plant resistant varieties. Fertilize and water regularly to promote vigorous growth. Immediately remove and destroy infected plants, including roots, and clear away garden debris in the fall. Wash hands and disinfect tools with a 10 percent bleach solution. Cucumber beetles spread bacterial wilt, so control them with the measures described on page 95. Because the fungi and bacteria persist in the soil a long time, don't site susceptible plants in an area that has been infected previously. Solarize the soil *(box, page 71).* *SUSCEPTIBLE PLANTS: CUCUMBERS, EGGPLANT, MELONS, PEPPERS, PUMPKINS, SQUASH, STRAWBERRIES, TOMATOES.*

Plant Selection Guide

This chart provides information on the culture and uses of 124 vegetables and fruits. "Days to maturity" applies to crops replanted yearly, either indoors or out, from seed, sets, roots, or tubers. For more information on each plant, refer to the encyclopedia that begins on page 106.

Plant	Cool Season Annual	Warm Season Annual	Hot Season Annual	Winter Hardy	Sun	Partial Shade	<1/2 Inch	1/2 to 2 Inches	>2 Inches	<1 Foot	1 to 2 Feet	>2 Feet	1 to 2 Feet	2 to 4 Feet	>4 Feet	<70 Days	70 to 100 Days	100 to 130 Days	>130 Days	Fresh	Frozen	Canned	Pickled	Jam/Preserves	Dried	Containers	Landscaping
ARTICHOKE 'GREEN GLOBE'		✓		✓	✓	✓		✓				✓		✓				✓		✓	✓		✓			✓	✓
ARUGULA	✓				✓	✓	✓			✓			✓			✓				✓							
ASPARAGUS 'JERSEY KNIGHT'				✓	✓				✓		✓			✓				✓	✓								✓
BASIL 'SPICY GLOBE'		✓			✓		✓			✓			✓			✓				✓					✓	✓	✓
BEAN, DRY 'BLACK TURTLE'		✓			✓			✓		✓				✓			✓			✓		✓			✓		
BEAN, DRY 'FRENCH HORTICULTURAL'		✓			✓			✓		✓				✓			✓			✓	✓	✓			✓		
BEAN, FAVA 'AQUADULCE'	✓				✓			✓		✓				✓			✓			✓	✓						
BEAN, FILET 'TAVERA'		✓			✓			✓		✓			✓			✓				✓							
BEAN, GREEN 'PROVIDER'		✓			✓			✓		✓			✓			✓				✓							
BEAN, GREEN 'TENDERCROP'		✓			✓			✓		✓			✓			✓				✓	✓	✓					
BEAN, LIMA 'FORDHOOK 242'		✓			✓			✓		✓				✓			✓			✓	✓	✓					
BEAN, POLE 'EMERITE'		✓			✓			✓		✓			✓			✓				✓	✓						
BEAN, POLE 'TRIONFO VIOLETTO'		✓			✓			✓		✓			✓			✓				✓	✓						
BEAN, PURPLE 'ROYAL BURGUNDY'		✓			✓			✓		✓			✓			✓				✓	✓						
BEAN, RUNNER 'SCARLET RUNNER'	✓				✓			✓		✓			✓			✓				✓					✓		✓
BEAN, YARDLONG 'GREEN POD'		✓			✓			✓		✓				✓		✓				✓	✓						
BEAN, YELLOW 'DORABEL'		✓			✓			✓		✓			✓			✓				✓	✓						
BEET 'DETROIT DARK RED'	✓				✓			✓		✓			✓			✓				✓	✓	✓	✓				
BEET 'GOLDEN'	✓				✓			✓		✓			✓			✓				✓	✓	✓	✓				
BLACKBERRY 'RANGER'			✓	✓	✓				✓		✓			✓				✓		✓	✓			✓			
BLACKBERRY 'THORNFREE'			✓	✓	✓				✓		✓			✓						✓	✓			✓			
BLACKBERRY 'YOUNG'			✓	✓	✓				✓		✓									✓	✓			✓			
BLACK-EYED PEA 'MISSISSIPPI SILVER'		✓			✓			✓		✓			✓			✓				✓	✓	✓			✓		
BROCCOLI 'EMPEROR'		✓			✓		✓			✓							✓			✓	✓						
BROCCOLI RABE	✓				✓			✓		✓			✓							✓	✓						
BRUSSELS SPROUT 'PRINCE MARVEL'	✓				✓			✓		✓				✓				✓		✓	✓						
CABBAGE 'EARLY JERSEY WAKEFIELD'	✓				✓	✓		✓		✓			✓			✓				✓			✓				
CABBAGE 'WISCONSIN ALL SEASONS'	✓				✓	✓		✓		✓			✓					✓		✓			✓				

	HARDINESS				LIGHT		PLANTING DEPTH			PLANT SPACING			ROW SPACING			DAYS TO MATURITY				WAYS TO USE							
	Cool Season Annual	Warm Season Annual	Hot Season Annual	Winter Hardy	Sun	Partial Shade	<1/2 to 1/2 inch	1/2 to 2 inch	>2 inches	<1 foot	1 to 2 feet	>2 feet	1 to 2 feet	2 to 4 feet	>4 feet	<70 days	70 to 100 days	100 to 130 days	>130 days	Fresh	Frozen	Canned	Pickled	Jam/Preserves	Dried	Containers	Landscaping
CABBAGE, CHINESE 'TWO SEASONS HYBRID'		✔		✔				✔			✔		✔							✔							
CARDOON				✔	✔			✔			✔		✔					✔		✔							
CARROT 'LITTLE FINGER'	✔				✔		✔			✔			✔			✔				✔	✔	✔				✔	✔
CARROT 'NAPOLI'	✔				✔		✔			✔			✔							✔	✔					✔	✔
CARROT 'TENDERSWEET'	✔				✔		✔			✔			✔							✔						✔	✔
CAULIFLOWER 'EARLY WHITE HYBRID'	✔				✔			✔			✔		✔			✔				✔	✔		✔				
CELERIAC 'BRILLIANT'		✔			✔	✔	✔				✔			✔				✔		✔							
CELERY 'UTAH 52-70R'		✔			✔		✔			✔				✔				✔		✔					✔		
CELTUCE	✔				✔	✔	✔			✔				✔						✔							
CHARD 'RHUBARB CHARD'		✔			✔	✔		✔		✔			✔							✔	✔					✔	✔
CHAYOTE			✔		✔	✔						✔						✔		✔							
CHICORY 'CERIOLO'	✔				✔	✔	✔			✔				✔						✔							
COLLARD 'GEORGIA'	✔				✔			✔			✔		✔					✔		✔	✔						
CORN 'EARLIVEE'			✔		✔			✔			✔		✔			✔				✔	✔	✔		✔			
CORN 'SENECA STARSHINE'			✔	✔	✔			✔			✔		✔				✔			✔	✔	✔		✔			
CORN 'STARSTRUCK'			✔		✔			✔			✔		✔				✔			✔	✔	✔		✔			
CORN SALAD 'COQUILLE'				✔	✔			✔		✔			✔							✔							
CRESS 'WINTER CRESS'	✔				✔	✔	✔			✔			✔							✔							
CUCUMBER 'BURPLESS'		✔			✔			✔				✔	✔							✔			✔				
CUCUMBER 'SALADIN'		✔			✔			✔			✔		✔							✔			✔				✔
CUCUMBER 'SPACEMASTER'		✔			✔			✔				✔	✔							✔			✔			✔	
EGGPLANT 'ICHIBAN'		✔			✔	✔		✔			✔			✔						✔							
ENDIVE 'TRES FIN'	✔				✔	✔	✔			✔			✔							✔							
FENNEL 'ZEFA FINO'	✔				✔		✔			✔				✔						✔							
GARLIC 'ELEPHANT GARLIC'				✔	✔	✔		✔	✔	✔								✔		✔					✔		
GARLIC 'SPANISH ROJA GARLIC'				✔	✔	✔		✔	✔	✔								✔		✔					✔		
HORSERADISH 'MALINER KREN'				✔	✔				✔	✔	✔		✔					✔		✔							
JERUSALEM ARTICHOKE 'FRENCH MAMMOTH WHITE'				✔	✔				✔		✔		✔					✔		✔							✔
JICAMA		✔			✔				✔		✔		✔					✔		✔							
KALE 'WINTERBOR'	✔			✔	✔	✔		✔			✔		✔			✔				✔	✔					✔	✔
KOHLRABI 'GRAND DUKE'	✔				✔	✔		✔		✔	✔		✔			✔				✔							
LEEK 'BROAD LONDON'	✔				✔	✔	✔			✔			✔					✔		✔	✔						

Table group headers: **HARDINESS** (Cool Season Annual, Warm Season Annual, Hot Season Annual, Winter Hardy) · **LIGHT** (Sun, Partial Shade) · **PLANTING DEPTH** (<½ inch, ½ to 2 inches, >2 inches) · **PLANT SPACING** (<1 foot, 1 to 2 feet, >2 feet) · **ROW SPACING** (1 to 2 feet, 2 to 4 feet, >4 feet) · **DAYS TO MATURITY** (<70 days, 70 to 100 days, 100 to 130 days, >130 days) · **WAYS TO USE** (Fresh, Frozen, Canned, Pickled, Jam/Preserves, Dried, Containers, Landscaping)

Variety	Cool Seas.	Warm Seas.	Hot Seas.	Winter Hardy	Sun	Part. Shade	<½ in	½–2 in	>2 in	<1 ft	1–2 ft	>2 ft	1–2 ft	2–4 ft	>4 ft	<70 d	70–100 d	100–130 d	>130 d	Fresh	Frozen	Canned	Pickled	Jam/Pres.	Dried	Contain.	Landscap.
LETTUCE 'LITTLE GEM'		✓			✓	✓	✓			✓			✓			✓				✓							
LETTUCE 'RUBY'		✓			✓	✓	✓			✓			✓			✓				✓					✓		
LETTUCE 'SUMMERTIME'		✓			✓	✓	✓			✓			✓			✓				✓							
LETTUCE 'TOM THUMB'		✓			✓	✓	✓			✓			✓			✓				✓							
MELON 'CASABLANCA'		✓			✓			✓				✓			✓		✓			✓	✓						
MELON 'PANCHA'		✓			✓			✓			✓				✓		✓			✓	✓						
MELON 'VENUS'		✓			✓			✓			✓				✓		✓			✓	✓						
MUSTARD GREENS 'SOUTHERN GIANT CURLED'	✓				✓		✓			✓			✓			✓				✓							
NASTURTIUM 'TIP TOP MIX'	✓				✓	✓	✓			✓			✓			✓				✓			✓			✓	✓
OKRA 'CLEMSON SPINELESS'			✓		✓			✓		✓	✓		✓							✓							
ONION 'ISHIKURA'	✓				✓			✓		✓			✓							✓	✓						
ONION 'NORTHERN OAK'	✓			✓	✓			✓		✓			✓					✓		✓	✓				✓		
ONION 'TEXAS GRANO 1015Y'	✓			✓	✓			✓		✓			✓					✓		✓					✓		
ORACH 'RED ORACH'	✓				✓		✓			✓			✓			✓				✓							
PAK-CHOI 'MEI-QUING CHOI'	✓				✓		✓				✓		✓			✓				✓							
PARSLEY 'MOSS CURLED FOREST GREEN'	✓			✓	✓	✓	✓			✓				✓						✓					✓	✓	
PARSNIP 'HOLLOW CROWN'	✓				✓		✓			✓								✓		✓							
PEA, GARDEN 'LITTLE MARVEL'	✓				✓			✓		✓			✓			✓				✓	✓	✓					
PEA, SNOW 'OREGON SUGAR POD II'	✓				✓			✓		✓			✓				✓			✓	✓						
PEA, SUGAR SNAP 'SUGAR DADDY'	✓				✓			✓			✓		✓			✓				✓							
PEANUT 'JUMBO VIRGINIA'			✓		✓			✓			✓		✓					✓		✓	✓						
PEPPER, CHILI 'LARGE HOT CHERRY'		✓			✓			✓			✓		✓					✓		✓	✓		✓				
PEPPER, SWEET 'CALIFORNIA WONDER'		✓			✓			✓			✓		✓					✓		✓	✓						
PEPPER, SWEET 'GYPSY'		✓			✓			✓			✓		✓				✓			✓							✓
POTATO 'NORGOLD RUSSET'		✓			✓				✓	✓			✓			✓				✓	✓					✓	
POTATO 'RED LA SODA'		✓			✓				✓	✓				✓			✓			✓	✓					✓	
POTATO 'RUSSET BURBANK'		✓			✓				✓	✓			✓					✓		✓	✓					✓	
PUMPKIN 'CONNECTICUT FIELD'		✓			✓			✓				✓		✓				✓		✓	✓						
PUMPKIN 'JACK BE LITTLE'		✓			✓			✓				✓		✓				✓		✓	✓						
RADICCHIO 'CASTELFRANCO'		✓			✓		✓			✓			✓							✓							
RADISH 'FRENCH BREAKFAST'	✓				✓		✓	✓		✓			✓			✓				✓							
RASPBERRY 'BLACK HAWK'				✓	✓	✓			✓			✓								✓	✓			✓			

	HARDINESS				LIGHT		PLANTING DEPTH			PLANT SPACING			ROW SPACING			DAYS TO MATURITY				WAYS TO USE							
	COOL SEASON ANNUAL	WARM SEASON ANNUAL	HOT SEASON ANNUAL	WINTER HARDY	SUN	PARTIAL SHADE	< 1/2 INCH	1/2 TO 2 INCHES	> 2 INCHES	< 1 FOOT	1 TO 2 FEET	> 2 FEET	1 TO 2 FEET	2 TO 4 FEET	> 4 FEET	< 70 DAYS	70 TO 100 DAYS	100 TO 130 DAYS	> 130 DAYS	FRESH	FROZEN	CANNED	PICKLED	JAM/PRESERVES	DRIED	CONTAINERS	LANDSCAPING
RASPBERRY 'NEWBURGH'			✓	✓	✓			✓				✓			✓					✓	✓		✓				
RASPBERRY 'WINEBERRY'			✓	✓	✓			✓				✓			✓					✓	✓		✓				✓
RHUBARB 'CHERRY RED'			✓	✓				✓			✓		✓							✓	✓		✓				
RUTABAGA 'IMPROVED PURPLE TOP YELLOW'	✓				✓			✓		✓			✓		✓					✓	✓						
SALSIFY 'MAMMOTH SANDWICH ISLAND'	✓				✓		✓			✓								✓	✓	✓							
SHALLOT 'SUCCESS'	✓			✓	✓			✓		✓			✓					✓	✓	✓							
SORREL			✓	✓	✓	✓	✓			✓			✓				✓			✓	✓					✓	
SOYBEAN 'PRIZE'		✓			✓			✓		✓			✓				✓			✓	✓			✓			
SPINACH 'MELODY'	✓			✓	✓	✓		✓		✓			✓			✓				✓	✓						
SPINACH, MALABAR 'ALBA'		✓			✓			✓			✓			✓			✓			✓						✓	✓
SPINACH, NEW ZEALAND		✓		✓	✓			✓		✓			✓			✓	✓			✓	✓					✓	
SQUASH, SUMMER 'PARK'S CREAMY HYBRID'		✓			✓			✓			✓		✓			✓				✓	✓						
SQUASH, SUMMER 'RAVEN'		✓			✓			✓			✓		✓			✓				✓	✓						
SQUASH, SUMMER 'SCALOPPINI'		✓			✓			✓		✓			✓	✓						✓	✓						
SQUASH, SUMMER 'SUNDANCE'		✓			✓			✓		✓			✓	✓						✓	✓						
SQUASH, WINTER 'BUTTERBUSH'		✓			✓			✓			✓			✓			✓			✓	✓						
SQUASH, WINTER 'CREAM OF THE CROP'		✓			✓			✓			✓		✓					✓		✓	✓						
SQUASH, WINTER 'SWEET DUMPLING'		✓			✓			✓			✓	✓						✓		✓	✓						
SQUASH, WINTER 'TURK'S TURBAN'		✓			✓			✓			✓	✓						✓		✓	✓						
STRAWBERRY 'ALEXANDRIA'		✓		✓	✓			✓	✓	✓								✓		✓			✓			✓	✓
STRAWBERRY 'PICNIC'		✓		✓	✓			✓	✓	✓								✓		✓	✓		✓		✓		
SUNFLOWER 'MAMMOTH'		✓			✓		✓				✓		✓			✓											✓
SWEET POTATO 'CENTENNIAL'			✓		✓			✓	✓			✓					✓			✓							
TAMPALA			✓		✓	✓		✓		✓			✓							✓							
TOMATILLO 'TOMA VERDE'		✓			✓			✓			✓	✓					✓			✓							
TOMATO 'BIG GIRL'		✓			✓		✓							✓			✓			✓		✓					
TOMATO 'EARLY CASCADE'		✓			✓		✓				✓		✓				✓			✓							
TOMATO 'HEINZ 1439'		✓			✓		✓				✓			✓				✓		✓		✓					
TOMATO 'SUGAR LUMP'		✓			✓		✓				✓			✓				✓		✓							
TOMATO 'VIVA ITALIA'		✓			✓		✓				✓		✓				✓			✓					✓		
TOMATO 'YELLOW CANARY'		✓			✓		✓				✓		✓				✓			✓					✓		
TURNIP 'TOKYO CROSS'	✓			✓	✓			✓		✓			✓			✓				✓	✓		✓				

Frost Dates in the U.S. and Canada

These maps indicate the average dates for the last spring frost and the first fall frost in various parts of the U.S. and Canada. Planting dates for most vegetables depend on when these frosts occur. A spring crop of radishes, for instance, can be sown 5 weeks before the last frost, while a fall crop can be sown as late as 4 weeks after the first frost. Cool-season crops like radishes can withstand some frost, but warm-season crops can be grown without protection only in the frost-free period between the year's last and first frosts. Used together, the maps and the information in the encyclopedia *(pages 106-152)* will help you choose vegetable varieties suited to your area and determine when to plant them. Be aware that specific frost dates vary widely within each region. For more precise figures, check with your weather bureau or extension service and keep a record of temperatures in your garden from year to year.

The two larger maps exclude Alaska; Alaska's dates are shown on the two smaller maps.

AVERAGE DATES OF LAST SPRING FROST

JUNE
MAY
APRIL
MARCH
FEBRUARY
JANUARY

AVERAGE DATES OF FIRST FALL FROST

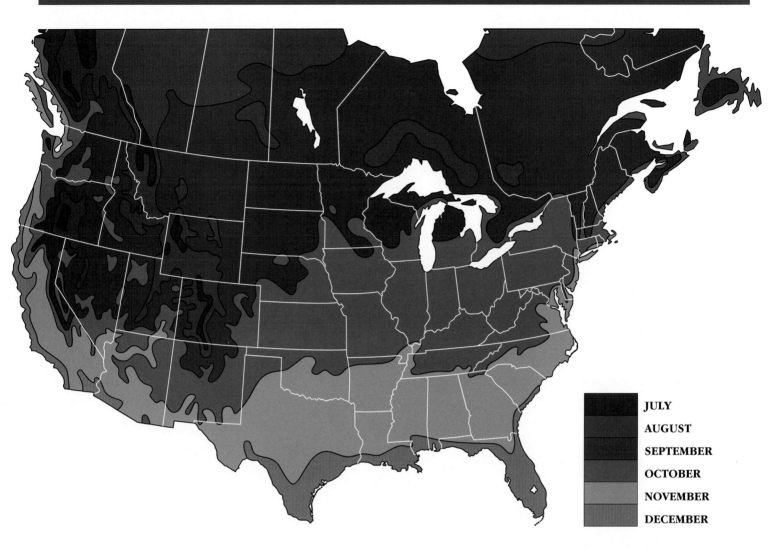

JULY
AUGUST
SEPTEMBER
OCTOBER
NOVEMBER
DECEMBER

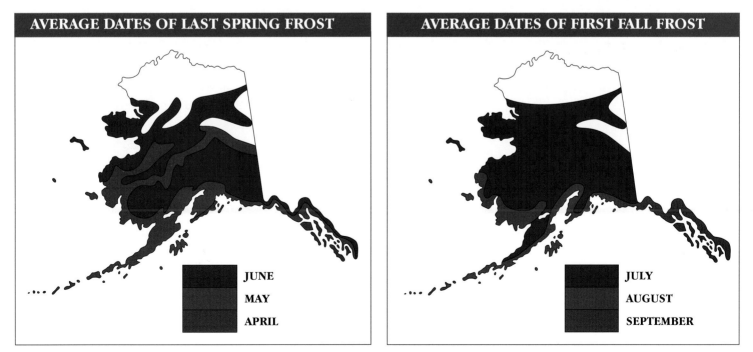

AVERAGE DATES OF LAST SPRING FROST

JUNE
MAY
APRIL

AVERAGE DATES OF FIRST FALL FROST

JULY
AUGUST
SEPTEMBER

Encyclopedia of Vegetables

A vegetable garden that is productive throughout the growing season depends on careful planning. With the right sequence of vegetables, even a small garden can yield bountiful harvests from the last spring frost, or even before, until after the first fall frost. In fact, you may be able to harvest fresh vegetables until the beginning of the next gardening year.

Presented here is a selection of season-spanning vegetables, along with several popular fruits, for maximizing harvests. Each entry begins with hardiness information to guide garden planning. Cool-season annuals include vegetables that can be sown or transplanted outdoors when the soil is cool and will withstand spring or fall frosts. In addition to true annuals, this category includes biennials such as Brussels sprouts and carrots that are commonly grown as annuals. Warm-season annuals germinate best when soil temperatures reach 65° to 70° F and will tolerate light frost. Hot-season annuals require very warm soil temperatures to germinate and both warm days and warm nights to develop and ripen. Winter-hardy vegetables are perennials in some climate zones, where they can be allowed to remain in the same garden spot from one year to the next. Some of these perennials can also be cultivated as cool-season annuals. Use the frost maps on pages 104-105 as a guide to the period in which you can expect the last hard spring frost and the first hard fall frost to occur in your area.

To further aid the planning process, each entry also lists the number of days from seed or transplanting to harvest. Check the relative days to maturity to determine when the crop will be ready for harvest and a successive crop can be seeded or transplanted to fill the space. Plant spacings indicate how much room to allow between plants for optimum growth. The descriptions also note which varieties are disease resistant, a highly desirable characteristic since such varieties are likely to produce well without spraying or other treatment.

ARTICHOKES

'Green Globe'

Hardiness: *Zones 8-11; warm-season annual*
Planting method: *direct sowing; rooted cuttings*
Plant spacing: *2 to 4 feet*
Light: *full sun to light shade*

Large, edible flower buds 4 to 6 inches across. Grown as perennials, artichokes are harvested in the spring; as annuals, they are harvested in the fall. The deeply lobed foliage makes artichokes attractive landscaping accents, and the buds and thistlelike flowers are prized in dried arrangements. Artichokes can be grown as container plants.

Selected varieties: 'Green Globe'—very prolific with buds in 100 days. 'Imperial Star'—spineless buds; performs well as an annual. 'Purple Sensation'—bronze-tinted buds.

Growing conditions: Artichokes need cool, moist summers and loose, constantly moist well-drained soil enriched with manure. When grown as annuals, they need at least 100 frost-free days. Plant cuttings 6 to 8 inches deep and 2 to 4 feet apart in spring if grown as an annual; where perennial, plant in spring or fall. To grow from seed as a perennial, sow seed outdoors ½ inch deep. Thin young plants to 6 inches, then thin again to stand 2 to 4 feet apart. For annual artichokes, start seed indoors 4 to 6 weeks before last frost date and transplant when the soil temperature reaches 70° F. Renew a perennial planting every 3 to 4 years. Plants yield six to 12 buds.

ARUGULA, ROCKET

Arugula

Hardiness: *cool-season annual*

Planting method: *direct sowing*

Plant spacing: *6 inches*

Light: *full sun to light shade*

Peppery young leaves in spring or fall provide leafy salad greens or a zesty garnish for pasta or other dishes. Add the spicy flowers of bolting plants to salads for color and flavor.

Selected varieties: No named varieties; sold as arugula. Rosettes of broad oval leaves ready in 35 to 45 days.

Growing conditions: Plant seeds ½ inch deep in wide rows in early spring and again in fall 4 to 8 weeks before the first frost date. Arugula can be grown outdoors in winter where temperatures do not go below 25° F. The heat and short nights of summer cause plants to bolt and leaves to become bitter. Pick outer leaves when they are 2 to 4 inches long to encourage new growth, or harvest entire plant; small weekly sowings prolong harvest. Handpick snails and slugs or use baited traps. Interplant arugula with taller cool-season vegetables such as peas or broccoli, and fill spaces left after a spring planting is harvested with warm-season crops such as green beans or eggplant.

ASPARAGUS

'Jersey Giant'

Hardiness: *winter-hardy Zones 3-8*

Planting method: *crowns; transplants*

Plant spacing: *15 to 18 inches*

Light: *full sun*

Succulent shoots ½ inch or more in diameter tipped with tight, tender buds rise from perennial rootstocks in spring. When the year's harvest ends, allow shoots to develop into 4- to 6-foot stems with ferny leaves. Plant lettuce or other low-growing cool-season crops where asparagus foliage will shade them.

Selected varieties: 'Argenteuil'—stems especially good for blanching white. 'Jersey Giant'—a hybrid with very high yields of large spears with purplish tips; resists rust and tolerates fusarium wilt, root rot, and crown rot. 'Jersey Knight'—high-yielding hybrid adaptable to many soil types; resistant to rust and tolerant of fusarium wilt, root rot, and crown rot. 'Mary Washington'—widely available rust-resistant variety producing crisp, deep green spears over a long season. 'UC157'—hybrid especially suited to areas with mild winters; produces clumps of three to five uniform spears with some tolerance of root rot and fusarium wilt.

Growing conditions: Plant crowns in spring when the soil temperature reaches 50° F or more, or in fall. Set crowns in trenches 1 foot deep lined with 3 to 4 inches of compost or well-rotted manure. When new shoots appear, cover them with 2 to 3 inches of a mixture of equal parts of soil and compost. As the

shoots elongate, continue adding more of the mixture until the trench is filled in. Mulch heavily with compost to suppress weeds. Although planting from crowns is the easiest method, asparagus can be started outdoors or indoors from seed that has been soaked for 2 days in tepid water before sowing. Seedlings started indoors are transplanted to the garden when 10 to 12 weeks old, after all danger of frost is past. To sow outdoors, plant seed ½ inch deep in soil that has warmed to the 70s. Asparagus takes 2 years to reach full production from roots and 3 years to reach picking size from seed. Harvest about one-third of the new shoots the first year after planting roots. Harvest established beds once or twice daily, cutting or snapping off 6- to 8-inch spears just above the soil line. Pick 2- to

'Mary Washington'

3-year-old beds over 4 weeks and older beds for as long as 10 weeks. To produce white spears, blanch shoots as they emerge by covering them with 8 to 10 inches of soil or straw and harvesting when the tips peek through. Asparagus beds remain productive for 20 years or more. Control asparagus beetles and spotted asparagus beetles by handpicking them or shaking them onto a sheet and destroying them, by releasing beneficial insects such as ladybeetles or parasitic wasps, and by cleaning up garden debris in fall. Asparagus is susceptible to crown or root rot, fusarium wilt, and rust; remove and destroy affected plants. Mature plants yield 15 to 25 spears each.

BASIL

'Purple Ruffles'

Hardiness: *warm-season annual*

Planting method: *direct sowing; transplants*

Plant spacing: *6 to 12 inches*

Light: *full sun*

Aromatic ½- to 2-inch leaves prized as culinary flavoring on bushy 6- to 24-inch plants from summer through fall. Grow basil to follow early spring vegetable crops, in containers, or in the landscape for the texture and fragrance of its foliage. Use basil fresh, dried, or frozen.

Selected varieties: 'Broadleaf'—large, pungent leaves. 'Cinnamon'—a taste and aroma of cinnamon. 'Dark Opal'—subtly flavored bronze-purple leaves. 'Genovese', also called 'Sweet Genovese'—upright plants suited to intensive culture. 'Green Ruffles'—fragrant, crinkled leaves. 'Lemon'—lemony, silver-green leaves. 'Licorice'—licorice-scented leaves. 'Piccolo', also called 'Fine Green'—small, fine-textured leaves. 'Purple Ruffles'—pungent ruffled and fringed purple leaves. 'Spicy Globe'—bushy mounds of small, aromatic leaves. All 80 to 90 days.

Growing conditions: Start basil indoors 6 weeks before the last frost or press the tiny seeds directly into the soil when night temperatures reach 50° F. Feed once in summer with a low-nitrogen fertilizer such as fish emulsion. Pinch flower buds off so leaves will maintain good flavor into fall.

BEANS, DRY

'Jacob's Cattle'

Hardiness: *warm-season annual*

Planting method: *direct sowing*

Plant spacing: *3 to 6 inches*

Light: *full sun*

Also called shelling beans. Successive plantings of bush or vining beans yield pods filled with ¼- to ¾-inch beans from summer through fall that are high in fiber and protein. Shell mature beans and use them fresh in side dishes, casseroles, and soups, or preserve them by freezing or canning. Alternatively, let pods dry on the plant, then shell and store beans. Soak dry beans to rehydrate and use like mature fresh beans.

Selected varieties: 'Adzuki'—small, dark red dry beans on 2-foot bushy plants in 118 days. 'Black Turtle'—bush variety with small black dry beans with a nutty flavor in 98 to 103 days. 'Cannellini'—vining pole bean with mildly flavored white to greenish white shelling beans in 50 to 60 days or dry beans in 80 days. 'French Horticultural'—disease-resistant heirloom 18-inch bush bean producing dry beans in 90 days. 'Great Northern'—prolific bush bean with oval, white dry beans in 85 days. 'Hutterite Soup'—heirloom bush bean with thick, yellowish white beans in 75 to 85 days. 'Jacob's Cattle', also called 'Dalmatian Bean'—heirloom 24-inch bush bean producing meaty, kidney-shaped white beans speckled maroon for shelling in 65 days or dry beans in 80 to 100 days. 'Pinto'—pole bean producing kidney-shaped

maroon-and-white-speckled dry seeds in 90 days. 'Soldier'—18-inch heirloom bush bean tolerant of both cool temperatures and drought with slender white dry beans splotched in brown in 85 days. 'Swedish Brown'—extremely hardy 15-inch heirloom bush bean producing quantities of small oval red-brown shelling beans with a small white eye in 65 days or dry beans in 85 days. 'Tongues of Fire'—ivory pods streaked with red producing shelling beans in 70 days. 'Vermont Cranberry'—heirloom bush variety with plump, mild white shelling beans swirled with maroon in

'Cannellini'

60 days and dry beans in 75 to 98 days. 'Yellow Eye'—prolific heirloom bush bean bearing white beans spotted with yellowish or tan eyes, good for shelling or dry beans.

Growing conditions: Plant seeds outdoors after the soil temperature has reached 65° F or more and all danger of frost is past, setting them 1 to 1½ inches deep after pretreating with a bacterial legume inoculant. Make several successive weekly plantings to prolong harvest. Provide trellises or other tall supports for vining pole beans. Mulch to suppress weeds and conserve moisture, which is essential while plants are flowering and seeds are developing in the pods. To harvest beans for shelling and using fresh or for freezing or canning, pick as seeds reach maturity and fill out the pods. Continuous picking of mature pods is essential for further pod production for shelling beans; plants stop producing as soon as even a few pods become overmature. To harvest dry beans, stop watering. When at least 90 percent of the leaves have fallen and at least two-thirds of the beans are dry, pull plants and spread them on tarpaulins or hang in a well-ventilated area to finish drying. When seeds can no longer be dented when bitten, they are ready to thresh; do this by flailing them in a cloth bag. Screen or winnow to remove pod debris. Remove and discard broken beans,

'Tongues of Fire'

freeze the remainder for several hours to destroy bean weevil larvae, then store in airtight containers for up to 3 years.

BEANS, FAVA

'Broad Windsor Longpod'

Hardiness: *cool-season annual*

Planting method: *direct sowing*

Plant spacing: *4 to 6 inches*

Light: *full sun*

Also called broad beans. Large, meaty seeds mature in long pods on erect bushy plants in late spring. Shell mature fava beans for using fresh or allow beans to dry for long-term storage.

Selected varieties: 'Aquadulce'—16-inch pods up to 2 inches wide filled with seven to eight large white beans in 85 days. 'Broad Windsor Longpod'—up to seven light green beans in 8-inch pods on heat-tolerant 3-foot plants in 85 days. 'Imperial Green Longpod'—20-inch pods in 84 days.

Growing conditions: Fava beans tolerate frost and grow best where spring weather remains cool for a long time. In hot weather, flowers will not set pods. Plant seed outdoors 4 to 6 weeks before the last spring frost, setting seeds 1 to 1½ inches deep after pretreating with a bacterial legume inoculant. Seeds may be broadcast or grown in wide rows. Provide twiggy branches or other supports among plants. Mulch to keep plants cool, suppress weeds, and conserve moisture. Continuous picking of mature pods encourages further production; plants stop producing as soon as even a few pods become overmature.

BEANS, FILET

'Tavera'

Hardiness: *warm-season annual*

Planting method: *direct sowing*

Plant spacing: *2 to 6 inches*

Light: *full sun*

Heavy crops of long, straight, elegantly thin green beans for fresh use in late spring through summer on upright, bushy plants.

Selected varieties: 'Astral'—miniature 3- to 4-inch beans on disease-resistant plants in 60 days. 'Finaud'—very thin 6- to 8-inch beans. 'Fin des Bagnols'—high yields of 7- to 8-inch beans. 'Tavera'—very thin, stringless 4- to 5-inch beans in 54 days. 'Triumph de Farcy'—straight 5- to 6-inch dark green beans in 48 days.

Growing conditions: Plant outdoors after all danger of frost is past and the soil temperature has reached 65° F, setting seeds 1 to 1½ inches deep. Mulch to conserve moisture and suppress weeds. Filet beans are best when they are ⅛ to ¼ inch in diameter. Pick every other day in hot weather and at least every 5 days but preferably more frequently in cool weather to prolong harvest over several weeks.

BEANS, GREEN

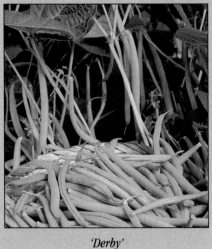

'Derby'

Hardiness: *warm-season annual*

Planting method: *direct sowing*

Plant spacing: *2 to 4 inches*

Light: *full sun*

Also called snap beans. Clusters of pods on compact 1- to 2-foot bushes can be harvested from early summer into fall when seed is sown in succession. Use green beans fresh or preserve them by freezing or canning.

Selected varieties: 'Blue Lake Bush'—6½-inch-long cylindrical pods produced all at once on disease-resistant plants in 58 days. 'Derby'—continuously produced cylindrical pods 7 inches long on vigorous bushes starting in 57 days over several weeks. 'Greencrop'—early crops of flat, stringless pods in 52 days. 'Harvester'—large crop of 5- to 6-inch curved, stringless pods on disease-resistant plants in 60 days. 'Jade'—large crop of straight 5- to 7-inch pods in 60 days. 'Provider'—early crop of 6-inch oval pods in 50 days on plants that resist disease, heat, and drought. 'Slenderette'—thin, stringless 5-inch pods on disease-resistant plants in 53 days. 'Stringless Greenpod'—stringless 6-inch cylindrical pods in 50 days. 'Tendercrop'—cylindrical 6-inch stringless pods on disease-resistant plants in 50 days. 'Tendergreen'—6-inch stringless pods on heat-tolerant plants.

Growing conditions: Plant outdoors after all danger of frost is past and the soil temperature has reached 65° F, set-

ting seeds 1 to 1½ inches deep after pretreating with a bacterial legume inoculant purchased from a seed supplier. The bacteria live in nodules on the roots of the plants and extract nitrogen from the air that helps the beans grow. The shallow roots of beans are easily damaged by cultivation, so control weeds by keeping the plants well mulched. Spacing plants closely also helps to suppress weeds.

Most varieties produce a single crop all at once, so plant weekly for a month to ensure successive harvests. Harvest green beans when pods snap crisply but before seeds start to form. Continuous

'Provider'

picking of pods encourages further production; plants stop producing flowers as soon as even a few pods go to seed.

BEANS, LIMA

'Burpee's Improved Bush'

Hardiness: *warm-season annual*

Planting method: *direct sowing*

Plant spacing: *2 to 4 inches*

Light: *full sun*

Starchy, delicately flavored beans on 1½- to 2-foot bushy plants or 7- to 12-foot vining plants from early summer into fall with successive plantings. Shell lima beans for using fresh or allow them to dry on plants for long-term storage.

Selected varieties: 'Baby Fordhook'—an early baby lima bush variety with three or four small light green beans in 3-inch pods in 70 days. 'Burpee's Best'—a high-yielding pole variety with three to five beans per pod in 92 days. 'Burpee's Improved Bush'—bush variety with four or five large beans in easily shelled 5½-inch pods in 75 days. 'Fordhook 242'—midseason bush variety with three or four very large, uniform beans per pod on heat-tolerant plants in 74 days. 'Henderson's Bush'—early baby lima bush variety with three or four small white beans per pod in 65 days. 'King of the Garden'—a vining pole variety with four or five creamy white or pale green beans per pod good for drying in 88 days.

Growing conditions: Plant outdoors after all danger of frost is past and the soil temperature has reached at least 65° F and preferably 75° F, setting seeds 1 to 1½ inches deep after pretreating with a bacterial legume inoculant, which can be purchased from most seed suppliers. Make several successive weekly plantings to prolong harvesting. Plant bush lima beans in double rows and provide supports among the plants to keep leaves and pods off the ground. Provide trellises or other tall supports for vining pole varieties. If the supports have been used previously for bean crops, treat them with a mixture of 10 parts water to 1 part household bleach to kill any disease organisms that may have overwintered. Mulch plants well and keep soil moist, especially while plants are flowering and beans are developing in the pods. Continuous picking of mature pods encourages further production for shelling beans; plants stop producing as soon as even a few pods become overmature and begin to dry.

To harvest dry beans, withhold water and allow at least two-thirds of the beans to dry, then pull out plants and spread on tarps or hang in a well-ventilated area

'Fordhook 242'

to finish drying. When seeds can no longer be dented when bitten, thresh by flailing them in a cloth bag. Screen or winnow to remove pod debris, freeze for several hours to destroy bean weevil larvae, and store in airtight containers for up to 3 years.

BEANS, POLE

'Trionfo Violetto'

Hardiness: *warm-season annual*

Planting method: *direct sowing*

Plant spacing: *3 to 6 inches*

Light: *full sun*

Vines up to 12 feet long produce green, yellow, or purple pods from summer into fall with successive plantings. Pole beans produce almost twice as many beans as green bush beans, making them an ideal choice for small spaces and intensive gardening.

Selected varieties: 'Blue Lake'—early-maturing variety with straight, round, stringless 5½-inch pods in 66 days. 'Emerite'—early, very slender stringless pods on very productive vines in 55 days. 'Kentucky Wonder'—flavorful beans with good texture for freezing in 65 days; can also be left on vine longer for dry beans. 'Kwintus'—long, flat pods that stay tender even when mature. 'Merchant of Venice', also called 'Meraviglia di Venezia'—flat, stringless golden yellow 3-inch pods filled with black seeds in 75 days. 'Trionfo Violetto'—an heirloom variety with attractive purple flowers that make it a good landscaping plant, followed by deep purple stringless beans in 62 days.

Growing conditions: Plant outdoors after all danger of frost is past and the soil temperature has reached 65° F, setting seeds 1 to 1½ inches deep after pretreating them with a bacterial inoculant, which can be purchased from most seed suppliers. The bacteria live in nodules on the roots of the plants and extract nitrogen from the air that helps the beans grow. Provide wooden or wire trellises, netting, tepee poles, or other supports for pole beans to climb. Disease organisms can overwinter on supports; reuse supports that beans have grown on in previous years only after sterilizing them with a mixture of 10 parts water to 1 part household bleach.

Beans have shallow roots that can easily be damaged by cultivation, so keep them well mulched to control weeds. It is important to keep plants well wa-

'Kentucky Wonder'

tered, especially when they are flowering and pods are developing. Harvest beans when pods snap crisply when broken but before seeds start to form. Continuous picking of mature pods encourages further pod production; plants stop producing flowers as soon as even a few pods go to seed. For dry beans, allow pods to mature and dry on plants in the garden. Thresh seeds from pods by flailing them in a cloth bag when seeds can no longer be dented when bitten.

BEANS, PURPLE

'Royal Burgundy'

Hardiness: *warm-season annual*

Planting method: *direct sowing*

Plant spacing: *3 to 6 inches*

Light: *full sun*

Produced from early summer to fall if sown successively, the colorful pods are easy to find among the foliage. Use purple-podded beans raw to add color to salads or hors d'oeuvres; they turn green when cooked.

Selected varieties: 'Royal Burgundy'—an insect-resistant variety with deep purple stringless, slightly curved 5½-inch pods in 54 days. 'Royalty'—bright purple, curving pods in 53 days. 'Sequoia'—flat purple pods filled with large, meaty seeds.

Growing conditions: Plant outdoors after the last spring frost, setting seeds 1 to 1½ inches deep. Make successive plantings over a month's time to extend harvest time into fall. Provide supports among the plants to keep beans up off the ground. Continuous picking of mature pods encourages further production; plants stop producing as soon as even a few pods become overmature.

BEANS, RUNNER

'Scarlet Runner'

Hardiness: *Zones 7-9; cool-season annual*

Planting method: *direct sowing*

Plant spacing: *3 to 6 inches*

Light: *full sun*

Long, flat fuzzy pods filled with colorful seeds develop from large, brilliantly colored flowers on long vines in summer and fall. Plants are perennial where winters are mild. Use immature runner bean pods fresh and mature pods as shell beans. Train runner bean vines on a trellis as a flowering screen.

Selected varieties: 'Painted Lady'—red-and-white flowers followed by 12-inch pods in 90 days; 'Scarlet Emperor'—red flowers followed by tender pods in 75 days; seeds mature more slowly than other varieties. 'Scarlet Runner'—edible red flowers in clusters of 20 to 40 blossoms followed by long, meaty pods filled with black-purple seeds in 90 days. Pods can also be picked before seeds mature and eaten fresh.

Growing conditions: Plant seeds 1 to 1½ inches deep after the last spring frost and make successive biweekly sowings to prolong harvest. Provide a trellis or other support for vines to climb and keep mulched. Continuous picking of mature pods encourages further production; plants stop producing flowers as soon as even a few pods become overmature. Mulch heavily over winter to protect roots in Zones 7-9.

BEANS, YARDLONG

'Green-Pod Yardlong'

Hardiness: *warm-season annual*

Planting method: *direct sowing*

Plant spacing: *8 to 12 inches*

Light: *full sun*

Also called asparagus beans. Quantities of extremely long, thin pods on vining plants in late summer and fall. Yardlong beans can grow as long as their name suggests but are tenderest when about 10 to 12 inches long. Eat raw or cooked.

Selected varieties: 'Green-Pod Yardlong' —2- to 3-foot, pencil-thin green beans in 75 days. 'Orient Wonder'—stringless 15- to 20-inch pods in 60 days. 'Purple-Pod Yardlong'—2- to 3-foot, very slender purple pods in 75 days.

Growing conditions: Yardlong beans require a long growing season and warm temperatures. Plant seeds outdoors after the last spring frost, setting them 1 to 1½ inches deep. Provide tall trellises or other supports for the vines to climb. Mulch to conserve moisture and suppress weeds. Continuous picking of pods encourages further production; plants stop producing flowers when any pods become overmature.

BEANS, YELLOW or WAX

'Pencil Pod Wax'

Hardiness: *warm-season annual*

Planting method: *direct sowing*

Plant spacing: *3 to 6 inches*

Light: *full sun*

Delicately flavored, buttery yellow pods develop on bushy plants from summer into fall with successive plantings. Use the colorful pods raw or cooked to brighten salads and side dishes or preserve them by freezing.

Selected varieties: 'Brittle Wax'—heavy crop of crisp 7-inch pods in 52 days. 'Cherokee'—heavy crop of stringless pods on disease-resistant plants in 50 days. 'Dorabel'—small 4- to 5-inch pods ready to pick in 57 to 60 days. 'Golden Rocky'—deep yellow 7-inch pods on cold-tolerant plants in 63 days. 'Goldenrod'—round, straight 6-inch pods with small seeds in 55 days. 'Pencil Pod Wax'—round, very crisp, slender 7-inch stringless pods in 55 days. 'Roc d'Or'—round, straight buttery tender pods on disease-resistant plants in 57 days. 'Roma Gold'—flat, stringless pods with plump seeds in 55 days. 'Wax Romano'—broad, flat beans with meaty seeds in 59 days.

Growing conditions: Plant wax beans outdoors after all danger of frost is past and the soil temperature has reached 65° F, setting seeds 1 to 1½ inches deep. Continuous picking of mature pods encourages further production.

BEETS

'Early Wonder'

Hardiness: *cool-season annual*

Planting method: *direct sowing*

Plant spacing: *2 to 4 inches*

Light: *full sun*

Sweet, tender red, yellow, or white roots and tangy greens are harvested from summer through fall. Varieties may be globe shaped or cylindrical. Both roots and greens can be used raw or cooked. The pigment in red beets is drawn out during cooking to color dishes.

Selected varieties: 'Albina Vereduna'—globe variety with mild white flesh and wavy greens in 60 days. 'Big Red'—globe variety with fine-textured roots and disease-resistant greens in 55 days. 'Burpee's Golden'—globe variety with reddish gold roots of excellent keeping quality in 55 days. 'Chioggia'—globe variety with rosy pink skin and white flesh marked with bright pink concentric rings and especially tasty greens. 'Cylindra'—cylindrical variety with long, 5- to 7-inch roots ideal for uniform slicing in 55 days. 'Detroit Dark Red'—globe variety with dark red roots in 60 days that store well. 'Early Wonder'—a globe variety with fine-grained 3-inch roots in 50 days. 'Formanova'—cylindrical variety with roots 6 to 8 inches long and 2½ inches in diameter in 50 days. 'Golden'—sweet, nonbleeding variety with deep yellow-orange flesh in 60 days. 'Long Season'—tapered variety with large roots and excellent storage qualities in 78 days. 'Lutz Green Leaf', also called 'Winter

Keeper'—tapered variety with succulent glossy greens with white stems and very sweet dark red roots with excellent keeping quality in 80 days. 'Red Ace'—vigorous, fast-growing globe variety with exceptionally sweet deep red roots in 53 days. 'Ruby Queen'—globe variety with smooth, deep red roots of uniform size in 54 days.

Growing conditions: Beets can be sown outdoors as soon as the soil can be worked. Soak seeds for 24 hours in warm water before setting them ½ inch deep in a loose, well-tilled soil rich in organic matter to allow growth of the long taproots. Fertilize at planting with a 5-10-10 organic fertilizer or very well rot-

'Golden'

ted manure. Mark rows of slow-germinating beets with quick-growing radishes for intensive cropping. Cover with floating row covers to help warm the soil and speed germination; row covers will also control insect pests on greens. Mulch to help provide the even moisture needed to produce sweet beets. Thin seedlings twice, first to stand 2 inches apart and later to stand 4 inches apart. Beets can be harvested anytime after they are half grown. For a fall crop, sow seed in mid- to late summer. Beet roots toughen when the temperature is 80° F or more. To avoid root rot, rotate beets with nonroot crops.

BLACKBERRIES

'Ebony King' Blackberry

Hardiness: *winter-hardy Zones 5-10*

Planting method: *bare root; containers*

Plant spacing: *3 to 5 feet*

Light: *full sun*

Juicy, sweet-tart berries 1 to 2 inches long in midsummer and sometimes again in fall on erect or trailing canes; except for a handful of varieties, blackberries and the closely related boysenberries, loganberries, and youngberries are notorious for the sharp thorns that line the canes. Both trailing and erect types produce canes that grow one year, then bear fruit and die the second year. The berries can be enjoyed fresh from the garden, baked into pies and other desserts, frozen, or made into preserves or wine. Blackberries and their relatives are long-lived, often remaining productive for as long as 20 years.

Selected varieties: Trailing varieties include: 'Boysen'—drought-resistant canes bearing very large 1½-inch, deep red to purple-black berries with a whitish bloom. 'Logan'—deep red to dusky maroon berries 1½ inches long on semierect canes; best suited to the West Coast. 'Lucretia'—early-ripening medium to large jet black fruit. 'Thornless Boysen'—very large, almost seedless, black-purple berries on thornless canes. 'Young'—large, round, wine-colored berries of exceptional juiciness and sweetness; does well on both the West Coast and the Gulf Coast. All trailing varieties are hardy in Zones 7-10.

Upright blackberry varieties include: 'Comanche'—midseason crop of very large glossy black berries. 'Darrow'—with early- to midseason crops of firm, inch-long fruits on virus-free, winter-hardy canes; Zones 5-10. 'Ebony King'—rust-resistant 3- to 4-foot canes bearing early-ripening purple-black fruits; Zones 5-10. 'Ranger'—with very early, very large yields of sweet berries ideal for fresh eating or winemaking. 'Thornfree'—late-ripening medium to large fruits on thornless 7- to 8-foot canes; Zones 7-10.

Growing conditions: Plant certified disease-free bare-root or container-grown plants in deep, fertile, moist but well-drained loam with a pH between 5.5 and 7.5, setting the top of the roots just be-

'Thornless Boysen'

low the soil line. From Zone 5 north set plants out in early spring, as soon as the soil can be worked. From Zone 6 south, set plants out in fall, winter, or spring. Plant upright types 3 feet apart in rows spaced 6 feet apart; trailing types should be planted 5 feet apart in rows 8 feet apart. For both types, cut the canes of newly planted bushes back to 6 inches from the ground. Water regularly and provide a deep mulch to suppress grass and weeds. For established erect varieties, prune the side branches of canes produced the previous year back to about 18 inches in early spring to encourage heavy fruit production in the coming season; the side branches of trailing varieties should be cut back to 12 inches. For both newly planted and established bushes, pinch off the tips of any new canes that are produced during the current season when they are about

3½ feet tall; pinching is important because it stimulates the canes to produce side branches and thus helps ensure heavy production the following year.

When the fruiting season is over, cut out all the canes that produced berries. Trailing types are most productive if their canes are trained in a fan shape on a support of horizontal wires. Harvest

'Logan'

blackberries after fruits turn from pink to red and finally deep glossy black-purple; the berries should be so ripe that they drop off at the slightest touch. Leave berries that are still firmly attached to ripen fully; otherwise they will be sour. A single plant yields 4 to 8 quarts of fruit.

BLACK-EYED PEAS

'California Blackeye #5'

Hardiness: *warm-season annual*

Planting method: *direct sowing*

Plant spacing: *2 to 4 inches*

Light: *full sun*

Also called cowpeas. White, cream, or tan ⅜- to ½-inch seeds with a dark spot, or eye, fill long clusters of pods at the top of bushy or semivining plants in summer through early fall. Harvest immature pods and cook like green beans, shell mature pods and use the peas fresh, or allow pods to dry on plants, then shell and store the beans.

Selected species and varieties: 'California Blackeye #5'—large seeds in pods up to 12 inches long on nematode- and wilt-resistant plants in 75 to 95 days. 'Mississippi Silver'—easy-to-shell cowpeas with 6-inch pods in 65 days. 'Pinkeye Purple Hull'—purple-eyed white cowpeas in 6- to 7-inch pods in 65 days; usually produces two crops a season.

Growing conditions: Plant after all danger of frost is past and the soil temperature reaches 70° F, sowing seeds ½ to 1 inch deep; seeds germinate in 10 to 14 days. Extend the harvest time with successive plantings. Fertilize soil before planting with phosphorus and potassium; adding nitrogen isn't necessary. Anthracnose, blight, powdery mildew, aphids, bean beetles, leafhoppers, mites, and nematodes may damage black-eyed peas and cowpeas.

BROCCOLI

'Green Comet'

Hardiness: *warm-season annual*

Planting method: *direct sowing; transplants*

Plant spacing: *12 to 24 inches*

Light: *full sun*

Tiny flowers packed into green or blue-green heads on thick, upright stalks in summer or fall. Some broccoli varieties tend to produce a single, large central head while others develop a smaller central head and multiple side shoots.

Selected varieties: 'Bonanza'—large central heads and many side shoots. 'De Cicco'—a very early, disease-resistant, highly productive variety with many side shoots. 'Emperor'—a heat- and disease-tolerant variety good for close spacing with dense 6- to 8-inch single heads. 'Green Comet'—a very fast maturing, disease-resistant variety with firm blue-green central heads and abundant side shoots. 'Green Valiant'—a cold-tolerant, disease-resistant variety. 'Oktal'—early variety with large, open heads and plentiful side shoots. 'Premium Crop'—a slow-to-bolt, disease-resistant variety with a central blue-green head and no side shoots. 'Romanesco Minaret'—pale green conical heads. 'Super Dome'—very productive compact plants ideal for close spacing. 'Waltham 29'—heat-tolerant, compact variety with a single head good for close spacing and growing in fall.

Growing conditions: Start broccoli indoors 6 to 8 weeks before the last frost and transplant to the garden 3 weeks before the last frost; otherwise, sow direct-

ly in the garden 1 to 2 weeks before the last frost. Sow fall crops 3 or 4 months before the first fall frost. Set seeds ¼ to ½ inch deep in a constantly moist but not wet soil enriched with compost or other organic matter. Cold snaps while heads are forming may cause production of small buttons of buds instead of large heads, and temperatures above 80° F may cause plants to bolt. Single-head varieties are generally best for summer harvest and side-shoot types for fall.

Fertilize at planting and again as heads begin forming with fish emulsion or a balanced 10-10-10 organic fertilizer. Mulch to retain soil moisture. Use paper

'Premium Crop'

collars to foil cutworms and floating row covers or parasitic wasps to thwart cabbageworms, flea beetles, cabbage loopers, and other cabbage pests. Remove plant tops and roots in fall to control soilborne diseases and wait 3 years before replanting broccoli in the same location.

To harvest, cut the large central head first to encourage production of a second crop of smaller side shoots. Soak heads in warm water with a small amount of added vinegar and salt to dislodge insects among the buds. One plant yields 1 to 2 pounds of broccoli.

BROCCOLI RABE

Broccoli Rabe

Hardiness: *cool-season annual*

Planting method: *direct sowing*

Plant spacing: *4 to 8 inches*

Light: *full sun*

Also called rapini. Tender greens with a mustardy tang and 1-inch broccoli-like florets in early summer or fall; a good choice for the winter garden in mild climates. Use the greens and florets raw in salads or cooked as a side dish. Despite its name, broccoli rabe is a member of the turnip family.

Selected varieties: None. Ruffled leaves and small florets on slender stalks ready to harvest in 40 days. Cut entire plant just as the flower buds are about to open.

Growing conditions: Start seed indoors 6 weeks before last frost or sow ½ inch deep outside in early spring; young plants tolerate light frost. Where summers are cool, plant in late summer or early fall for a late fall crop. In milder climates, plant in late fall for a winter crop. Water generously and fertilize 2 to 3 weeks after plants are well established. In windy locations, protect stems from damage by mounding soil around the base of plants or tying plants to stakes. Broccoli rabe is a heavy feeder; rotate with legumes such as peas or beans and renew the soil with a generous amount of compost before planting. Harvest leaves when they are 4 to 6 inches long and cut florets with 2 to 3 inches of stem. A 10-foot row will produce about 3 pounds of greens over a 2- to 4-week period.

BRUSSELS SPROUTS

'Jade Cross'

Hardiness: *cool-season annual*

Planting method: *transplants; direct sowing*

Plant spacing: *18 to 24 inches*

Light: *full sun*

Firm, blue-green flower buds resembling miniature cabbages growing in a spiral up tall stalks in mid- to late fall in northern gardens and from late fall through winter in milder climates. Frost improves the flavor of the sprouts. Use them fresh or frozen cooked as a side dish.

Selected varieties: 'Jade Cross'—extremely cold-tolerant variety with abundant, closely spaced sprouts in 115 days. 'Prince Marvel'—very early crop of small, sweet sprouts with creamy white centers in 95 days. 'Rubine'—a late-maturing variety with tiny red sprouts in 130 days.

Growing conditions: Brussels sprouts require a long growing season and are best harvested after the first fall frost, so work backward from that date to determine when to sow seed outdoors or to set out transplants. Plants started indoors from seed will be ready to plant outside in 4 to 8 weeks. For direct sowing, plant seed ½ inch deep in soil enriched with compost, and mulch plants to conserve moisture. Do not plant where other members of the cabbage family have grown for at least 3 years. Harvest sprouts from the bottom of the stalk upward when they are 1 inch or more across. Fresh sprouts will keep for several weeks if the entire plant is pulled up and stored in a cool location. One plant produces 50 to 100 sprouts.

CABBAGE

'Stonehead'

Hardiness: *cool-season annual*

Planting method: *transplants; direct sowing*

Plant spacing: *12 to 24 inches*

Light: *full sun or filtered sun*

Common cabbage has firm, dense heads of succulent green or red leaves in spring, summer, or fall. Plant early varieties for spring crops of small to medium 3- to 4-pound heads, midseason varieties with medium to large heads weighing 5 to 8 pounds for spring or fall crops, or slow-maturing late varieties with large heads weighing up to 12 pounds or more for fall crops. Savoy cabbage has crinkled leaves that are more tender and milder in flavor than the common cabbage varieties.

Selected varieties: Green-leaved varieties include: 'Copenhagen Market'—midseason variety with heads in 72 days that last well in the garden. 'Danish Ballhead'—late-season variety with 6- to 8-pound heads that store well in 105 days. 'Earliana'—very early variety with 2-pound heads in 60 days. 'Early Flat Dutch'—midseason variety with split-resistant, flattened heads in 85 days. 'Early Jersey Wakefield'—disease-resistant early variety with small conical heads that tolerate close spacing in 63 days. 'Emerald Cross Hybrid'—early variety with round heads with blue-green outer leaves and creamy centers in 63 days. 'Golden Acre'—early disease-resistant variety with round light green heads in 64 days. 'Late Flat Dutch'—late variety with flat 10- to 12-pound heads in 100 days. 'Stonehead'—

early variety with blue-green leaves packed into extremely dense 3-pound heads that keep well in the garden in 60 to 70 days. 'Wisconsin All Seasons'—disease-resistant late variety with excellent storage quality in 94 days.

Red-leaved varieties include: 'Crimson'—midseason variety that stores well in the garden in 82 days. 'Lasso'—early vari-

'Ruby Ball'

ety with solid 2- to 4-pound heads in 70 days. 'Red Acre'—insect-tolerant, split-resistant midseason variety with 3- to 4-pound heads on compact plants in 76 days. 'Ruby Ball'—midseason variety with round 3- to 4-pound heads that keep well in the garden in 68 days. 'Ruby Perfection'—split-resistant midseason variety with solid, round red heads in 85 days.

Savoy varieties include: 'Chieftain Savoy'—midseason variety with round, 4- to 5-pound heads of crinkled leaves. 'Julius'—late variety with blue-green leaves in 3- to 5-pound heads with sweet flavor in 90 days. 'Savoy Ace'—midseason variety with delicately flavored leaves in 78 days.

Growing conditions: Start spring crop early cabbages indoors 4 to 8 weeks before the last frost, planting seeds ¼ to ½ inch deep. Transplant to garden soil enriched with compost after all danger of frost is past and mulch to conserve moisture. Direct sow midseason cabbages as soon as all danger of frost is past. For fall crops, direct sow late cabbages at least 100 days before the first fall frost. Plant spring varieties with small heads 12 to 15 inches apart, medium-sized midseason varieties 15 to 24 inches, and large fall varieties 24 inches apart. Close spacing produces smaller heads and increases

the tendency of mature heads to split.

Keep cabbages constantly moist but not soggy and fertilize every 2 to 3 weeks with fish emulsion or other organic fertilizer with at least 10 percent nitrogen. Use paper collars to foil cutworms, water sprays to remove aphids. Use Bt, handpicking, floating row covers, or parasitic wasps to thwart cabbageworms, flea beetles, cabbage loopers, and other insect pests. To minimize clubroot and other soil-borne diseases, do not plant cabbages where other cabbage family members have been planted for at least 3 years.

Harvest cabbages anytime after heads form. Root pruning on one side of the plant will delay splitting and prolong garden storage; in addition, growth is slowed. Harvesting spring varieties when

'Chieftain Savoy'

the heads are softball-sized while leaving five or six large outer leaves attached to the stalk stimulates plants to produce a second crop of small heads in fall. Cabbage tolerates light frost. Heads harvested in fall will keep several weeks or more in a cool, humid place. Common green cabbages store better than red or savoy.

CABBAGE, CHINESE

'Blues'

Hardiness: *cool-season annual*

Planting method: *transplants; direct sowing*

Plant spacing: *10 to 18 inches*

Light: *full sun*

Also called celery cabbage. Vase-shaped heads of crinkly leaves with succulent ribs and mild, sweet flavor in early summer or fall. Use Chinese cabbage in salads, soups, or steamed as a side dish.

Selected varieties: 'Blues'—small disease-resistant, slow-to-bolt heads in 50 days, especially good for spring planting. 'Jade Pagoda'—disease-resistant hybrid with upright green heads with yellow hearts in 68 days. 'Monument'—tall, dense heads with creamy white centers in 80 days. 'Orient Express'—a very early, heat-resistant variety with crisp, peppery flavor in 43 days. 'Two Seasons Hybrid'—oval, slow-to-bolt heads in 62 days, good for spring or fall crops.

Growing conditions: Start Chinese cabbage indoors 8 to 10 weeks before the last frost, setting seed ½ inch deep in peat pots to transplant directly into garden soil enriched with compost. Choose locations where cabbage family members have not grown for at least 3 years and mulch to conserve moisture. Harvest heads before the increasing length of summer days causes plants to bolt. For fall crops, sow seed for leafy varieties 7 weeks and heading varieties 10 to 12 weeks before the first frost. Tie heads loosely with string to blanch hearts for milder flavor.

CARDOON

Cardoon

Hardiness: *Zones 5-9*

Planting method: *direct sowing; transplants*

Plant spacing: *1½ to 2 feet*

Light: *full sun*

Crunchy roots and thick, succulent leaf midribs in fall on perennial thistlelike plants that can also be grown as annuals. Use mature midribs or cubed roots blanched and marinated in salads and antipasto and parboiled or battered and fried as a side dish.

Selected varieties: Usually sold without a varietal name; silver-gray foliage on plants to 8 feet tall in 120 to 150 days.

Growing conditions: Start cardoon indoors 10 weeks before the last frost or sow directly in the garden 1 to 2 weeks before the last frost in a rich, constantly moist but well-drained loam. Space transplants or thin seedlings to stand 1½ to 2 feet apart. Approximately a month before first frost, when plants are 3 feet tall or more, blanch stalks by tying them together with twine and wrapping with paper or burlap. Leaves will blanch in 3 to 4 weeks. Harvest by cutting stems just below the crown. Discard tough outer leaves and trim leaves from the thick midribs before cooking. Plants will grow taller and stronger the second year. If you grow cardoon as an annual, pull up the whole plant and use the roots as well as the midribs for cooking.

CARROTS

'Gold Pak'

Hardiness: *cool-season annual*

Planting method: *direct sowing*

Plant spacing: *2 to 4 inches*

Light: *full sun*

Sweet, crisp red-orange roots with fine-textured flesh surrounding a pithier core from late spring through fall and into winter with successive plantings. The deeper the color, the higher the vitamin content. Choose among several carrot shapes and sizes depending on soil type. Imperator types with long, slender roots need deeply tilled, loose soils. Cylindrical Nantes types and thick, blocky Chantenay and Danvers types will grow where soils are heavy or rocky. Use the very short ball-shaped and baby varieties in extremely heavy soils. The short Nantes, Chantenay, and Danvers types can be grown in pots. Plant carrots in a border among ornamental annuals or perennials, where the lacy foliage will be an attractive filler. It also makes a pretty addition to bouquets.

Selected varieties: Long varieties include: 'Gold Pak'—pencil-thin tapered roots up to 10 inches long in 76 days. 'Imperator'—slender, tapering 8-inch roots in 77 days. 'Sweetness II'—very sweet and juicy 6- to 8-inch cylindrical roots in 73 days; 'Tendersweet'—slender, coreless roots 7 inches or longer in 75 days.

Medium varieties include: 'Artist'—thick, blunt 7- to 8-inch roots in 65 days that retain exceptional sweetness even through winter storage. 'Coreless

Nantes'—almost coreless blunt-tipped 6-inch roots in 65 days; 'Danvers Half Long'—crisp, cylindrical 6- to 7-inch roots that will grow in heavy soils in 75 days, good for canning and storing; 'Nantes'—small-cored cylinders of sweet flesh 1½ inches thick and 6 to 7 inches long in 65 days; 'Nantes Half Long'—slim, blunt-tipped 6- to 7-inch cylindrical roots with small cores in 70 days; 'Napoli'—with early maturing, slim blunt

'Danvers Half Long'

7-inch roots that tolerate crowding in 66 days. 'Red Cored Chantenay', also called 'Goldinhart'—stocky, blunt-tipped 4- to 5-inch roots up to 2½ inches wide in 65 days that are good for canning and freezing and grow well in heavy soils. 'Royal Chantenay'—with deep red-orange color in thick, tapering roots up to 8 inches long in 70 days. 'Scarlet Nantes'—bright red-orange cylindrical roots with dependably sweet flavor and very small cores in 68 days. 'Touchon'—a very sweet Nantes-type carrot up to 7 inches long with high moisture content, ideal for juicing.

Ball-shaped carrot varieties include: 'Parmex'—very early ½- to 1-inch roots with exceptionally good flavor in 50 days. 'Planet'—deep orange 1½-inch roots in 55 days. 'Thumbelina'—roots ½ to 1½ inches in diameter with sweet flesh and thin skin that needs no peeling in 60 to 70 days.

Finger carrot varieties include: 'Baby Spike'—early-maturing tapered roots only 3 to 4 inches long and ½ inch in diameter in 52 days. 'Little Finger'—3½-inch roots 1 inch in diameter in 60 days. 'Minicor'—sweet, very slender, blunt-tipped 6- to 7-inch roots in 55 days.

Growing conditions: Sow carrots ¼ to ½ inch deep in well-tilled, loose loam. Begin sowing 2 to 4 weeks before the last frost, making successive sowings every 2 to 3 weeks until midsummer for continuous harvesting. To speed germination, soak seed for 24 hours, then freeze for 1 week before sowing. Mix the tiny seeds with sand for easier handling. Thin seedlings to stand 2 to 3 inches apart in blocks or rows. Use thinnings in soups or stews. Carrots can be harvested young or allowed to mature. Keep dirt mounded around shoulders to prevent them from turning green. Forked roots indicate injury by stones, hairy carrots indicate an overfertile soil, and twisted roots indicate inadequate thinning. Excessive moisture from heavy rains or heavy watering after a

'Thumbelina'

period of drought can cause roots to crack. Store carrots in the garden through the winter by covering them with a deep mulch of straw or leaves anchored with black plastic to keep the ground from freezing. A 10-foot row yields 10 to 15 pounds of carrots.

CAULIFLOWER

'Snow Crown'

Hardiness: *cool-season annual*

Planting method: *transplants; direct sowing*

Plant spacing: *18 to 36 inches*

Light: *full sun*

Mounds of immature white or purplish flower buds called curds packed tightly into broad, domed heads on upright plants in early summer or fall. Use cauliflower raw for crudités or in salads. Purple cauliflower makes a colorful raw garnish but loses its tint when cooked.

Selected varieties: 'Early Snowball'—medium-sized heads on compact plants in 60 days. 'Early White Hybrid'—early maturing variety with tight outer leaves that naturally blanch curds in 52 days. 'Green Goddess'—easy-to-grow variety with yellow-green curds that do not require blanching. 'Self Blanche'—tight outer leaves ensure naturally creamy white curds for fall crops in 71 days. 'Snow Ball'—early-maturing variety with medium-sized heads in 55 days. 'Snow Crown'—early maturing, vigorous variety for spring or fall crops in 50 days. 'Violet Queen'—looser, broccoli-like purple heads with milder flavor for fall harvest in 54 days.

Growing conditions: Plant heat-sensitive cauliflower for early spring or late fall crops when it will have the cool daytime temperatures between 57° and 68° F it requires to produce heads. For spring crops, start transplants indoors 6 to 8 weeks before the last frost date and move outdoors into a rich garden soil

amended with compost or other organic matter around the time of the last frost. Light frost does not harm transplants, but after a hard frost they may produce "buttons," immature heads only an inch or two across. Mulch to conserve moisture. For a late fall or early winter crop, sow seeds ½ inch deep 10 to 15 weeks before the first frost.

Keep cauliflower constantly moist but not soggy and fertilize every 2 to 3 weeks

'Snow Ball'

with fish emulsion or other organic fertilizer with at least 10 percent nitrogen. Use paper collars to foil cutworms, water sprays to remove aphids. Use Bt, handpicking, floating row covers, or parasitic wasps to thwart cabbageworms, flea beetles, cabbage loopers, and other brassica insect pests. To minimize clubroot and other soil-borne diseases, do not plant cauliflower where other cabbage family members have been planted for at least 3 years.

Exposure to sun will discolor the curds. When the heads of varieties that are not self-blanching reach softball size, pull the outer leaves together over the curds and secure them with a rubber band or string. This covering will blanch the curds and keep them tender. The leaves of self-blanching varieties may need to be tied over the curds if heat wilts them. Harvest as soon as heads are full and firm; overmature heads become coarse or discolored. Each cauliflower plant produces a 1- to 2-pound head. A 10-foot row produces some four to seven heads, depending on spacing.

CELERIAC

'Brilliant'

Hardiness: *warm-season annual*

Planting method: *transplants*

Plant spacing: *12 inches*

Light: *light shade to full sun*

Also called celery root. Ball-shaped roots with a nutty flavor that are harvested in fall when they are 2 to 4 inches in diameter. Shred celeriac raw for salads or cook like celery, which is a close relative.

Selected varieties: 'Brilliant'—smooth 3- to 4-inch roots with a creamy white interior in 110 days. 'Large Smooth Prague'—buff-colored roots in 110 days.

Growing conditions: Sow celeriac seeds ⅛ inch deep indoors 6 to 8 weeks before the last frost and keep them covered with a damp cloth until seedlings emerge. Transplant after all danger of frost is past into a constantly moist but well-drained soil enriched with compost, setting seedlings 12 inches apart. Feed at planting time and during the growing season with a balanced organic 5-10-10 fertilizer. Celeriac requires constant, even moisture and daytime temperatures between 55° and 85° F to grow. Harvest celeriac when roots are between 2 and 4 inches in diameter. Trim leaves and stems close to root and discard. Roots keep well in the garden under heavy mulch for up to a month after the first frost. They can also be stored in damp sand at 40° F in a root cellar or other cool location. A 10-foot row yields 6 to 10 pounds of celeriac.

CELERY

'Utah'

Hardiness: *warm-season annual*

Planting method: *transplants*

Plant spacing: *6 to 9 inches*

Light: *full sun to light shade*

Crisp, succulent stalks enclosing a pale, leafy heart in early summer or fall. Use celery in salads, for hors d'oeuvres, as a side dish, and as an aromatic flavoring in soups and stews.

Selected varieties: 'Fordhook Giant'—stocky 15- to 18-inch plants ready to harvest in 120 days. 'Giant Pascal'—thick stalks, creamy hearts, and dark green foliage on 2-foot plants in 125 days. 'Golden Self-Blanching'—very early variety with golden yellow, almost stringless 2-foot stalks in 85 days. 'Utah 52-70 R Improved'—dark green stalks with excellent keeping quality on 26-inch disease-resistant plants in 105 days.

Growing conditions: Sow celery seeds ¼ inch deep indoors 6 to 8 weeks before last frost. When seedlings are about 4 inches tall and all danger of frost is past, transplant them to a constantly moist but well-drained garden soil enriched with compost; a pH between 5.8 and 6.7 is ideal. Set seedlings 6 to 9 inches apart. Sow seed directly in the garden in late spring for a fall crop. Feed at planting and about once a month during the growing season with a balanced 5-10-10 organic fertilizer. Celery requires daytime temperatures between 55° and 85° F to grow.

CELTUCE

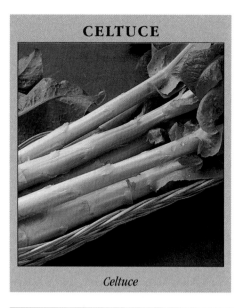

Celtuce

Hardiness: *cool-season annual*

Planting method: *direct sowing; transplants*

Plant spacing: *12 inches*

Light: *full sun to light shade*

Tender spring leaves and succulent midribs on mature leaves in late spring to early summer. Use the tasty young leaves in salads or cook them as spring greens. Midribs have a consistency like that of artichoke hearts. Peel and eat them raw or cooked; they can be substituted in recipes calling for celery or asparagus. In frost-free areas, grow celtuce as a winter green.

Selected varieties: Sold only as celtuce; has rosettes of puckered, lobed leaves ready to eat in 45 days; the midribs are ready to harvest in 90 days.

Growing conditions: Start celtuce seeds indoors 4 weeks before the desired transplanting date, setting seeds ½ inch deep. Transplant outdoors as early as 4 weeks before the last frost, in time for the crop to mature before hot weather arrives. Celtuce prefers a loose soil amended with compost or other organic matter. Celtuce can also be sown directly outdoors 4 to 6 weeks before last frost for spring crops and 8 weeks before first frost for fall crops. Sow seed in wide bands and thin when seedlings are 2 inches tall. Provide ample water to keep leaves from becoming bitter and to keep midribs succulent.

CHARD, SWISS CHARD

'Rhubarb'

Hardiness: *warm-season annual*

Planting method: *direct sowing*

Plant spacing: *6 to 12 inches*

Light: *full sun to light shade*

Smooth or crinkled broad leaves with thick, crunchy midribs from late spring to fall. Actually a type of beet that lacks an edible root, chard is heat tolerant and provides a reliable crop of vitamin-rich greens throughout the summer, when many other greens bolt. Leaves have a flavor reminiscent of spinach, while the midribs are prepared like celery or asparagus. Some varieties may overwinter as perennials in milder climates. Plant chard in containers in a kitchen garden and use red-ribbed varieties in an edible landscape with carrots, nasturtiums, and other attractive vegetables and herbs.

Selected varieties: 'Fordhook Giant'—fleshy leaves with creamy white midribs up to 2½ inches across in 60 days. 'Large White Ribbed'—wide white midribs and veins on deep green, smooth leaves in 60 days. 'Lucullus'—pale green leaves and white stems in 60 days. 'Perpetual Spinach'—early variety with smooth, dark green leaves and very little midrib, ideal for cooking greens, in 50 days. 'Rhubarb'—thick, reddish green leaves and brilliant ruby red midribs and veins in 60 days. 'Swiss Chard of Geneva'—winter-hardy variety for year-round culture with large, celery-like midribs in 60 days.

Growing conditions: Sow chard outdoors just after the last frost, setting seeds ½ inch deep in well-drained soil enriched with organic matter; chard does not transplant well. It can be planted at any time throughout spring and summer up until 8 weeks before the first fall frost and is ideal for succeeding spring crops such as peas. Thin seedlings to stand 6 to 12 inches apart and use thinnings in salads and soups. Maintain a constant moisture level for the sweetest, most succulent leaves and midribs. Pick outer leaves continuously to keep new young leaves coming on, or cut entire plants 2 inches above the crown when leaves reach 6 inches or taller; plants will regrow from the deep, strong roots in 3 to 4 weeks for

'Lucullus'

harvesting again. Cutting plants back whenever leaves become too tough or coarse will stimulate them to produce tender young leaves. A 10-foot row yields approximately 5 pounds of chard.

CHAYOTE

Chayote

Hardiness: *Zones 8-10*

Planting method: *direct sowing*

Plant spacing: *10 to 15 feet*

Light: *full sun*

Also called vegetable pear. A member of the squash family with furrowed, pear-shaped green fruits on climbing vines in late summer to fall. Grow as a hot-season annual north of Zone 8. Use the mild-flavored young fruits like summer squashes and mature fruits like winter squashes. The single large seed has a nutty flavor. Harvest young shoots of established plants and prepare like asparagus or dig the large roots and use like potatoes. Also called mirliton or christophene.

Selected varieties: No named varieties; sold as chayote. Young fruits ready to harvest in 90 days and ½- to 1-pound mature fruits in 180 days.

Growing conditions: For each vine, plant an entire fruit, laying it at an angle with the stem end slightly exposed above the soil level. Ideal soil pH is between 5.5 and 6.5. Plant in pairs to ensure pollination needed for fruit set and provide a trellis, wall, or other support for the fast-growing vines to climb. Keep well watered. Begin harvesting when young fruits are 4 to 6 inches in length. Chayote can be stored in a cool location for up to 2 to 3 months. A well-grown vine typically bears about 35 fruits but may yield as many as 100 in ideal conditions.

CHICORY

'Spadona'

Hardiness: *cool-season annual*

Planting method: *direct sowing*

Plant spacing: *8 inches*

Light: *full sun*

Tart or bitter leaves for mixed green salads and spring flower stalks that are eaten raw or cooked like asparagus. For sweeter flavor, harvest the inner leaves when they are small—no more than 6 inches long—and discard the outer leaves. Chicory is milder in cool weather.

Selected varieties: 'Ceriolo'—tight 2- to 3-inch rosettes of tender medium green leaves in 40 days. 'Dentarella', also called 'Catalogna'—succulent stalks and dandelion-shaped leaves in 65 days; sometimes called asparagus chicory. 'Puntarella'—thick, twisted 12- to 18-inch flower stalks. 'Spadona', also called 'Lingua di Cane'—smooth, toothed, pale green leaves in 40 days.

Growing conditions: Plant chicory seeds ½ inch deep in well-drained, moderately fertile soil in early spring or in late summer to early fall for harvesting in fall, winter, or spring. Thin plants to stand 8 inches apart. Cut individual leaves as needed with scissors or harvest the entire head. Harvest flower stalks when they are 6 inches tall, cutting them at soil level.

COLLARDS

'Georgia'

Hardiness: *cool-season annual*

Planting method: *direct sowing*

Plant spacing: *12 to 18 inches*

Light: *full sun*

Tall rosettes of thick blue-green leaves with a mild cabbagelike flavor in summer or fall. Frost sweetens the flavor. Cook collards as a side dish or use in soups.

Selected varieties: 'Georgia'—heat-tolerant variety with loose rosettes of white-veined leaves in 70 to 80 days. 'Vates'—thick, broad leaves on compact, bolt-resistant plants in 75 days.

Growing conditions: A member of the cabbage family, collards tolerate heat better than kale and are more cold tolerant than cabbage, two closely related vegetables. Plant seed ½ inch deep outdoors 3 to 4 weeks before the last frost for harvesting from spring through summer or in midsummer for a fall crop. Collards may overwinter in mild climates.

Keep collards constantly moist but not soggy and fertilize every 2 to 3 weeks with fish emulsion or other organic fertilizer with at least 10 percent nitrogen. To minimize soil-borne diseases, do not plant collards where other members of the cabbage family have been planted for at least 3 years. Young leaves are ready to pick in 40 days. Twelve plants will supply a family of four with summer and fall greens.

CORN

'Silver Queen'

Hardiness: *hot-season annual*

Planting method: *direct sowing*

Plant spacing: *12 to 14 inches*

Light: *full sun*

Sweet, juicy yellow, white, or bicolored starchy kernels lining cylindrical cobs on stalks up to 9 feet tall in mid- to late summer. Plant breeders have improved both the taste and the keeping quality of sweet corn by manipulating the gene that makes sweet corn sweet to produce "sugar-enhanced" varieties that have a higher initial sugar content and a storage life 3 to 5 days longer than standard varieties. Also the result of breeding programs are "supersweet" varieties that have twice the sugar content of standard varieties and a storage life up to 10 days longer. Choose early, midseason, and late-maturing varieties for a succession of sweet corn through the end of summer. Sweet corn freezes well for long-term storage. Popcorn varieties are higher in starch and lower in sugar than sweet corn. The ears are harvested after the stalks have dried.

Selected varieties: Sweet corn varieties include: 'Burgundy Delight'—a midseason variety with bicolored kernels on 8-inch ears wrapped in burgundy-colored husks in 80 days. 'Butter and Sugar'—early variety with bicolored kernels on 7½-inch ears in 70 days. 'Earlivee'—early yellow variety with ears in 63 days, making it a good choice for short-season gardens or a succession planting to follow spring crops such as peas or spinach. 'Golden Cross Bantam'—popular yellow hybrid with 8-inch ears in 85 days. 'Platinum Lady'—drought-resistant midseason variety with white kernels on 8-inch ears in 78 days. 'Silver Queen'—extremely sweet and tender late-season, blight-and-wilt-resistant white variety with 9-inch ears in 92 days.

Sugar-enhanced varieties include: 'Bodacious'—midseason variety with yellow kernels on 8-inch ears in 80 days. 'Clockwork'—vigorous midseason variety that will germinate in cool soil with bicolored kernels on 8-inch ears in 78 days. 'Double Gem'—early variety that

'Lancelot'

will germinate in cool soil with tender, bicolored kernels on blocky, 8-inch ears in 70 days. 'Duet'—midseason variety with bicolored kernels on 9-inch ears wrapped in burgundy-tinged husks in 74 days. 'Lancelot'—wilt-resistant, drought-tolerant bicolored variety with 9-inch ears in 80 days. 'Miracle'—late season, rust-resistant variety with yellow kernels on large 9½-inch ears in 84 days. 'Pristine'—midseason variety with very sweet white kernels on 8½-inch ears in 76 days. 'Seneca Starshine'—early white variety with 8½-inch ears of exceptional keeping quality in 70 days. 'Sugar Buns'—early hybrid with creamy yellow kernels on 7½-inch ears in 70 days. 'Tuxedo'—wilt-resistant and drought-tolerant midseason yellow variety with 8½-inch ears in 74 days.

Supersweet varieties include: 'Early Xtra Sweet'—early yellow hybrid with 9-inch ears in 70 days. 'How Sweet It Is'—midseason white variety with 8-inch ears in 88 days. 'Northern Xtra-

Sweet'—early variety with yellow kernels on 7½-inch ears in 67 days. 'Skyline'—early bicolored variety that germinates in cool soil with very sweet kernels on 8-inch ears in 70 days. 'Starstruck'—a late-maturing variety

'Early Xtra Sweet'

with bicolored kernels on 8- to 9-inch cobs in 92 days.

Popcorn varieties include: 'Giant Yellow'—tender yellow kernels in 105 days. 'Mini-Blue'—stubby 2- to 4-inch ears with tiny blue kernels for decorative use or popping in 100 days. 'Robust 20-70'—late-maturing yellow variety with high popping volume in 98 days. 'White Cloud'—late white variety with 5-inch ears in 95 days. 'Yellow Hybrid'—deep yellow kernels in 89 days.

Growing conditions: Corn needs a long, hot summer for good growth; days to maturity are a less reliable measure of when a variety will ripen than the number of hot days. Plant seeds 1 to 2 inches deep when the temperature of the soil is at least 60° F, in late spring to early summer; supersweet varieties need very warm, moist soil to germinate well. Row covers help to speed the germination and growth of early varieties in cool soil. Since corn is pollinated by the wind, sow seed in blocks of at least four rows to ensure good pollination. If you are planting more than one variety, choose varieties with maturity dates at least 14 days apart to avoid cross-pollination. If space allows, you can also prevent cross-pollination by planting different varieties at least 250 feet apart.

Thin plants to stand 12 to 14 inches apart; closer spacing lowers yields and encourages fungal diseases. When the

first sowing is knee high, plant a second variety to extend the harvest season. To ensure that ears on the edges of the blocks get pollinated, strip pollen from the tassels and sprinkle it on the silks. Provide ample water throughout the growing season and feed corn with a balanced 5-10-10 organic fertilizer when stalks are knee high and again when silks become visible at the tips of the ears. Rotate corn with other crops to control both pests and diseases.

Harvest sweet corn 3 weeks after silks appear; the highest ear on the stalk

'How Sweet It Is'

ripens first. Allow popcorn stalks to dry, then harvest ears, pull husks back, and hang in a well-ventilated area to finish drying. Sweet corn and popcorn produce one or two ears per stalk.

CORN SALAD, MACHE

'Vit'

Hardiness:	*winter-hardy Zones 5-9*
Planting method:	*direct sowing*
Plant spacing:	*2 inches*
Light:	*full sun*

Mounded rosettes of tender smooth greens with a mild nutty flavor prized for salads in spring or fall in northern gardens and throughout the winter in mild regions. Also called lamb's lettuce.

Selected varieties: 'Big Seed', also called 'Grosse Graine'—smooth, round, bright green leaves in 45 days. 'Coquille'—cold-tolerant variety with spoon-shaped, cupped leaves in 45 days. 'D'Etampes'—prominently veined, smooth, round leaves on compact, cold-tolerant plants good for overwintering. 'Elan'—short, smooth shiny upright leaves; especially suitable for fall and winter crops where the weather is cold and wet because of its mildew resistance. 'Verte des Cambrai'—pest-resistant and very cold tolerant compact rosettes of 3- to 4-inch flat round leaves in 60 days. 'Vit'—very vigorous variety with long, glossy leaves and a minty flavor, especially good for overwintering.

Growing conditions: Plant corn salad ½ inch deep in very early spring 2 to 4 weeks before the last frost or in late summer to early fall; corn salad grows best at temperatures below 75° F. Keep constantly moist. Mulch fall crops lightly after frost to keep them growing into winter. Fall-planted corn salad will resume growth the following spring.

CRESS

Watercress

Hardiness:	*Zones 6-9; cool-season annual*
Planting method:	*transplants; direct sowing*
Plant spacing:	*4 inches*
Light:	*full sun to light shade*

Plants of three different species that go by the same common name because their leaves have a similar peppery flavor. Two of these cresses grow in ordinary garden soil, while the third is an aquatic plant that requires constant moisture. Use any of the cresses for garnishes, add to sandwiches for a crunchy bite, and add to salads to complement the blander taste of tender lettuces. Sprout cress seeds for use in salads, sandwiches, stir-fry dishes, and casseroles.

Selected species: Curly cress, also called broadleaf cress, garden cress, mountain grass, peppergrass (*Lepidium sativum*)—cool-season annual with finely cut, tightly frilled leaves in 10 to 21 days; seeds are especially recommended for sprouting. Watercress (*Nasturtium officinale*)—aquatic perennial with broad, mildly pungent leaves and succulent stems in 60 days. Winter cress, upland cress (*Barbarea verna*)—hardy biennial grown as a cool-season annual with smooth leaves on 6- to 8-inch stalks in 60 days.

Growing conditions: Plant curly cress 4 to 6 weeks before the last frost. Make successive sowings every 2 weeks until 2 weeks after the last frost for a continuous supply of fresh greens until plants bolt in summer heat. Sow fall crop starting 2 to

4 weeks before the first frost; plants will tolerate severe frost. Harvest by snipping stems about an inch above the plant's base; the plant will send up new growth two or three times. Indoors, sprout seeds on wet paper towels, cover with glass, and keep warm until seeds sprout, then grow on to about 4 inches tall, keeping towels constantly moist.

Sow winter cress ¼ inch deep in full sun to light shade in late fall or winter. Keep soil constantly moist but not wet. Thin to 4 inches. Harvest leaves from winter until

Upland Cress

late spring or early summer, when they become bitter. Seed can also be sown in early spring for harvest in 7 weeks.

Sow watercress indoors in containers, pressing seeds into the soil and covering containers with glass or plastic until seeds germinate. Transplant seedlings to individual pots, then transplant to constantly moist soil on bank of a pond or stream in full sun 2 to 4 weeks before the last frost; weight roots down with pebbles until they anchor themselves. Pinch plants back when they are 6 inches tall. Alternatively, grow watercress indoors in a container set in a saucer of water that is changed daily; when grown in soil, watercress needs indirect light to keep from becoming bitter. Pinch flower buds off; leaves become bitter if plants are allowed to bloom.

CUCUMBERS

'Marketmore 76'

Hardiness: *warm-season annual*

Planting method: *transplants; direct sowing*

Plant spacing: *12 inches*

Light: *full sun*

Oblong, cylindrical, mildly flavored succulent fruits with green skins on climbing vines or low bushy plants. Use juicy 8- to 10-inch slicing cucumbers fresh in salads and as a garnish. Crisp, stubby varieties, including dwarf cornichon types, have been specially bred for making pickles and relishes. Dwarf bush cucumbers require only one-third the space of vining types and are ideal for small garden plots or containers. Allow cucumber vines to sprawl in the garden among cornstalks or train vines on trellises or fences for edible landscaping. Gynecious varieties, which bear only female flowers, are noted for their very high yields. To ensure pollination and fruit production of gynecious cucumbers, plant at least one monoecious variety—that is, a type that bears both male and female flowers.

Selected varieties: Cornichon types include: 'Verte de Massy'—with very slim, 4-inch, bumpy fruits.

Bush types include: 'Bush Pickle'—heavy crop of early-maturing 4- to 5-inch fruits on compact 24-inch plants in 45 days. 'Salad Bush'—disease- and wilt-resistant plants with 8-inch fruits in 58 days. 'Spacemaster' 7- to 8-inch cucumbers in 62 days on compact, mosaic-resistant plants suitable for containers or hanging baskets.

Pickling types include: 'Boston'—extremely prolific vines with early crop of smooth 6- to 7-inch tapered fruits in 58 days. 'Early Green Cluster'—large crop of deep green, 5- to 6-inch fruits suitable for pickling or slicing in 55 days. 'Gherkin'—2- to 3-inch fruits ideal for sweet pickles in 60 days. 'Little Leaf'—very disease resistant, high-yielding vines with small fruits in 70 days. 'Miss Pickler'—gynecious variety producing a large crop of uniform fruits. 'Saladin'—large crop of knobby, crisp 4- to 5-inch fruits on mildew- and disease-resistant gynecious vines in 55 days.

Slicing types include: 'Burpee Hybrid II'—gynecious plants producing straight 8-inch fruits in 55 days. 'Burpless'—somewhat disease-tolerant hybrid with 10- to 12-inch fruits that are more easily digested than those of other varieties, in

'Salad Bush'

62 days. 'Early Pride'—large crop of 8½-inch fruits on mildew- and mosaic-resistant vines in 55 days. 'Early Surecrop'—vigorous, mildew-resistant variety with 8- to 9½-inch fruits in 58 days. 'Fanfare Hybrid'—disease- and mildew-resistant semidwarf with slender, 8- to 9-inch fruits in 63 days. 'Marketmore 76'—vines with exceptional disease resistance producing 8-inch fruits in 67 days. 'Poinsett 76'—early to midseason variety with wilt and mildew resistance bearing 7½-inch fruits in 63 days. 'Slicemaster'—early crop of 8-inch fruits on disease- and wilt-resistant gynecious vines in 55 days. 'Straight Eight'—slightly striped 8-inch fruits in 63 days. 'Sweet Slice'—very mild burpless 10- to 12-inch fruits on disease- and mildew-resistant vines in 63 days. 'Sweet Success'—mildew-resistant

vines bearing seedless, burpless 14-inch fruits in 54 days.

Growing conditions: Start cucumbers indoors 4 to 6 weeks before the last frost or direct sow 2 to 3 weeks after last frost, setting seed 1 inch deep in rows and thinning plants to stand 12 inches apart. Alternatively, plant five to six seeds in hills spaced 6 feet apart and thin to two

'Burpless'

to three plants. If you have planted a gynecious (female) variety with a monoecious pollinator, be sure to mark the pollinator so it is not accidentally thinned out. Monoecious cucumbers have green seeds, and gynecious types have beige seeds. There should be 1 pollinator plant for every 5 or 6 female plants. Provide ample water. Mulch to conserve moisture and reduce fruit rot. Plant disease-resistant varieties; remove and destroy any infected plants.

Pick cucumbers often to keep vines productive. They are ready to harvest when the flower falls off the blossom end. For best flavor and texture, pick them promptly, before seeds enlarge and toughen; a yellowish tinge at the blossom end signals an overmature fruit. Use a sharp knife to cut cucumbers from the vine to avoid injury to stems. Twenty-five plants yield approximately 30 pounds of cucumbers.

EGGPLANT

'White Egg'

Hardiness: *warm-season annual*

Planting method: *transplants; direct sowing*

Plant spacing: *18 to 24 inches*

Light: *full sun*

Glossy, smooth-skinned, shiny deep purple to lavender or white fruits with mild-flavored, soft flesh. Depending on the variety, fruits range in size from 1 to 12 inches or more. The low-growing, small-fruited varieties make excellent container plants. All parts of the plant except the fruits are poisonous.

Selected varieties: 'Bambino'—very heavy yields of rounded purple fruits only 1 to 2 inches in diameter on disease-resistant foot-high plants 60 days after transplanting. 'Black Beauty'—heavy yield of glossy black-purple, almost round fruits 80 days after transplanting. 'Classic'—long, slim, glossy black-purple fruits on vigorous plants 76 days after transplanting. 'Ichiban'—slender fruits 12 inches long and 1½ inches in diameter 58 days after transplanting on bushy 3-foot plants ideal for small gardens. 'Neon'—large yield of cylindrical, dark pink fruits completely free of bitterness 60 days from transplanting. 'Slim Jim'—slender 4- to 6-inch lavender to deep purple fruits on compact plants with handsome lavender-tinged foliage 75 days after transplanting, suitable for containers. 'Violette di Firenze'—large oblong to round deep lavender fruits, sometimes with white stripes. 'White Egg', also called 'Osterei' or 'Easter Egg'—clusters of 2- to 3-inch oval white fruits 52 days after transplanting on bushy 2-foot plants ideal for containers.

Growing conditions: Eggplant requires long, warm seasons to mature. In areas with a long growing season, sow seed ¼ to ½ inch deep directly in the garden when soil temperature is 70° F. Elsewhere, start indoors 8 to 10 weeks before last frost and set plants out about 2 to 3 weeks after the last frost, when night temperatures will remain above 50° F. Space plants 18 to 24 inches apart in

'Black Beauty'

rows 3 feet apart and stake to keep fruits growing straight. Use floating row covers to speed the growth of transplants and control insects. Feed biweekly with a side dressing of fish emulsion or manure tea and water well, especially from flowering through harvest. To control verticillium wilt, do not plant eggplant where tomatoes, peppers, or strawberries have grown the year before. Avoid working among plants after smoking to prevent introduction of tobacco mosaic virus. Harvest eggplant before the skin loses its shine; an overmature eggplant is dull and likely to be bitter. Cut the stem with shears or a knife and clip eggplant from stems; pick continuously to keep plants producing. A 10-foot row yields 7 or 8 pounds of eggplant.

ENDIVE and ESCAROLE

'Batavian'

Hardiness: *cool-season annuals*

Planting method: *direct sowing*

Plant spacing: *8 to 12 inches*

Light: *full sun to light shade*

Tender, piquant greens with distinctively different leaf shapes. Endive has rather slender, curly, finely cut leaves in loose, flat rosettes, while the broad, somewhat twisted or ruffled leaves of escarole form open, upright heads. Endive and escarole are most often used in salads but are also delicious cooked as side dishes or in soup. The gourmet vegetable called Belgian endive is actually not an endive but a type of chicory.

Selected varieties: Endive types include: 'Green Curled Ruffec'—a cold-tolerant endive good for fall planting with lacy dark green outer leaves and a creamy white heart in prostrate rosettes 15 to 17 inches across in 95 days. 'Salad King'—vigorous endive variety with deeply cut, curly dark green leaves with a pale green heart in spreading 2-foot plants that withstand light frost and are heat resistant and slow to bolt in 100 days. 'Tres Fin', also called 'Fine Curled'—lacy dark green leaves with a white midrib and creamy blanched heart in 60 to 70 days on spreading 10- to 12-inch plants that are slow to bolt.

Broad-leaved escarole types include: 'Batavian'—crumpled yellow-green outer leaves with fleshy, white midribs surrounding creamy white hearts in 85 days. 'Cornet d'Anjou'—loose head of very broad leaves with fan-shaped midribs in spring or fall that can be blanched to mellow its flavor.

Growing conditions: Plant endive and escarole for spring or fall crops; in summer leaves become bitter and plants go to seed. Sow spring crops outdoors 4 weeks before the last frost, setting seed ¼ inch deep; sow fall crops in midsummer. Space plants that will be blanched 8 inches apart; otherwise allow 12 inches between plants. Overcrowding encourages rot. Interplant escarole and endive among herbs and lettuce or in the shade of tomatoes. Keep the soil constantly moist and side-dress biweekly with weak manure tea or fish emulsion. In warm weather, escarole types are prone to

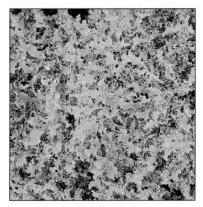

'Salad King'

bitterness, which can be prevented by blanching. To blanch, tie the outer leaves together around the inner heart for 2 to 3 weeks. In humid climates blanching may cause rot.

To harvest, pick individual leaves or cut entire plant at the soil line. If only the central core of leaves is removed and outer leaves are left in place, plants will sprout a new, smaller center in 3 to 4 weeks.

FENNEL

'Mammoth'

Hardiness: *cool-season annual*

Planting method: *direct sowing*

Plant spacing: *6 to 8 inches*

Light: *full sun to light shade*

Also known as Florence fennel. Broad-ribbed overlapping leafstalks that swell into a large white bulbous base with a licorice-like flavor and a crisp texture. Use raw in salads or hors d'oeuvres or cooked as a side dish. The feathery blue-green foliage can be used as an aromatic flavoring. Also called finochio or sweet anise. Be sure the seeds you purchase are *Foeniculum vulgare* var. *azoricum.* The closely related sweet fennel, *F. vulgare* var. *dulce,* is an herb valued for its leaves and seeds. It lacks the large bulb of Florence fennel.

Selected varieties: 'Mammoth'—firm, creamy white bulbs in 75 days. 'Zefa Fino'—less tendency to bolt than other varieties; matures in 65 to 75 days.

Growing conditions: Sow seeds ¼ inch deep 2 to 3 weeks before the last frost, as soon as the soil can be worked. Overmature bulbs become woody, so plant successive crops for a prolonged harvest of young bulbs until hot weather causes plants to bolt. Sow again in late summer for a fall harvest; fennel tolerates light frost. Hill soil around plant base as the bulb swells to blanch it and make it tender. Harvest when bulbs are 2 to 3 inches across, cutting just below the soil surface; the remaining stump will produce shoots that can be used for seasoning.

GARLIC

'California Silverskin'

Hardiness: *Zones 3-8*

Planting method: *cloves*

Plant spacing: *3 to 6 inches*

Light: *full sun to light shade*

Plump, pungently aromatic bulbs composed of wedge-shaped cloves in midsummer. Softneck garlic varieties produce medium-sized, intensely flavored cloves surrounding several overlapping inner layers of small bulbs. These varieties have good keeping quality and are excellent for braiding. Stiffneck garlic, the most cold-hardy type, produces both underground bulbs composed of four to six mildly flavored, easy-to-peel cloves with no inner layer and clusters of tiny bulblets atop coiled stalks called scapes; save the bulblets for planting the next year's crop. Elephant garlic has very large, mild bulbs that are delicious raw or baked whole. Use spring greens like chives and cut flowers for bouquets.

Selected varieties: 'California Silverskin'—softneck garlic with pearly white, sometimes yellow-veined bulbs composed of up to 20 cloves; excellent keeping quality. 'Elephant Garlic'—large 2½- to 3-inch bulbs composed of four to six enormous cloves. 'German Red'—stiffneck type with bright purple ¼-pound bulbs composed of up to 12 yellow-fleshed cloves. 'German White Stiffneck'—a stiffneck type with five to six plump cloves forming large bulbs. 'Italian Purple'—stiffneck garlic producing medium-sized bulbs striped with purple;

biting flavor. 'New York Strains'—very cold hardy softneck garlic with a purple blush on papery white skins. 'Rocambole'—stiffneck garlic type with fat, mild-flavored bulbs. 'Spanish Roja Garlic'—softneck type with a particularly sharp, biting flavor. Spring plantings of all types mature in 120 to 150 days; fall plantings mature the following summer.

Growing conditions: Separate garlic cloves and plant them with the pointed tip up about 1½ to 2 inches deep in com-

'German White Stiffneck'

post-enriched soil starting 6 weeks before first frost and continuing until early winter; alternatively, plant in early to midspring. Mulch to prevent heaving. Garlic will grow in light shade, producing smaller bulbs than it does when grown in full sun. Spring-planted crops also yield smaller bulbs. Pinch the coiled scapes of stiffneck garlic as they appear to produce larger bulbs instead of a dual crop of bulbs and bulblets. Harvest by forking out of ground in summer when tops begin to yellow. Use bruised bulbs immediately or freeze. Cure unblemished bulbs for several days on screens in a well-ventilated place, then braid them, hang in bunches, or put in mesh bags and store in dry, cool area until needed.

HORSERADISH

'Maliner Kren'

Hardiness: *Zones 3-8*

Planting method: *root cuttings*

Plant spacing: *18 inches*

Light: *full sun*

Thick, forked white roots in fall through early winter. Peeled horseradish grated into white wine vinegar or distilled vinegar keeps several weeks for use as a hot, pungent flavoring for meats and sauces. Use young leaves as a salad green.

Selected varieties: 'Maliner Kren', also called 'Bohemian'—straight roots up to 18 inches long in 150 days.

Growing conditions: Plant small horseradish roots or 6-inch thin root cuttings taken from larger roots 2 to 3 inches deep in spring as soon as the ground can be worked. Even moisture produces the best roots. Dig roots anytime after a hard frost from fall until early spring, before growth resumes. Be careful to remove the entire root. Horseradish sprouts from any remaining root sections to become an invasive garden pest; plant in a bottomless bucket or wooden frame to restrain its spread. Grate roots for immediate use or store whole roots in sawdust or sand in a cool location; use small roots to start the next season's crop. Where growing seasons are short, plant horseradish roots in fall for harvest the following year. Though a winter-hardy perennial, horseradish is usually grown as a cool-season annual since older roots become woody and are less flavorful than young ones.

JERUSALEM ARTICHOKES

'French Mammoth White'

Hardiness: *Zones 6-9*

Planting method: *root cuttings*

Plant spacing: *12 to 24 inches*

Light: *full sun*

Small, knobby, round tubers with a crunchy texture and nutty flavor from late summer through fall. Peel Jerusalem artichokes and slice raw for salads, use like water chestnuts, or prepare like potatoes. During the growing season the tall foliage can serve as a screen for the vegetable garden.

Selected varieties: 'French Mammoth White'—clumps of egg-sized tubers in 110 to 150 days and stout 6- to 10-foot stalks bearing 3-inch yellow blossoms resembling sunflowers.

Growing conditions: Plant small whole tubers or pieces of Jerusalem artichoke with two or three eyes each 4 to 6 inches deep in spring, allowing 3 feet between rows. Jerusalem artichoke thrives in a dry, infertile soil, so water and fertilize sparingly. Remove flower buds as they form to encourage greater root growth. Dig tubers as needed or store in sand in a cool location. They can also be mulched and stored in the ground over the winter. Jerusalem artichoke sprouts readily from any tubers or pieces remaining in the ground and can become an invasive pest.

JICAMA

Jicama

Hardiness: *hot-season annual*

Planting method: *transplants*

Plant spacing: *1 to 2 feet*

Light: *full sun*

Large, round tubers with crispy, sweet white flesh resembling water chestnuts in fall. Slice jicama into fruit or vegetable salads, use in place of crackers for hors d'oeuvres, or fry like potatoes. Leaves, flowers, and seeds and ripe seed pods are all poisonous.

Selected varieties: Sold only as jicama, a climbing vine with large, heart-shaped leaves, pealike purple flowers, and a single rounded to heart-shaped tuber up to 6 inches in diameter with smooth, brown-gray skin in 120 to 180 days.

Growing conditions: Start jicama seeds indoors 8 to 10 weeks before last frost and set transplants outdoors into a loose, fertile soil enriched with compost as soon as soil warms; soak seeds for best germination. Provide a trellis or other support for vines. Pinch growing tips when vines reach 3 feet and remove all flower buds to produce the largest tubers. Dig tubers before the first frost. Jicama requires a 9-month growing season to reach full size; roots grown in a shorter growing season will be proportionally smaller.

KALE

'Dwarf Blue Curled Scotch Vates'

Hardiness: *cool-season annual*

Planting method: *direct sowing; transplants*

Plant spacing: *8 to 12 inches*

Light: *full sun to light shade*

Dense rosettes of ruffled and curled succulent leaves in multiple shades of green and blue-green with a mild cabbage flavor in spring or fall that is at its best in fall when a touch of frost sweetens flavor. Greens can even be harvested beneath a blanket of snow for a fresh winter vegetable. Use spring thinnings and crunchy young kale leaves in salads or as a garnish. Cook greens in soups, side dishes, and casseroles, discarding the tough midrib before preparing. The bold rosettes are attractive accents in beds, borders, or containers.

Selected varieties: 'Blue Siberian'—dwarf variety with ruffled blue-green leaves in open rosettes up to 2 feet across in 70 days. 'Dwarf Blue Curled Scotch Vates'—very early variety with tightly curled leaves on low-spreading 12- to 14-inch plants from seed in 55 days; not as cold tolerant as other varieties. 'Red Russian', also called 'Ragged Jack'—heirloom variety with wavy, oak-like leaves on tall plants that turn from blue-green to deep purple-red when touched by frost in 48 days. 'Winterbor'—very cold tolerant variety with curly green leaves in 60 days on large plants 3 feet tall and 2 feet wide that regrow vigorously when picked for a continuing harvest.

Growing conditions: For spring crops, plant seed outdoors 4 to 6 weeks before the last frost, setting seeds ½ inch deep in rows 2 to 3 feet apart. Make successive sowings that will mature before hot weather induces semidormancy and leaves become bitter and tough. For fall and winter crops, make successive sowings starting 6 to 8 weeks before the first frost. Plant kale in moist, well-drained fertile loam enriched with compost and use mulch to retain moisture. Feed growing plants every 2 weeks with fish emulsion or any other balanced organic

'Red Russian'

fertilizer that provides ample nitrogen to support leaf growth. To minimize clubroot and other soil-borne diseases, do not plant kale where other members of the cabbage family have been planted for at least 3 years.

To harvest, remove outer leaves for a continuous supply of greens or cut whole plant at the soil line. Kale can be stored over winter in the garden and harvested as needed. It will keep for several weeks after cutting if refrigerated. A 10-foot row produces about 5 pounds of kale.

KOHLRABI	**LEEKS**	**LETTUCE**

'Early Purple Vienna'

'Large American Flag'

![Lettuce]

'Buttercrunch'

Hardiness: *cool-season annual*

Planting method: *transplants; direct sowing*

Plant spacing: *4 to 6 inches*

Light: *full sun to light shade*

Hardiness: *cool-season annual*

Planting method: *transplants; direct sowing*

Plant spacing: *4 to 6 inches*

Light: *full sun to light shade*

Hardiness: *cool-season annual*

Planting method: *direct sowing; transplants*

Plant spacing: *4 to 14 inches*

Light: *full sun to light shade*

Pale green or purplish bulbs with a very mild cabbagelike flavor in late spring or fall. Eat young kohlrabi raw out of hand like apples, slice into salads, or steam or parboil for side dishes.

Selected varieties: 'Early Purple Vienna'—greenish white flesh beneath purple skin in 60 days, recommended for fall planting. 'Early White Vienna'—an especially cold tolerant variety with 2-inch pale green bulbs in 55 days, recommended for fall planting. 'Grand Duke'—small bulbs with crisp, tender white flesh on compact plants in 45 days, especially recommended for spring planting.

Growing conditions: For a spring crop, sow seed indoors in peat pots 6 to 8 weeks before setting outdoors anytime from 5 weeks before the last frost until 2 weeks after in soil enriched with compost. For a fall crop, sow seeds ½ inch deep outdoors in mid- to late summer; light frost improves flavor. Harvest when bulbs are 2 inches across; older bulbs become woody and fibrous. Kohlrabi can be grown in light shade but if so produces elongated, rather than round, bulbs that aren't as crisp in texture. A 10-foot row yields 5 to 8 pounds of bulbs.

Thick white stems and broad, flat green leaves with a mild onion flavor in fall and winter. Use like onions for flavoring, garnishes, salads, soups, and side dishes.

Selected varieties: 'Alaska'—thick, sweet stems, good for overwintering, in 125 days. 'Blue Solaise'—short 4- to 6-inch stems in 140 days. 'King Richard'—early variety maturing in 75 days; will withstand frost to 20° F but is not winter hardy. 'Large American Flag', also called 'Broad London'—1- to 1½-inch-thick stems, very cold tolerant and excellent for overwintering, in 120 days. 'Winter Giant'—very tall, thick stems, good for overwintering.

Growing conditions: For fall harvest, sow leeks ¼ inch deep indoors 8 to 12 weeks before the last frost date. Bury transplants up to their leaf joints in a narrow trench 8 to 12 inches deep. As leeks grow, gradually fill trench in to develop thick, blanched stalks. For a winter or early spring crop, sow seed of cold-hardy varieties outdoors from late spring to early summer. Where winter temperatures fall below 20° F, mulch with 12 to 18 inches of straw or leaves. Leeks will also keep for up to 8 weeks if dug before the ground freezes and packed in damp sand or sawdust in a cool place. A 10-foot row yields up to 30 pounds of leeks.

Loose rosettes or firm heads of delectable leaves from spring to early summer and again from early to late fall when a succession of different varieties is planted. Crisphead varieties have tight, firm heads that are blanched at the center. They require a very long growing season and are lowest in nutrients of all lettuce types. Butterhead or Boston varieties have tender, easily bruised leaves folded into loose heads with creamy blanched centers; they contain vitamins A and C as well as calcium and iron. Leaf or bunching varieties form open rosettes of curly, puckered leaves that are easy to grow, mature quickly, and are very nutritious, with high levels of vitamins A and C, and calcium. The stiff, erect leaves of romaine or cos varieties fold into upright heads that blanch at their centers; more heat tolerant than other types, they are similar nutritionally to leaf varieties.

Lettuce reigns as the supreme green in salads. Sauté lettuces alone or with other greens as a side dish, add whole or shredded leaves to soups, tuck into sandwiches, or use as a garnish.

Selected varieties: Crisphead varieties, also called Batavian or iceberg lettuces, include: 'Great Lakes'—a cold-tolerant, slow-to-bolt variety with crisp, juicy leaves in 82 to 90 days. 'Iceberg'—

creamy blanched centers and deep green outer leaves in 85 days. 'Ithaca'—bolt-resistant variety best for spring crops in 72 days. 'Red Grenoble'—slow-to-bolt spring lettuce with wine red leaves to cut as needed when young or allow to develop into heads. 'Rosy'—slow-to-bolt variety with burgundy-tinged leaves in small heads. 'Summertime'—very bolt resistant medium-sized heads of crisp leaves in 68 days.

'Green Ice'

Butterhead or Boston lettuce varieties include: 'Bibb'—3½-inch heads of deep green leaves in 75 days. 'Buttercrunch'—thick, dark green leaves in firm heads with buttery yellow centers on heat-resistant plants in 53 to 65 days. 'Dark Green Boston'—tight heads of deep green leaves in 70 days. 'Four Seasons', also called 'Merveille des Quatre Saisons'—large 16-inch heads of bronze-tinged outer leaves around a tender, pale green inner heart in 49 to 65 days; best for spring planting because of its tendency to bolt. 'Tom Thumb'—firm miniature heads of medium green leaves ideal as an individual serving in 52 to 60 days.

Leaf or bunching lettuce varieties include: 'Black-Seeded Simpson'—fast-growing, heat-tolerant variety with crisp, highly frilled leaves in 45 days. 'Green Ice'—very slow to bolt rosettes of sweet, deep green, crinkled leaves in 45 days. 'Oakleaf'—deeply lobed, tender leaves on slow-to-bolt plants in 45 to 55 days. 'Prizehead'—frilly red-tinged leaves in large, loose heads in 48 days. 'Red Sails'—bolt-resistant variety with large crumpled leaves fringed with red in broad, open heads up to a foot across in 45 days. 'Ruby'—heat-tolerant variety

with frilled, curly leaves shading from deep burgundy to pale green in 47 days. 'Salad Bowl'—rosettes of bright green, frilly leaves in 60 days in cool weather, ideal for spring planting.

Romaine or cos lettuce varieties include: 'Cimarron Red'—compact heads of much-crinkled, red-tinged leaves in 58 days. 'Little Gem', also called 'Diamond Gem'—crisp miniature heads 4 inches across and 6 inches tall with creamy blanched centers in 45 to 56 days. 'Paris Island Cos'—thick-ribbed, dense 12-inch-tall heads with blanched hearts in 65 days. 'Rosalita'—thick-ribbed summer lettuce with oval, curly leaves in dense heads in 62 days. 'Rouge d'Hiver'—very large heads of broad, deep red leaves enfolding crisp hearts, best for fall planting, in 60 days. 'Winter Density'—extremely frost-tolerant cross between

'Oakleaf'

cos and butterhead types good for fall planting in 65 days.

Growing conditions: Plant lettuce seeds ¼ to ½ inch deep outdoors in a moisture-retentive, compost-enriched soil as soon as the ground can be worked in spring. In areas where the cool growing season is short, start seeds of long-season crisphead, butterhead, and romaine crops 4 to 6 weeks before the last frost date. Lettuce is very shallow rooted; keep soil evenly moist for continuous growth and sweetest flavor. Loosehead and butterhead varieties tolerate light shade, especially as summer heat approaches. Lettuce grows best in cool soil at cool temperatures. Make small successive sowings of different varieties for a continuous supply of lettuce until summer temperatures of 85° F cause plants to

bolt to seed and leaves to become bitter. Sow again in early fall when daytime temperatures become cool again.

Proper thinning of lettuces is critical to success; thin crisphead or butterhead varieties to stand 12 to 14 inches apart, leaf or romaine varieties to stand 4 to 6 inches at first and later to 6 to 10 inches apart

'Red Sails'

depending on the variety. Use thinnings in salads or transplant to another spot for a later harvest. To harvest, pull up the entire head of crisphead or butterhead lettuces. Pick outer leaves of loosehead or cos varieties as they mature or cut entire plant off at the base; it will regrow a second, smaller crop of leaves. A 10-foot row yields 10 heads of head lettuce or 9 pounds of leaf lettuce.

MELONS

'Earlisweet' Muskmelon

Hardiness: *warm-season annual*

Planting method: *transplants; direct sowing*

Plant spacing: *18 to 36 inches*

Light: *full sun*

Round or oval fruits with sweet, juicy, often aromatic flesh enclosed in a hard rind on sprawling vines. Muskmelons, sometimes incorrectly called cantaloupes, have a deeply ribbed, heavily netted rind and orange flesh with a musky aroma. Charentais-type cantaloupes, or true cantaloupes, are small, round orange-fleshed melons with smooth rinds and no netting. Honeydew, Crenshaw, and casaba melons are large, smooth-skinned melons with pale green or orange flesh that has a fruity rather than a musky aroma. Oval or round, smooth-skinned watermelons have deliciously sweet and exceptionally juicy, crisp red or yellow flesh with seeds scattered throughout rather than in the central seed cavity found in other types of melons.

Selected varieties: Netted muskmelon types include: 'Alaska'—with very early oval melons with deep salmon flesh in 72 days. 'Ambrosia'—3- to 5-pound melons with thick peach-colored flesh and small seed cavities on disease-resistant vines in 86 days. 'Casablanca'—mildew-resistant vines bearing 4-pound melons with soft-textured, juicy, creamy white flesh tinged with pink in 85 days. 'Earlisweet'—very early maturing 5-inch fruits with deep salmon flesh in 70 days, resistant to fusarium wilt. 'Hale's Best Jumbo'—4-pound

melons with thick salmon flesh on drought-tolerant vines in 86 days. 'Hearts of Gold'—extremely sweet salmon-fleshed melons with small seed cavities in 90 days. 'Musketeer'—compact vines only 2½ to 3 feet long bearing 3-pound fruits with fragrant, light orange flesh in 90 days. 'Super Market'—wilt- and mildew-resistant vines bearing 4-pound melons with thick, bruise-resistant rinds and juicy orange flesh in 84 days. 'Sweet Bush'—very compact vines ideal for small gardens bearing 2-pound melons in 74 days. 'Topmark'—wilt-resistant oval melons with orange flesh and a small seed cavity in 90 days.

Charentais-type cantaloupes include: 'Alienor'—round, 2-pound fruits with

'Alaska' Muskmelon

pale, smooth skins and deep orange flesh in 90 days or sooner if vines are pruned to force earlier maturity. 'Charentais'—exceptionally sweet heirloom variety from France that ripens in 75 to 85 days even in cool areas. 'Pancha'—wilt- and mildew-resistant vines bearing 2-pound fruits with aromatic flesh in 80 days. 'Savor'—2½-pound melons with pale gray-green skin and deliciously aromatic flesh on disease-resistant vines in 78 days.

Honeydew melons include: 'Earlidew'—vigorous, disease-tolerant vines recommended for gardens in the East and Midwest with fruits that have aromatic, pale yellow-green flesh in 75 to 80 days. 'Orange Flesh'—late-maturing 4- to 6-pound round melons with sweet salmon-colored flesh in 90 days; 'Venus'—with heavy crops of 5½-inch oval fruits with a golden yellow rind enclosing bright green sweet flesh in 88 days.

Watermelon varieties include: 'Black

Diamond'—enormous round melons up to 50 pounds each with dark green skins and bright red flesh in 90 days. 'Bush Baby II'—very compact, space-saving vines bearing round 10-pound melons in 80 to 90 days. 'Charleston Gray'—wilt-

'Orange Flesh' Honeydew Melon

resistant and drought-tolerant vines with 28- to 35-pound melons that store well in 90 days. 'Crimson Sweet'—round 25-pound melons with skin striped light and dark green and firm, deep red flesh on disease-resistant vines in 80 days. 'Redball Seedless'—round 12-pound melons with glossy green skin and only a few white, edible seeds in 80 days. 'Sugar Baby'—10-inch round fruits with red flesh in 80 days. 'Yellow Baby'—small melons up to 7 inches in diameter with crisp yellow flesh in 80 days.

Miscellaneous melons include: 'Casaba Golden Beauty'—7- to 8-pound oval melon with wrinkled golden skin, white flesh, and a small seed cavity in 110 days. 'Crenshaw'—large, oval melons up to 14 pounds each with very tender peach-colored flesh and a small seed cavity in 90 days. 'Galia'—a tropical melon with pale green, very sweet flesh and a flavor reminiscent of banana in 75 days. 'Jaune des Canaries'—oval melon with slightly wrinkled green skin turning yellow when ripe and whitish green flesh in 100 to 110 days. 'Passport'—3½- to 4-pound tropical melon with thick, juicy pale green flesh with a banana-like aroma in 70 to 78 days.

Growing conditions: Start melons indoors 4 to 6 weeks before the last frost or direct sow 2 to 3 weeks after the last frost, setting seed ½ inch deep in rows and thinning plants to stand 18 to 36 inches apart. Allow 4 to 6 feet between rows. For direct sowing, plant five to six seeds in hills spaced 6 feet apart after the soil has warmed and thin to two to three plants. Choose compact bush-type vines for gardens that lack space for sprawling melon vines.

Melons grow best when the soil temperature is 70° F or more and need hot, dry weather in late summer and early fall to produce good fruit; air or soil temperatures below 50° F cause damage. Use black plastic mulch to warm soil and

'Crimson Sweet' Watermelon

keep fruits clean. Water well during early stages of growth and when plants are blooming and pollinating. Use floating row covers to protect young plants from insect pests but remove row covers when plants blossom so flowers will be pollinated. After fruit sets, withhold water unless conditions become very dry in order to concentrate sugars in the fruits, which need 2 to 3 weeks to ripen.

Powdery mildew attacks melon seedlings and vines with heavy fruit set in cool, damp weather; once leaves become mildewed, fruit will not ripen. Melons do not ripen off the vine.

Thumb pressure at the blossom end causes ripe cantaloupes to slip from their vines. Harvest tropical melons as the deep green skin changes to buff-yellow. Watermelons are ripe when the tendril closest to the fruit stem on the vine browns or when the part of the rind resting on the ground turns yellow. Each vine produces two to four fruits.

MUSTARD GREENS

'Florida Broadleaf'

Hardiness: *cool-season annual*

Planting method: *direct sowing*

Plant spacing: *4 to 6 inches*

Light: *full sun*

Smooth or highly frilled leaves with a pungent flavor in early spring or late fall. Pick young leaves to add zest and crunch to salads; parboil mature leaves for side dishes or use as a garnish.

Selected varieties: 'Florida Broadleaf'—smooth, lobed oval leaves with a white midrib in 45 days. 'Fordhook Fancy'—heat-tolerant variety with rather mild-flavored, deeply curled and fringed leaves in 40 days. 'Green Wave'—bright green leaves with tightly frilled edges in 45 days. 'Osaka Purple'—mild-flavored, broad dark purple leaves with white veins in 40 days, extremely slow to bolt. 'Red Giant'—red and green crinkled leaves up to 18 inches tall on very productive plants in 45 days. 'Southern Giant Curled'—light green leaves with frilly edges 45 to 50 days, cold tolerant and resistant to bolting.

Growing conditions: Sow mustard seeds outdoors ¼ to ½ inch deep in a compost-enriched soil as soon as the ground can be worked in spring. In mild-winter areas, sow a second crop 6 to 8 weeks before the first fall frost. For tender leaves, keep evenly moist and harvest leaves while young, cutting them as needed. A 10-foot row yields 10 pounds of mustard greens.

NASTURTIUM

'Whirlybird Mix'

Hardiness: *cool-season annual*

Planting method: *direct sowing*

Plant spacing: *4 to 10 inches*

Light: *full sun to light shade*

Brightly colored, 2- to 3-inch edible flowers and round, succulent leaves with a peppery flavor reminiscent of watercress on compact mounds or trailing stems in summer and fall. Use young leaves in salads or sandwiches and flower buds or mature petals as a colorful garnish for salads. Pickle buds or immature green seeds and use like capers. Use nasturtiums as edible ornamentals in beds, borders, and hanging baskets.

Selected varieties: 'Glorious Gleam Mixture'—deep gold to scarlet blossoms on trailing 2-foot stems. 'Jewel Mixed'—yellow, orange, red, and pink double flowers on 12-inch plants. 'Tip Top Mix'—apricot, gold, and scarlet flowers on compact 12-inch plants. 'Whirlybird Mix'—rose, gold, orange, and mahogany flowers in 12-inch mounds. All varieties bloom in 50 to 60 days.

Growing conditions: Start nasturtiums indoors 2 to 3 weeks before the last heavy frost or sow outdoors after danger of heavy frost is past, setting seeds ½ inch deep. Thin plants to stand 4 to 10 inches apart. Nasturtiums tolerate drought and poor or alkaline soils. Remove and discard the bitter pistils before eating the flowers.

OKRA

'Annie Oakley'

Hardiness: *hot-season annual*

Planting method: *direct sowing; transplants*

Plant spacing: *18 to 24 inches*

Light: *full sun*

Smooth or ribbed pods, often with spines, on erect bushy plants. The pods thicken soups, gumbos, and stews and are delicious served as a side dish. The dried pods are lovely in dried flower arrangements.

Selected varieties: 'Annie Oakley'—large crop of pods on dwarf 3- to 4-foot plants in 55 days. 'Burgundy'—plants to 4 feet with ornamental red-veined leaves and burgundy-colored pods in 60 days that retain their color after cooking. 'Clemson Spineless'—with spineless pods on 5-foot plants in 56 to 65 days.

Growing conditions: Sow okra seed ½ inch deep outdoors after soil temperatures reach 60° F; presoaking improves their germination rate. Thin dwarf plants to stand 18 inches apart, others to 24 inches. Okra grows best at temperatures between 70° and 85° F; where the warm growing season is short, start okra seeds indoors 4 to 6 weeks before setting outdoors, and mulch with black plastic to warm the soil. Feed regularly and keep constantly moist for succulent pods. Wear gloves and a long-sleeved shirt while snipping pods from plants. Pick young, tender pods 3 to 4 inches long every 2 or 3 days to keep plants producing. A single plant produces 50 to 200 pods.

ONIONS

'Granex Yellow'

Hardiness: *Zones 3-9*

Planting method: *direct sowing; transplants; sets*

Plant spacing: *2 to 3 inches*

Light: *full sun*

Pungently sweet, crisp bulbs, thickened stems, and piquant hollow greens in summer or fall depending on the type. Onion bulb formation is sensitive to day length. Plant short-day varieties as a winter bulb crop in mild-winter areas or for small pickling onions farther north. Grow long-day varieties for bulbs in northern gardens or for bunching onions in milder areas. Delicately flavored chives grow as a perennial in Zones 3-9. Egyptian onions form small bulbs at the tips of their stems rather than underground. Bunching onions have either very small bulbs or no bulb at all and are perennials in Zones 3-9.

Onions are the soul of many dishes. Use them as flavorings or as cases for stuffings. Cream, fry, escallop, boil, steam, or glaze them for side dishes. Slice them raw for salads, sandwiches, crudités, and garnishes. Pickle small onions or freeze chopped or whole small onions. Grow chives in pots indoors or out.

Selected varieties: Short-day varieties include: 'Granex Yellow'—very mild bulbs in 162 days. 'Red Granex'—slow-to-bolt bulbs with mild red flesh in 162 days. 'Red Hamburger'—slightly flattened bulbs with red-and-white flesh excellent eaten raw in 95 days. 'Texas Early Grano'—sweet jumbo bulbs best for fresh use in

175 days. 'Texas Grano'—large disease-resistant bulbs with thick rings of soft, white flesh in 168 days. 'Texas Grano 1015Y', also called 'Texas Supersweet' —heat- and drought-tolerant variety with very sweet softball-sized bulbs in 175 days. 'Yellow Bermuda'—extremely sweet white flesh in thick rings in 92 days.

Long-day varieties include: 'Ailsa Craig' —exceptionally large, early bulbs with pale yellow skins in 110 days. 'Early Yellow Globe'—uniform yellow onions that store well in 100 days. 'Northern Oak' —white flesh and heavy, dark brown skins for excellent storage quality in 108

'Walla Walla'

days. 'Sweet Sandwich'—large globes 3½ inches across with sweet yellow flesh in 112 days. 'Walla Walla'—mildly flavored, sweet jumbo bulbs in 110 to 120 days spring seeded, 300 days fall seeded. 'White Sweet Spanish'—very mild, sweet white bulbs with good keeping quality in 110 days. 'Yellow Sweet Spanish'—very mild, sweet yellow-fleshed bulbs up to a pound each in 110 days.

Egyptian onions—very cold hardy perennials that form small bulbs at the tips of the thick, hollow stems in lieu of flowers and a smaller number of bulbs underground in 180 days.

Green onion varieties, also called scallions or bunching onions, include: 'Beltsville Bunching'—very hardy variety for spring or fall planting in 65 days. 'Evergreen Long White', also called 'Nebuka'—good for overwintering in 60 days. 'Ishikura'—bulbless, long white stems and blue-green tops in 66 days.

Growing conditions: Grow onions from seeds, transplants, or sets depending on the length of the growing season and the type of onions desired. Plant short-day varieties in fall to produce bulbs the following summer; plant long-day varieties in spring for onions in fall. Plant bunching onions in spring or fall for use throughout the season. Plant perennial Egyptian onions in spring or fall; divide clumps every 3 or 4 years to maintain vigor. Sow seeds of bunching onions or long-day onions ½ inch deep in a fertile, moisture-

'Ishikura'

retentive soil enriched with compost or manure 4 to 6 weeks before last frost as soon as the ground can be worked in spring. Thin to stand 2 to 3 inches apart in rows 1 to 2 feet apart. For larger bulbs in a shorter time, start seeds indoors 12 weeks before setting out; transplants can be moved outdoors up to a month before the last frost. Small, dry onions called sets are the most reliable way to produce large bulbs, particularly for long-day varieties. Plant sets in early spring.

Harvest bulb onions by pulling them when half of their tops have fallen over. When the tops are completely wilted, snip them off 1½ inches above the bulbs, wipe off dirt and any loose skins, and continue to dry for 2 weeks or more in a dry area with good ventilation. Store the dry onions at 35° to 50° F. Harvest Egyptian onions when the tops begin to wilt and dry; dry for storage, pickle, or freeze. Bulb and bunching onions yield about 10 pounds per 10 feet of row.

ORACH

'Green Orach'

Hardiness: *cool-season annual*

Planting method: *direct sowing*

Plant spacing: *6 to 10 inches*

Light: *full sun*

Also called mountain spinach. Arrow-shaped leaves with a mild spinachy flavor in erect 1- to 4-foot clumps from spring into summer. Slower to bolt than spinach, orach is a good warm-weather alternative. Use tender young orach leaves in mesclun mixtures of young greens, and older leaves cooked or as a salad green mixed with lettuces; the red and yellow cultivars retain their tints when cooked. The seed heads are attractive additions to floral arrangements.

Selected varieties: 'Green Orach'—sweet, juicy leaves that do not become bitter as they age. 'Red Orach'—red-tinted stems and leaves. 'Yellow Orach'—golden leaves. All varieties ready to pick in 40 days.

Growing conditions: Sow orach seeds outdoors ½ inch deep when the soil temperature reaches 50° to 60° F. Keep soil moist. Make successive sowings throughout spring for a continuous supply of mesclun greens. Pick 6-inch leaves for mesclun; use leaves a foot or longer for summer salads or for cooking. Pinch out flower heads as they appear to encourage continued leaf growth. Orach tolerates both light frost and summer heat.

PAK-CHOI or BOK CHOY

'Mei Quing Choi'

Hardiness: *cool-season annual*

Planting method: *direct sowing*

Plant spacing: *8 to 12 inches*

Light: *full sun*

Broad rosettes of upright leaves with thick, succulent stalks that have a mildly pungent flavor. Pak-choi is essential in stir-fry dishes. Uncooked, the crisp stalks can be used like celery or carrots with dips and sauces.

Selected varieties: 'Lei Choi'—heat-tolerant variety with crunchy, celery-like white 8- to 10-inch stalks and deep green leaves in 47 days. 'Mei Quing Choi'—baby pak-choi with very tender pale green 6- to 8-inch stalks and leaves in 45 days; frost tolerant, heat tolerant, and slow to bolt.

Growing conditions: Sow pak-choi seeds outdoors as soon as ground can be worked in spring, setting seeds ½ inch deep and thinning plants to stand 8 to 12 inches apart. Pak-choi needs cool temperatures for best growth and goes to seed as days lengthen and weather warms. Plant a second crop in fall 50 to 60 days before first frost. Pak-choi will tolerate light frost. Harvest by cutting stems just above the soil line.

PARSLEY

Flatleaf

Hardiness: *Zones 8-9; cool-season annual*

Planting method: *direct sowing; transplants*

Plant spacing: *8 to 10 inches*

Light: *light shade to full sun*

Flat or crisply curled bright green leaves with a pungent flavor on strong stems from spring through fall, sometimes overwintering in milder climates. Interplant vitamin-rich parsley among lettuces, tomatoes, or peppers, or plant in containers to move indoors to a sunny window sill in winter. Use fresh or dried parsley for seasoning or as a breath-freshening edible garnish. Use fresh parsley for sauces such as salsa verde.

Selected varieties: Flatleaf, also called Italian, plainleaf, single leaf—flat, glossy, intensely flavored leaves excellent for cooking or drying. 'Krausa'—very frilly leaves especially pretty for garnishes. 'Moss Curled'—finely curled, deeply cut dark green leaves on compact plants. All 75 to 80 days.

Growing conditions: Sow parsley seed ¼ inch deep outdoors 2 to 4 weeks before the last frost after presoaking seeds in warm water for 24 hours or rubbing them between two sheets of sandpaper to break seed coats. Remove flowers to keep new leaves coming. Plants cut to the ground in fall may regrow the following spring. Sow seed in late summer for an early spring harvest.

PARSNIPS

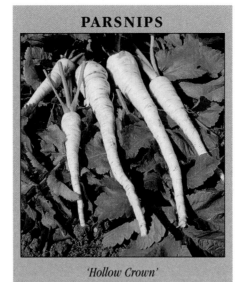

'Hollow Crown'

Hardiness: *cool-season annual*

Planting method: *direct sowing*

Plant spacing: *2 to 3 inches*

Light: *full sun*

Tapering white roots resembling carrots with a fine texture and sweet, nutty flavor that mature in late fall and can be stored in the garden through winter. Parsnips can be baked, steamed, grilled, sautéed, or prepared in many of the same ways as carrots or potatoes. Parboiling, however, dissolves and draws out the sugars in the roots, leaving them bland tasting.

Selected varieties: 'Harris Early Model'—short, stocky 12-inch roots with wide shoulders in 120 days. 'Hollow Crown'—exceptionally sweet, fine-grained roots up to 18 inches long in 125 days.

Growing conditions: Sow parsnip seeds in very early spring as soon as the ground can be worked. Soak seeds for 24 hours before setting them ½ to 1 inch deep in soil that has been tilled to a depth of 12 to 18 inches. Mulch to conserve moisture; lack of water causes roots to toughen. Begin harvesting after the first hard fall frost has sweetened the flavor. Store parsnips in the garden over the winter under a 12-inch mulch of hay or leaves anchored under black plastic. Harvest all of the previous season's parsnips by early spring before new growth begins; after that point roots toughen. A 10-foot row yields about 8 pounds of parsnips.

PEANUTS

'Early Spanish'

Hardiness: *hot-season annual*

Planting method: *direct sowing; transplants*

Plant spacing: *12 inches*

Light: *full sun*

Pods or shells filled with richly flavored kernels under bushy plants. Male flowers appear among the upper leaves; the smaller female flowers, on short stalks near the plant's base. Each fertilized female flower develops a peg, or stem, that grows downward and into the soil; the pods are produced underground on the pegs. Eat shelled peanuts raw, roasted, or boiled or grind them for nut butter.

Selected varieties: 'Early Spanish'—heavy-yielding plants with early-maturing pods with two to three kernels each in 105 days. 'Jumbo Virginia'—large crop of pods with one or two large kernels on 18-inch plants in 120 to 135 days.

Growing conditions: Pretreat pods or individual peanuts with skins intact with a bacterial inoculant and plant 1 inch deep in a heavy soil or 2 or more inches deep in a loose, sandy soil after it has warmed in the spring. Where growing seasons are short, start peanuts indoors in individual peat pots and plant out after all danger of frost is past in soil prewarmed under black plastic mulch; remove the plastic mulch to allow pegs access to the soil. Thin plants to stand 12 inches apart. Harvest after the foliage turns yellow but before the first frost, pulling plants up and hanging by roots to dry before removing pods. A single plant yields 40 to 50 pods.

PEAS

'Sugar Snap'

Hardiness: *cool-season annual*

Planting method: *direct sowing*

Plant spacing: *1 inch*

Light: *full sun*

Plump, sweet, round green seeds in long pods that are edible in some varieties on vining or bushy plants in early spring or late fall. Garden or shelling peas have thick, stringy, inedible pods that contain long rows of up to 11 large peas. Snow peas are raised primarily for their thin, succulent edible pods. Exceptionally sweet sugar snap peas offer both plump seeds and thick-walled, edible pods. Among the first fruits of the spring garden, fresh garden peas are a tonic eaten raw out of hand or in salads; they are delicious parboiled or steamed for use in side dishes, soups, and stews. Use snow peas in Oriental cuisine or as an hors d'oeuvre. Prepare sugar snap peas like garden peas or snow peas. Freeze surplus peas for long-term storage.

Selected varieties: Garden or shelling pea varieties include: 'Alaska'—the earliest garden pea with a heavy yield of 2½-inch pods containing six to eight peas on 2-foot plants in 56 days. 'Alderman', or 'Tall Telephone'—late-maturing 5- to 6-foot vine with large peas in easy-to-shell pods in 76 days. 'Green Arrow'—large crop of 4-inch pods with up to 11 peas each on disease-resistant plants in 70 days. 'Lincoln'—vigorous 2-foot vines with 3½-inch pods filled with up to nine plump peas excellent for freezing in 67

days. 'Little Marvel'—dependable crop of very early 3-inch pods on 18-inch plants in 63 days. 'Petit Provencal'—heavy crop of 2½-inch pods filled with six or seven tiny, sweet peas, or *petit pois,* on bushy plants in 60 days. 'Progress No. 9'—4-inch pods containing up to seven peas each on short, 15-inch vines in 62 days. 'Wando'—both heat- and cold-tolerant with very heavy crop of 3-inch pods containing seven to eight peas in 67 days, ideal for late-season crops in northern gardens. 'Waverex'—semiclimbing 18-inch vines bearing pods filled with seven or eight tiny, sweet peas, or *petit pois.* Snow or sugar pea varieties include:

'Green Arrow'

'Carouby de Maussane'—vigorous 5-foot vines with long, flat 5½-inch pods up to an inch wide in 65 days. 'Dwarf Gray Sugar'—pale green 2½- to 3-inch pods on 2½-foot vines in 63 days. 'Mammoth Melting Sugar'—disease-resistant 4-foot vines with broad pods in 72 days. 'Oregon Giant'—disease-resistant compact plants with broad, inch-wide pods up to 5 inches long filled with large, sweet peas in 70 days. 'Oregon Sugar Pod II'—heavy yields of crisp 4- to 5-inch pods, often in pairs, on nonclimbing dwarf vines in 70 days.

Sugar snap pea varieties include: 'Cascadia'—3-inch, thick-walled, juicy pods filled with sweet peas on compact plants in 58 days. 'Sugar Ann'—bushy, early-maturing variety with succulent 2½-inch pods on nonclimbing dwarf vines in 52 days. 'Sugar Bon'—disease-resistant, compact 2-foot plants with 3-inch pods in 56 days. 'Sugar Daddy'—stringless sugar snap peas on compact bushy 2-foot plants in 65 days. 'Sugar Snap'—3-inch pods on climbing 6-foot vines in 62

days. 'Super Sugar Mel'—thick 4-inch pods on 3-foot vines in 68 days.

Growing conditions: Sow peas ½ to 1 inch deep and 1 inch apart in spring 6 weeks before the last frost date or in fall 6 weeks before the first frost date. Sprinkle planting holes or trenches with a bacterial legume inoculant. Peas are a cool-

'Little Marvel'

weather crop that will tolerate temperatures as low as 25° F without protection and even lower temperatures when started under floating row covers. They grow best at daytime temperatures between 50° and 60° F. Do not thin; peas grow best in crowded stands. Provide trellises, netting, or other supports for vines to climb or lay twiggy brush among bush types to support plants and keep pods off the ground. Weed carefully, as disturbing roots causes blossoms and even pods to drop.

Harvest garden peas when pods are bulging and before there is any sign of yellowing or shriveling. Pick snow peas and sugar snap peas just as seeds begin to form; overmature pods become fibrous and tough. Pick daily to encourage vining peas to continue producing; most bush varieties mature their pods all at once for a single picking. For continuous harvest, select varieties with different maturity dates. A 10-foot row yields approximately 5 to 10 pounds of peas.

PEPPERS

'Golden Bell'

Hardiness: *hot-season annual*

Planting method: *transplants; direct sowing*

Plant spacing: *18 to 24 inches*

Light: *full sun*

Succulent, fleshy, thin-skinned fruits, some mild and sweet, others hot, on bushy plants in late summer. Mildly flavored bell peppers are usually harvested at their immature green stage but can be left on plants to ripen to yellow, red, or purple and become even sweeter; use bell peppers as edible food cases, sliced raw in salads, or sautéed or parboiled as a flavoring. Most hot, or chili, peppers are picked after they ripen to red or yellow; use them in ethnic dishes. Surplus peppers can be chopped and frozen, dried, or pickled for long-term storage. The days to maturity for the peppers described below are counted from the date transplants are set out in the garden.

Selected varieties: Sweet bell pepper varieties include: 'Bell Boy'—a disease-resistant hybrid with thick-walled, glossy green fruits 3½ inches in diameter in 70 days that ripen to red. 'California Wonder'—thick-walled pepper 3 inches in diameter in 75 days. 'Cherry Sweet', also called 'Red Cherry'—1½-inch, slightly tapered peppers in 78 days especially recommended for pickling. 'Chocolate Belle'—blocky 4-inch fruits with chocolate brown skin and red flesh in 75 days. 'Cubanelle'—slender, tapering 6-inch-long pale green peppers 2½ inches wide at the shoulders in 65 days. 'Golden

Bell'—blocky three- or four-lobed peppers in 70 days that ripen to a deep gold. 'Gypsy'—disease-resistant variety with wedge-shaped 5-inch fruits in 65 days that mature from pale green to deep yellow. 'New Ace'—4-inch fruits in 62 days for short-season areas. 'Purple Beauty'—blocky fruits with deep purple skin in 70 days, ripening to red. 'Whopper Improved'—disease-resistant, almost square 4-inch peppers in 71 days. 'Yolo Wonder'—disease-resistant plants with 4-inch squarish peppers in 75 days.

Chili, or hot, pepper varieties include: 'Anaheim TMR 23'—with tapering, flat peppers 8 inches long by 1½ inches wide in 77 days, milder flavored than most chilies and usually picked while still green. 'Ancho', also called 'Poblano'—relatively mild with 5- to 6-inch dark green to red peppers in 65 to 75 days.

'Anaheim'

'Habañero'—extremely hot, dark green pepper 1 to 2 inches long ripening to pinkish orange in 85 to 95 days. 'Hungarian Wax'—tapering three-lobed 6-inch-by-2-inch peppers that mature from pale yellow to bright red with a medium-hot flavor 65 to 75 days. 'Jalapeño'—tiny, extremely hot cone-shaped peppers 3 inches long in 70 to 80 days that are usually picked green before they ripen to red. 'Large Hot Cherry'—heavy crop of hot, slightly conical 1½-inch fruits ripening from green to red in 75 days, recommended for pickling. 'Numex Big Jim'—medium hot 10-inch red peppers in 80 days. 'Serrano Chile'—extremely hot conical peppers 2½ inches long and ½ inch across in 75 days that turn from green to red. 'Super Cayenne'—very hot, slim 4-inch peppers in 70 days that turn from

green to red. 'Super Chili'—very hot, conical pale green fruits growing upright on bushes and maturing to orange then red in 70 days. 'Thai Hot'—very compact plants with extremely hot ¾ to 1-inch green fruits that ripen to red in 75 days.

'Hungarian Wax'

Growing conditions: Start pepper plants indoors 8 to 10 weeks before night temperatures stay reliably above 55° F, setting seeds ½ inch deep; in areas with a long growing season, peppers can be sown directly in the garden. For disease prevention, avoid planting where other peppers, tomatoes, or eggplant has grown in the past 3 years. Peppers grow best when night temperatures are 62° F or more and daytime temperatures are 75° F or less. Temperatures below 55° F or above 85° F will cause blossoms to drop; although plants will recover, the crop will be smaller. Chili peppers require warmer soil for germination and growth than bell peppers; warm soil with black plastic before setting plants out in spring.

Pick bell peppers while still green and immature, while they are changing color, or when they have fully ripened to yellow, red, or purple. Fully ripe bell peppers have more sweetness and flavor than green ones. With a few exceptions, most chilies are left on plants to ripen fully before being snipped from plants. Continuous picking encourages continued fruiting.

POTATOES

'Red La Soda'

Hardiness: *warm-season annual*

Planting method: *seed potatoes*

Plant spacing: *10 to 14 inches*

Light: *full sun*

Round or oblong firm-textured tubers, sometimes with colorful skins or flesh, from early summer to fall with successive planting of different varieties. Early-season varieties mature with thin skins tender enough to rub off when the potatoes are first harvested. Midseason and late-season or storage potatoes can be dug as thin-skinned "new" potatoes for immediate use or allowed to mature in the ground until their skins are fully set and cannot be rubbed off, then stored for fresh use over several months. Baby new potatoes are excellent boiled in their skins to eat whole or to slice into salads. Mature potatoes can be boiled, baked, fried, mashed, and escalloped in a myriad of flavorful ways. Home gardeners can enjoy potatoes with colorful yellow, blue, or purple flesh seldom available except in markets offering gourmet vegetables.

Selected varieties: Early-season varieties include: 'Irish Cobbler'—very early oblong tubers with smooth white skins and creamy white flesh in 65 days. 'Norgold Russet'—scab-resistant smooth, oblong, brown-skinned tubers with golden netting and flaky, moist flesh excellent for baking in 65 days. 'Red Norland'—scab-tolerant round potatoes with thin red skins and crisp white interiors in 65 days. 'Yukon Gold'—scab-resistant round or slightly oval potatoes with yellow skins and flavorful, buttery golden yellow flesh in 65 days with good keeping quality.

Midseason varieties include: 'Beltsville' —vigorous plants resistant to nematodes, scab, and wilt with white flesh and excellent keeping quality. 'Katahdin'—scab-resistant plants adapted to varied climate and soil conditions producing round tubers with tan skins and white flesh. 'Kennebec'—blight-resistant plants with heavy yields of smooth-textured, round all-purpose potatoes in 80 days. 'Purple Marker'—disease-resistant plants producing medium-sized oval potatoes with deep purple-blue skins and flesh in 80 days. 'Red La Soda'—heat- and drought-tolerant round to oblong tubers

'Irish Cobbler'

with bright red skins and firm white flesh ideal for boiling in 80 days. 'Russet Burbank', also called 'Idaho Russet'—long, cylindrical, slightly flattened tubers with heavily netted brown skins and dry, flaky white flesh in 80 days. 'Russian Banana'—disease-resistant plants producing small to medium-sized fingerling potatoes with yellow skins and waxy pale yellow flesh. 'Viking Purple'—dark purple skins mottled red or pink over smooth-textured white flesh good for boiling in 80 days.

Late-season varieties include: 'Purple Peruvian'—long, narrow ½- to ¾-pound fingerling potatoes with deep purple skins, purple flesh, and purple-tinted foliage. 'Red Pontiac'—thin red skins over firm, white flesh with a light waxy texture good for boiling, midseason to late; excellent storage quality and also good harvested early for new potatoes.

Growing conditions: Use certified virus-free seed potatoes to plant a crop. An acid soil inhibits the growth of the potato scab virus. Early varieties are planted out 6 to 8 weeks before the last frost date, as soon as the ground can be worked in spring. Before planting, the seed potatoes should be sprouted, or "chitted." About 2 weeks before the date they will be set out, put them in a single layer in a

'Purple Peruvian'

shallow box with the eyes facing up. Set the box in a cool, frost-free room in indirect light until the potatoes produce short, stubby 1-inch sprouts. Plant whole seed potatoes the size of an egg or cut larger ones into egg-sized sections at least a day in advance so the cut surfaces can dry and be more resistant to rot. Set the seed potatoes 10 to 14 inches apart in trenches 6 to 8 inches deep; rows should be 2 feet apart. Cover the seed potatoes with no more than 4 inches of soil. Keep soil evenly moist. When stems are 8 inches high, hill more soil around plants, leaving 4 inches of the stems exposed. Hill twice more at 2-week intervals. Hilling in this fashion is essential because the tubers form on underground stolons produced along the stems.

Plant mid- and late-season potatoes directly in the garden, without sprouting, or chitting, 1 to 4 weeks before the last frost. Set them 3 to 4 inches deep in rows 2 feet apart. Hill the soil as described above.

Where soil is hard or rocky, potatoes can be grown under mulch. Place seed potatoes in shallow trenches and cover with a loose layer of straw, leaves, or dried grass clippings 6 to 10 inches deep; as stems elongate and plants emerge through mulch, add more mulch as though hilling soil as described above, taking care that tubers are covered at all times. Alternatively, grow potatoes in tall bottomless boxes, wooden cribs, barrels, or wire cages. Plant seed potatoes 6 to 8 inches apart and cover with 4 inches of soil; as plants grow taller, hill soil, compost, or mulch around the stems at 2-week intervals as described above.

Harvest potatoes anytime for new potatoes, carefully digging into soil to find small potatoes up to 2 inches in diameter. To harvest main crop potatoes, cut off vines, then wait 2 weeks before digging. To dig, use a garden fork, carefully

'Red Pontiac'

lifting soil starting 1½ to 2 feet out from the plant's crown and taking care not to spear tubers. Use cut or bruised tubers immediately. Allow intact, unbruised tubers to dry for 1 or 2 weeks in a dark, well-ventilated area at 60° F, then store at 40° F in wooden boxes, burlap bags, or other well-ventilated containers. Check occasionally and remove any rotting potatoes. One plant yields between 2 and 10 pounds of potatoes.

PUMPKINS

'Big Max'

Hardiness: *warm-season annual*

Planting method: *transplants; direct sowing*

Plant spacing: *2 to 4 feet*

Light: *full sun*

Globe-shaped fruits filled with deep orange, firm-textured flesh and edible seeds on strong, sprawling vines. The large varieties are ideal for Halloween jack-o'-lanterns; the medium-sized ones, for side dishes, soups, and pies. Hollow out miniature pumpkins as containers for soups or stuffings or use them like decorative gourds in arrangements. Roasted pumpkin seeds, particularly the hull-less varieties, make a nutritious snack.

Selected varieties: 'Atlantic Giant'—huge, deeply ribbed fruits weighing up to several hundred pounds in 125 days. 'Baby Bear'—disease-resistant vines with small, slightly flattened fruits only 6 inches across and 3½ to 4 inches tall with fine-textured flesh and hull-less seeds in 105 days. 'Big Max'—enormous 50- to 100-pound fruits with thick orange flesh in 120 days, excellent for carving. 'Connecticut Field'—large 20- to 25-pound fruits with dark orange skins and slightly flattened shapes, good for carving. 'Jack Be Little'—six or seven miniature fruits only 3 inches across and 2 inches high on each vine in 95 days, ideal for decorations. 'Jack O' Lantern'—medium-sized, tall 7- to 9-pound pumpkins up to 9 inches across in 100 days. 'Lumina'—10- to 12-pound fruits up to 10 inches in diameter with creamy white skin and orange

flesh in 110 days. 'Small Sugar Pie', also called 'New England Pie', 'Early Small Sugar'—5- to 6-pound fruits with very sweet, fine-textured yellow-orange flesh, excellent for pies, in 100 days.

Growing conditions: Plant pumpkin seeds outdoors after the last frost, setting seeds ½ to 1 inch deep, and thin to stand 2 to 3 feet apart in rows 4 to 6 feet apart for bush types and 3 to 4 feet apart in rows 8 to 12 feet apart for vining types. Alternatively, plant five or six seeds in hills spaced 4 feet apart for bush types and 8 feet apart for vining types and thin to two or three plants. Pumpkin seeds can be started indoors 4 or 5 weeks before the last frost date in peat pots that are planted directly

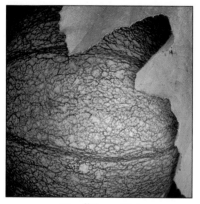

'Small Sugar Pie'

in the garden. Mulch with black plastic to warm the soil and conserve water. Water well during early growth and fruit set; standing water on maturing fruits invites rot. Ensure good pollination by transferring pollen from male to female (with swollen stems just below the blossoms) flowers with a soft brush. When vines are 2 to 3 feet long and fruits are just beginning to develop, pinch shoots to stimulate larger fruit growth. For large exhibition pumpkins, allow only one fruit to develop per vine. Raise maturing pumpkins off the ground on boards to prevent rot. Harvest pumpkins when their skins harden or after frost has killed the vines. Pumpkins will store well for up to a year if skins are undamaged.

RADICCHIO	RADISHES	RASPBERRIES

'Castelfranco'

'Easter Egg'

'Fall Red'

Hardiness: *cool-season annual*

Planting method: *direct sowing*

Plant spacing: *12 inches*

Light: *full sun*

A type of chicory with loose rosettes or small heads of green or red, slightly bitter leaves in spring, summer, or fall, depending on the region. Use as a garnish and to add color and flavor to salads.

Selected varieties: 'Augusto'—deep burgundy frost-resistant and bolt-resistant heads in 70 days. 'Castelfranco'—heirloom variety with loose red-and-white-marbled heads in 85 days. 'Early Treviso'—deep burgundy heads with white veins in 80 days. 'Giulio'—easy-to-grow white-veined burgundy heads in 80 days, ideal for spring planting. 'Red Verona'—heirloom variety with bright red, baseball-sized heads veined in white in 100 days.

Growing conditions: Sow radicchio outdoors, setting seed ½ inch deep and thinning plants to 12 inches. In Zones 3-7, plant radicchio in spring. Harvest leaves as needed during summer, then cut plants back to an inch or so above the ground in late summer or early fall to stimulate roots to produce small heads in 4 to 6 weeks. Where winter temperatures do not go below 10° F, sow seed for leaves in early spring followed by heads in early summer. 'Castelfranco' and 'Giulio' form heads without cutting back, and 'Early Treviso' often does so. Seed can also be sown from midsummer to early fall for a fall crop.

Hardiness: *cool-season annual*

Planting method: *direct sowing*

Plant spacing: *1 to 6 inches*

Light: *full sun*

Zesty roots in spring or fall. The large winter radishes, which are ready to harvest in fall, are stronger in taste and keep longer than spring varieties. Use as garnishes, hors d'oeuvres, or sliced in salads.

Selected varieties: Spring varieties include: 'Champion'—red, very cold hardy. 'Cherry Bell'—crisp red globes. 'Giant White Globe'—white, mildly flavored. 'Early Scarlet Globe'—very early, mildly flavored red globes. 'Easter Egg'—red, white, purple, and violet roots. 'French Breakfast'—thick, cylindrical red roots with white tips. 'Plum Purple'—bright purple cylinders. 'White Icicle'—tapered white roots. All in 25 to 30 days.

Winter varieties include: 'Misato Rose'—sweet pink flesh. 'Munich Bier'—pungent white cylinders. 'Round Black Spanish'—black exterior, white flesh. 'Tokinashi'—strongly flavored white roots 8 or more inches long. All in 50 to 60 days.

Growing conditions: Sow ½ inch deep in fertile, moisture-retentive soil. Sow spring radishes successively from 5 weeks before the last frost until 4 weeks after; thin plants to 1 to 2 inches apart. Sow winter radishes from midsummer until 8 weeks before the first frost; thin to 4 to 6 inches apart. Keep both well watered and mulch in hot weather so roots won't be tough or unpleasantly strong.

Hardiness: *Zones 4-7*

Planting method: *bare root; containers*

Plant spacing: *4 to 6 feet*

Light: *full sun to light shade*

Juicy, plump red, pink, golden, or black-purple berries on arching biennial canes growing from perennial rootstocks. Select varieties with maturity dates that provide fruit from early summer through frost. Standard red raspberries produce a single crop of fruit on 2-year-old canes; everbearing red raspberry canes bear fruit twice, once in the fall of their first year and again in the spring of their second year. Extremely fragile, delicately flavored yellow raspberries may be golden to pale pink. Black raspberries have a distinctly musky flavor and scent. Raspberries will spread rapidly via suckers along an underground network of rootlike stems.

Highly perishable, raspberries are most delectable straight from the garden. They can be frozen for long-term storage, although berries become mushy when thawed. Use berries in pies, desserts, jams, and jellies. Besides producing fruit, Japanese wineberry is a handsome ornamental for winter color.

Selected varieties: Red and yellow raspberry varieties include: 'Canby'—standard variety with midsummer crop of fleshy, deliciously flavored red berries on thornless canes. 'Chief'—very early crop of small red fruits, recommended for the Midwest. 'Fall Gold'—very hardy plants with golden yellow berries that have a high sugar content. 'Fall Red'—everbearing variety with large, extremely sweet berries, producing a larger crop in fall than in summer; good for areas with a short growing season. 'Heritage'—everbearing variety with firm, conical bright red berries, producing a larger crop in summer than in fall. 'Latham'—medium-

'Heritage'

sized red fruits on very hardy, adaptable plants. 'Newburgh'—standard disease-resistant variety with firm, large red berries in midsummer on short plants that need no support. 'Taylor'—standard variety with conical, somewhat tart red berries on vigorous plants that sucker freely. 'Viking'—heavy crop of red berries on very tall canes.

Black raspberry varieties include: 'Allen'—large crop of large, firm, very sweet berries all at once in midsummer. 'Black Hawk'—late midseason crop of large, firm, glossy berries on disease- and drought-resistant plants. 'Bristol'—large, very flavorful, nearly seedless berries on mosaic-resistant plants. 'John Robertson'—plump, juicy large berries on very hardy plants.

Hybrids include: Wineberry, also called Japanese wineberry—raspberry-blackberry hybrid with small, mildly flavored cherry red berries on attractive arching canes lined with soft red bristles that provide welcome color in the winter garden.

Growing conditions: Use only certified disease-free plants and never dig plants from the wild, since they may introduce viruses into the garden. Raspberries prefer deep, fertile loam enriched with compost. Plant rootstock with the top of the roots just below the soil line. Space plants 4 to 6 feet apart in rows 6 to 7 feet

apart. Water regularly and provide a deep mulch to suppress grass and weeds. For the largest yields and easier picking, provide 3-foot-high wire trellises for vines to trail over. Cover canes with coarse ¾- to 1-inch netting to protect ripening berries from birds.

Remove spent fruiting canes of standard red or yellow raspberry varieties after berries are harvested; prune the summer-fruiting canes of everbearing varieties after harvest. Remove weak suckers, leaving only two or three strong canes per foot of row.

To prune black and purple raspberries, remove old or weak canes, leaving three

'Bristol'

or four strong canes per foot of row. Prune lateral branches on the previous year's canes back to about 6 inches for black raspberries or 10 inches for purple raspberries in late winter to early spring to encourage heavy fruit production later in the season. Pinch tips of new shoots when they are about 18 to 24 inches tall to encourage lateral branching for the next season's crop.

Harvest raspberries when the fruits soften and pull away easily from the stem. Use or process immediately as fruits are highly perishable. A mature plant yields about 1½ quarts of berries.

RHUBARB

'Cherry Red'

Hardiness: *Zones 3-8*

Planting method: *root divisions*

Plant spacing: *2 to 3 feet*

Light: *full sun*

Tart, juicy leafstalks in clumps in spring. Also called the pie plant, rhubarb is one of the earliest spring fruits for pies, cobblers, jams, and jellies. Rhubarb foliage is highly toxic and must be stripped off when the stalks are harvested.

Selected varieties: 'Cherry Red'—heavy yields of stalks that are cherry red outside, green inside. 'Valentine'—thick 12- to 24-inch stalks that retain their red color when cooked.

Growing conditions: Rhubarb needs at least 2 months of freezing weather and does not tolerate temperatures higher than 90° F. Start plants from root divisions purchased from suppliers or taken from plants at least 3 years old in late fall or very early spring; each division should have at least two eyes, or large buds. Set divisions 2 inches deep and space them 3 feet apart. Rhubarb can also be started from seed, but plants are usually not of the same quality and take a year longer to mature. Allow roots to become established the first year; harvest no more than 20 percent of the stalks the second year. Harvest stalks 1 inch or more in width from plants 3 years old or more over a 6- to 8-week period; do not remove more than half of the plant's stalks at one time. Each plant yields 10 to 20 stalks.

RUTABAGAS

'Improved Purple Top Yellow'

Hardiness: *cool-season annual*

Planting method: *direct sowing*

Plant spacing: *6 to 8 inches*

Light: *full sun*

Also called Swedish turnips. Large globe-shaped, 2- to 3-pound roots with mild, sweet, fine-grained yellow flesh and pungent leaves from fall into winter. Serve rutabaga roots mashed, baked, or fried, and boil or steam the greens.

Selected varieties: 'American Purple Top'—5- to 6-inch beige-yellow roots with purple crowns in 90 days. 'Improved Purple Top Yellow'—round to oblong roots that store well in 90 days. 'Laurentian'—round roots with pale yellow crowns that store well in 105 days.

Growing conditions: Sow rutabagas ½ inch deep 12 to 14 weeks before the first fall frost and thin seedlings to stand 6 to 8 inches apart. To control soil-borne diseases, don't plant rutabagas where they or any other members of the cabbage family have been grown within 3 years. Keep soil constantly moist but not soggy. Harvest rutabagas after several frosts have sweetened the roots, cutting off all but 1 inch of the leaves. To store roots, dip them in melted paraffin floating on top of warm water to prevent wrinkling. Store in a root cellar at 40° F. Rutabagas can also be overwintered in the garden under a thick layer of mulch but may become woody. A 10-foot row yields about 10 pounds of roots.

SALSIFY

'Mammoth Sandwich Island'

Hardiness: *cool-season annual*

Planting method: *direct sowing*

Plant spacing: *2 to 4 inches*

Light: *full sun*

Also known as oyster plant. Tapering white roots resembling parsnips from fall through winter. Salsify, which has a mild flavor reminiscent of oysters, can be served boiled and mashed, fried, or be added to soups.

Selected varieties: 'Mammoth Sandwich Island'—roots 8 or more inches in length and about 1½ inches in diameter in 120 days.

Growing conditions: Sow salsify ¼ to ½ inch deep in spring in loose, well-tilled soil with all stones removed. Do not use manure when preparing salsify beds because the high nitrogen content results in hairy roots. Scratching wood ashes into the soil or watering with seaweed emulsion while roots are forming encourages thicker roots. Thin seedlings to 2 to 4 inches apart and mulch to keep soil evenly moist. Frost improves the flavor of salsify. Dig roots with a garden fork or shovel and store in moist peat or sand in a root cellar at 40° F. Alternatively, store salsify roots in the garden, covering them with a 12-inch mulch of straw or leaves. Harvest all roots by the following spring before new growth begins. A 10-foot row yields 10 to 20 pounds of salsify.

SHALLOTS

'Success'

Hardiness: *Zones 6-9; cool-season annual*

Planting method: *sets*

Plant spacing: *6 inches*

Light: *full sun*

Small, round bulbs with a delicate onion flavor from summer through fall or tender scallions in spring. Shallots are prized for the unique, mild accent they add to many gourmet dishes.

Selected varieties: 'Atlantic'—clumps of plump bulbs with yellow-tan skins. 'Success'—small bulbs with reddish brown skins. Both in 120 to 150 days.

Growing conditions: Grow shallots from tiny bulbs called sets, setting them out in fall in mild climates or as soon as the ground can be worked in spring elsewhere. Place sets with their tips barely above the soil in a rich, deep garden loam enriched with compost and keep evenly moist. Young shallots can be pulled for use like scallions. If allowed to mature, sets multiply into clusters of small bulbs each up to an inch across. When tops begin to yellow and wither in fall, pull shallots and allow to dry in a well-ventilated area. Remove dirt and loose skins, clip stems an inch above the bulbs, and store dried bulbs for up to a year. Each set produces eight to 12 shallots.

SORREL

Sorrel

Hardiness: *Zones 3-9; cool-season annual*

Planting method: *direct sowing; transplants*

Plant spacing: *8 inches*

Light: *full sun to light shade*

Clumps of lemony, slightly sour leaves from spring through early summer. Mix tangy young leaves with blander greens for salads. Chop the more strongly flavored older leaves as an herbal garnish or flavoring or cook them as a side dish. Leaves can also be frozen for later use.

Selected varieties: Usually sold simply as sorrel—broad, arrow- or shield-shaped, upright leaves in spreading clumps to 18 inches tall in 60 to 70 days from seed.

Growing conditions: Start sorrel indoors 2 to 3 weeks before the last heavy frost or outdoors as soon as the soil can be worked in spring, setting seed ⅛ inch deep. Sorrel grows best in fertile, moist, well-drained soil and develops the best flavor in cool weather; it is slower to bolt in light shade. Side-dress annually with compost or well-rotted manure. Pick outer leaves continuously as they reach 4 to 6 inches in length, leaving the center rosette intact. Pinch off flower buds as they appear to prolong the supply of tangy, young leaves. Cut plants to the ground after the spring harvest for a second crop of young leaves in fall. Renew sorrel beds by division every 3 to 4 years in spring or fall. Growing sorrel as an annual will limit its invasive tendency.

SOYBEANS

'Prize'

Hardiness: *warm-season annual*

Planting method: *direct sowing*

Plant spacing: *3 to 6 inches*

Light: *full sun*

Small, fuzzy pods in heavy clusters on bushy, erect plants in late summer. Shell mature soybeans and use them fresh or for canning or freezing. Pods can also be allowed to dry, then shelled for long-term storage. Dry soybeans are used in cooking like other dry beans and are also sprouted for salads, stir-frying, and stuffings.

Selected varieties: 'Edible Early Haku-cho'—early maturing variety 1 foot tall for fresh use in 65 days. 'Prize'—large pod clusters with two to four beans per pod suitable for fresh use in 85 days or dried in 100 days.

Growing conditions: Dry soybeans require a long growing season, but early varieties are suitable for shelling beans in northern gardens. After all danger of frost is past and the soil temperature is 65° F or more, plant seed that has been treated with a bacterial inoculant 1 inch deep. Plant in double rows, keep well watered, and mulch to conserve moisture. In windy areas, provide supports among plants. Harvest shelling beans before seeds turn from green to yellow. Harvest dry soybeans before pods shatter and release their seeds, then thresh like other dry beans *(pages 108-109)*.

SPINACH

'Tyee'

Hardiness: *cool-season annual*

Planting method: *direct sowing*

Plant spacing: *2 to 3 inches*

Light: *full sun to light shade*

Smooth or crinkled leaves in upright clumps from early to late spring or in fall. Use spinach in salads or for soups, side dishes, and stuffings.

Selected varieties: 'Bloomsdale Long Standing'—thick, deeply crinkled leaves on slow-to-bolt plants. 'Imperial Spring'—smooth leaves on fast-growing, upright plants resistant to mildew. 'Indian Summer'—crinkled leaves on slow-to-bolt, disease-resistant plants. 'Melody'—thick, somewhat crinkled leaves that are resistant to mold and blight. 'Space'—slow-to-bolt hybrid with smooth, deep green leaves on upright, slow-to-bolt plants resistant to viruses and mildew. 'Tyee'—deeply crinkled leaves on upright, extremely bolt-resistant plants tolerant of mildew. All in 35 to 40 days.

Growing conditions: Sow spinach ½ inch deep outdoors in early spring, repeating every 10 days for an extended supply of greens. Keep well watered. Plant 4 to 6 weeks before the first frost for a fall crop. In mild areas it will winter over and produce a very early spring crop. Plants go to seed as weather warms and days lengthen, but bolting can be delayed by siting later sowings in the shade of taller plants. Smooth varieties require less washing than savoyed types. A 10-foot row produces 4 to 6 pounds of spinach.

SPINACH, MALABAR

'Alba'

Hardiness: *warm-season annual*

Planting method: *transplants; direct sowing*

Plant spacing: *12 inches*

Light: *full sun*

Mild-flavored 4- to 6-inch leaves on 6- to 10-foot vines throughout summer. Use Malabar spinach leaves fresh in salads, cooked like spinach, or as a thickening agent in soups or sauces. Use the handsome vines in an edible landscape, either trained on a trellis or fence or cascading from hanging baskets.

Selected varieties: 'Alba'—thick, dark green leaves. 'Rubra'—dark green leaves with red stems and veins. Both in 70 to 100 days.

Growing conditions: Start Malabar spinach indoors 8 weeks before the last frost or sow directly in the garden in late spring to early summer after the soil has warmed to at least 65 ° F. Plant seeds 1 inch deep in humus-enriched soil and keep soil moist. Thin plants to 12 inches apart and provide supports for vines to climb. Malabar spinach requires warm temperatures to grow and will not bolt in hot weather like spinach. Begin picking young leaves for salads before vines reach maturity. Pinch tips to encourage branching, and remove any flower blossoms to prolong leaf production.

SPINACH, NEW ZEALAND

New Zealand Spinach

Hardiness: *Zones 9-11; warm-season annual*

Planting method: *direct sowing; transplants*

Plant spacing: *12 inches*

Light: *full sun*

Small clumps of thick, succulent leaves with a flavor reminiscent of spinach on trailing heat-resistant vines in summer and fall. Use New Zealand spinach fresh in salads or cooked as a hot-weather substitute for spinach. The plants are an attractive addition to an edible landscape. Use them as a ground cover, train on trellises, or plant in hanging baskets.

Selected varieties: No named varieties; sold as New Zealand spinach—mildly flavored triangular leaves on pest-free plants in 55 to 70 days

Growing conditions: Soak seeds overnight before planting ½ to 1 inch deep. In Zones 9-11, seeds should also be chilled for 1 to 2 days before sowing directly outdoors. From Zone 8 north, sow seed outdoors 2 weeks before the last frost. For transplants, sow seed in peat pots and set them directly in the garden to minimize transplant shock, after all danger of frost is past. Pick leaves when they are young, harvesting frequently to encourage continued growth. In warm climates plants often seed themselves. A 10-foot row yields about 5 pounds of New Zealand spinach.

SQUASH, SUMMER

'Early Golden Summer'

Hardiness: *warm-season annual*

Planting method: *direct sowing; transplants*

Plant spacing: *18 inches to 7 feet*

Light: *full sun*

Mild-tasting, tender-skinned fruits on sprawling vines or compact, bushy plants ideal for small gardens. Summer squashes are grouped according to shape. The crookneck summer squashes have bumpy surfaces and narrow, curved necks. The flat, round, scallop squashes have pretty fluted edges. Straightneck varieties have narrow stem ends and bulbous blossom ends. The zucchini types are uniform cylinders, often speckled and slightly ribbed.

Summer squashes, especially the scallop varieties, are delectable harvested as baby vegetables, before seeds enlarge and harden. Whether half-grown or larger, the mild flavor of summer squashes mingles well with other vegetables in salads or hors d'oeuvres, soups, or side dishes. Hollow squashes out to serve as edible casings for a variety of meat or vegetable dishes.

Selected varieties: Crookneck squashes include: 'Crescent'—vigorous, adaptable vines bearing early-maturing bright yellow fruits in 45 days. 'Early Golden Summer'—vining variety producing a large crop of bumpy yellow fruits that freeze well in 53 days. 'Sundance'—creamy yellow, miniature oval fruits on compact, bushy plants in 50 days. 'Yellow Crookneck'—bumpy-skinned, deep yellow fruits with buttery flavor and firm flesh beginning in 58 days and continuing over a long season when picked often.

Scallop varieties include: 'Early White Bush', also called 'White Patty Pan'—flattened, creamy white fruits in 60 days. 'Patty Green Tint'—a very early variety with pale green fruits on bushy plants in 52 days, exceptionally tender if picked when about 2 to 3 inches across. 'Scallopini'—extremely productive compact,

'Sunburst'

bushy plants bearing early-maturing small, round dark green fruits with a nutty flavor in 50 days. 'Sunburst'—compact, bushy plants with numerous flat golden yellow fruits with a green sunburst pattern at the stem and blossom ends in 48 days.

Straightneck varieties include: 'Early Prolific'—heavy yield of yellow fruits in 50 days, best picked when about 6 inches long. 'Park's Creamy Hybrid'—compact plants only 18 inches across with heavy yields of creamy yellow 6- to 8-inch fruits in 48 days and throughout summer. 'Seneca'—high yield of cylindrical, bright yellow fruits in 51 days. 'Sundrops'—smooth-skinned golden fruits in 50 days, best harvested when 2 inches across.

Zucchini varieties include: 'Black Eagle'—very dark green slender fruits with creamy flesh in 53 days. 'Cocozelle'—very prolific vines with fruits attractively striped in pale and dark green in 55 days. 'Condor'—early crop of glossy deep green fruits flecked with pale green on bushy plants in 48 days. 'Gold Rush'—bushy plants with bright yellow fruits in 50 days. 'Greyzini'—slightly tapered light green fruits in 50 days. 'Milano'—bushy plants bearing dark green fruits ready to

harvest in 42 days. 'Raven'—very early crop of deep green fruits in 42 days with delicate flesh even in more mature fruits.

Growing conditions: Plant seed outdoors 1 inch deep after all danger of frost is past and when soil has warmed to 70° F. Thin bush types to stand 18 to 36 inches apart and vining types to stand 3 to 7 feet apart. Alternatively, plant five to six seeds in hills 3 to 4 feet apart and thin to two or three plants. Summer squash can also be started indoors 3 to 4 weeks before the last frost. For a fall crop, sow seeds 8 to 10 weeks before the first frost. To save space, train vining varieties against trellises or fences.

Pick summer squashes while still immature for fine-textured flesh with tender seeds; mature fruits become pithy and have woody seeds that must be removed before cooking. Keep vines picked clean

'Black Eagle'

to encourage greater fruit production. Three or four vigorous summer squash plants may produce 60 to 75 pounds of summer squash over the season.

'Cream of the Crop'

Hardiness: *warm-season annual*

Planting method: *direct sowing; transplants*

Plant spacing: *18 inches to 7 feet*

Light: *full sun*

Hard-skinned fruits with firm-textured flesh around a large seed cavity in an array of colors, shapes, and sizes. Acorn squash has heart-shaped, deeply ribbed fruits with sweet, somewhat dry orange flesh. Butternut squash fruits have bulbous blossom ends with small seed cavities and long, fleshy necks. Hubbard squash has teardrop- or pear-shaped fruits with rough, ribbed blue-gray skin and yellow-orange flesh. The light yellow flesh of spaghetti squash is composed of moist, slightly crunchy strands that can be sauced like pasta. Sweet-potato squashes have extremely sweet, fine-grained flesh. Turban squashes are flattened globes, sometimes with contrasting splotches of color and buttonlike protrusions at their blossom ends.

Bake or parboil as a side dish; hollow smaller varieties as containers for other vegetables, soups, or stuffings; or add to soups and stews. Winter squash stores well if the skin is undamaged; the cooked flesh freezes well. The colorful varieties make attractive decorations.

Selected varieties: Acorn squash varieties include: 'Bush Table'—bushy plants only 3 feet across bearing deeply ribbed, dark green 5-inch fruits with fine-textured orange flesh in 80 days. 'Cream of the Crop'—compact, bushy vines with

2-pound cream-colored fruits with a nutty flavor in 82 days. 'Table Ace'—compact plants with a very early crop of deep green fruits in 70 days. 'Table Queen'—large vines with deep green, almost black 1½-pound fruits with yellow flesh in 80 days.

Butternut varieties include: 'Butterbush'—thin-skinned fruits with deep red-orange flesh on compact, bushy

'Early Butternut'

plants 4 feet in diameter in 75 days. 'Early Butternut'—very productive vines with thick-necked, light tan fruits in 85 days. 'Ponca'—long-necked tan fruits with very small seed cavities in 83 days. 'Waltham'—fruits with sweet, dry flesh in 85 days.

Hubbard varieties include: 'Blue Hubbard'—12- to 20-pound pear-shaped blue-gray fruits with rough-textured, ribbed skin and fine-grained yellow-orange flesh in 120 days. 'Golden Hubbard'—oval, 10-pound, orange-skinned fruits in 105 days.

Spaghetti squash varieties include: 'Tivoli'—cream-colored fruits on compact, bushy plants in 100 days. 'Vegetable Spaghetti'—oblong 2- to 3-pound fruits in 100 days that store well.

Sweet-potato squash varieties include: 'Delicata'—short vines with slender, oblong 1½- to 2-pound cream-colored fruits marked with green stripes and filled with very sweet orange flesh in 100 days, good for baking, stuffing, and storage. 'Sweet Dumpling'—medium-length vines bearing small 4-inch, slightly flattened fruits with very sweet, tender flesh in 100 days, ideal for individual servings.

Turban squash varieties include: 'Buttercup'—flattened, blocky, deep green 3- to 5-pound fruits with a gray button at

the blossom end and with sweet, fine-textured deep orange flesh in 105 days. 'Turk's Turban'—turban-shaped, bright orange fruits streaked green and white in 100 days.

Growing conditions: Plant winter squash outdoors after the last frost, setting seeds ½ to 1 inch deep. Thin bush types to stand 18 to 36 inches apart and vining types to stand 3 to 7 feet apart. Alternatively, plant five or six seeds in hills spaced 4 feet apart; thin each hill to two or three plants. Winter squash can also be started indoors 3 to 4 weeks before the last frost date. Mulch with black plastic to warm the soil and conserve water. Water well during early growth and fruit

'Sweet Dumpling'

set. When vines are 2 to 3 feet long and fruits are just beginning to develop, pinch shoots to stimulate the production of large fruits.

Harvest winter squashes when the skin hardens to the point where it is difficult to nick with a fingernail; leave several inches of stem attached to prevent rot during storage. Acorn, hubbard, and turban squashes bear two to four fruits per plant; spaghetti squash bears five to nine fruits per plant.

STRAWBERRIES

'Chandler'

Hardiness: *Zones 4-7*

Planting method: *direct sowing; runners*

Plant spacing: *15 inches*

Light: *full sun*

Juicy, fragrant, conical or wedge-shaped red berries in late spring, summer, or fall. Alpine strawberries form neat mounds of toothed foliage and are ideal for edging a vegetable garden or an ornamental border. Garden varieties, which send out plentiful runners that quickly spread into large mats, are categorized according to the time they set fruit. June-bearing varieties produce a single large crop of late-spring or early-summer berries. Everbearing varieties produce two crops, one in summer and another in fall; usually one crop is heavier than the other. Because they are not influenced by day length, the "day-neutral" varieties produce a continuous supply of berries from summer through fall.

Strawberries are at their best eaten fresh from the garden and are the basis of innumerable delicious desserts including shortcakes, pies, and tortes. Excess berries can be frozen or made into jams and jellies. Plant garden strawberries in containers and hanging baskets.

Selected varieties: Alpine strawberry varieties include: 'Alexandria'—inch-long, very sweet conical berries, somewhat larger than other alpine strawberries. 'Frais de Bois'—tiny golden, red, or deep crimson fruits with a fruity perfume on very cold hardy plants. 'Reugen Improved'—slim, elongated, very fragrant fruits continuously from early summer through fall, with the heaviest crop in fall.

Garden varieties include: 'Big Red'—June-bearing variety with glossy conical

'Sparkle'

fruits that are a deep red throughout. 'Chandler'—everbearing variety with flat, wedge-shaped berries on plants that produce numerous runners. 'Earli-glow'—June-bearing variety producing a large, very early spring crop of medium to large deep red berries. 'Ever Red'—everbearing variety with large conical fruits that are deep red throughout. 'Ozark Beauty'—everbearing variety with large, rich red, exceptionally sweet berries. 'Picnic'—everbearing strawberry that produces sweet, medium-sized fruits in just 4 months from seed. 'September Sweet'—disease-resistant day-neutral variety with very sweet, medium-sized berries from June through September, with the heaviest yield in fall. 'Serenata'—everbearing variety with deep pink rather than the typical white flowers followed by glossy red berries. 'Sparkle'—a single, large, late-summer crop of firm, flavorful berries on disease-resistant, hardy plants. 'Sure Crop'—June-bearing, drought-tolerant, disease-resistant variety with a reliably heavy yield of very large berries. 'Tribute'—day-neutral variety steadily producing plump, slightly acidic fruits with excellent flavor on disease-resistant plants. 'Tristar'—day-neutral variety with firm, sweet red berries on wilt- and mildew-resistant plants; ideal for hanging baskets.

Growing conditions: Select virus-free strawberry plants and set them out in spring or fall in a loose, fertile soil en-

riched with organic matter. Plant in raised beds where soils are heavy or clayey. Set bare-rooted stock in the ground with the soil line where the roots and crown meet. Plants set with their crowns below the soil line will rot, and those set too shallow will die because their roots are exposed. Mulch plants to control weeds and reduce rot. Alpine strawberries and some garden strawberries can also be started from seed sown indoors 2 to 3 months before the danger of frost passes and they can safely be planted outdoors.

Grow strawberries in mats or hills. For mats, set plants out 15 inches apart in

'Sure Crop'

rows 3 to 4 feet apart. Allow the runners to fill the area but keep a pathway open between rows for access. For hills, set plants 1 foot apart in double or triple rows spaced 12 inches apart; keep a pathway between each group of rows. Cut off all runners produced the first summer.

Remove old plants and renew strawberry beds when berry production slows. Everbearing varieties usually need renewing every year or every other year. June-bearing strawberries may remain productive for as long as 5 years.

SUNFLOWER

'Mammoth Russian'

Hardiness:	*warm-season annual*
Planting method:	*direct sowing*
Plant spacing:	*18 inches*
Light:	*full sun*

Tasty, oil- and protein-rich seeds from late summer to fall in heavy seed heads that follow attractive white or yellow flowers on tall stalks. Eat sunflower seeds raw or roasted as a snack and add them to salads or breads.

Selected varieties: 'Aztec Gold'—early-maturing variety with seed heads up to 11 inches across on 6-foot plants in 68 days. 'Grey Stripe', also called 'Giant Grey Stripe'—20-inch seed heads filled with large, thin-shelled seeds on 8- to 12-foot stalks in 85 days. 'Mammoth'—seed heads crammed with thin-shelled, meaty seeds on 6- to 12-foot stalks in 80 days. 'Mammoth Russian'—disease-resistant 8- to 12-foot plants with 12-inch heads filled with large, richly flavored striped seeds in 80 days.

Growing conditions: Plant seeds directly in the garden after all danger of frost is past, setting them ½ inch deep and thinning them to 18 inches apart. Tall stalks with heavy seed heads may need staking. Cover seed heads with cheesecloth to protect ripening seeds from birds and animals. Harvest seed heads when the back of the head dries or frost has killed foliage. Cut with 1 foot of the stalk attached and hang or lay on newspaper to finish drying in a well-ventilated area. Store seeds in airtight containers.

SWEET POTATOES

'Centennial'

Hardiness: *warm-season annual*

Planting method: *plants*

Plant spacing: *12 inches*

Light: *full sun*

Tapered tubers with sweet, moist, highly nutritious orange or red-orange flesh in fall. Enjoy baked or parboiled for side dishes, casseroles, and pies. Sweet potatoes are most easily started from small plants purchased from a nursery.

Selected varieties: 'Centennial'—fast-maturing variety with baby tubers ready to harvest in 90 to 100 days. 'Georgia Jet'—large red-skinned potatoes in 90 to 100 days. 'Jewell'—prolific variety with coppery red skins and fine-textured flesh in 100 days. 'Vardaman'—potatoes with deep orange flesh on compact, bushy plants in 100 days.

Growing conditions: Sweet potatoes are heat- and drought-resistant and need to grow where night temperatures will not drop below 60° F. Set certified virus-free plants out after all danger of frost is past and the soil is warm. Plant them in mounds of loose soil 6 to 10 inches high. Harvest sweet potatoes when vines yellow in fall. If an unseasonable frost is predicted before harvest, protect plants with floating row covers. Tubers must be harvested immediately if plants are nipped by frost. Cure tubers in a warm, humid, well-ventilated area for 8 to 10 days, then store at 55° to 60° F. A 10-foot row yields about 10 pounds of tubers.

TAMPALA

Tampala

Hardiness: *hot-season annual*

Planting method: *direct sowing*

Plant spacing: *6 inches*

Light: *full sun*

Tangy red- or green-leaved vegetable that resembles spinach but thrives in hot weather and can be sown successfully for harvesting all summer. Use tender young tampala leaves in salads, soups, and side dishes, either alone or combined with other greens.

Selected varieties: No named varieties; sold only as tampala. Heart-shaped 4-inch leaves ready to cut in 40 to 55 days on drought-tolerant, bushy plants.

Growing conditions: Sow tampala seeds ¼ inch deep after all danger of frost is past in a well-drained garden soil, working a balanced 5-10-5 organic fertilizer into the soil before planting. Tampala requires warm soil and high temperatures for best growth. When seedlings are 4 inches tall, thin to stand 6 inches apart; use thinnings in salads and soups. When plants reach 6 to 8 inches in height, harvest by cutting the entire plant at the soil line. For a continuous harvest of young, tender leaves, make successive sowings every 2 weeks until a month before the first frost date.

TOMATILLOES

Tomatillo

Hardiness: *warm-season annual*

Planting method: *transplants*

Plant spacing: *18 to 24 inches*

Light: *full sun*

Also called Mexican ground cherries. Round fruits encased in thin, papery husks on broad, bushy plants up to 4 feet tall. Tomatilloes are piquant when picked green and tangily sweet when they ripen and turn yellow. A staple in Mexican cuisine, tomatilloes are used fresh, depending on their degree of ripeness, for savory sauces and dishes such as salsa verde or for dessert toppings, jams, and preserves. Cooked tomatilloes freeze well.

Selected varieties: 'Goldie', also called 'Golden'—¾-inch berries ripening in 75 days. 'Toma Verde'—firm-textured 1½-inch pale green sweet-sour berries in 60 to 80 days.

Growing conditions: Start tomatillo seeds indoors 3 to 6 weeks before the last frost, setting seeds ½ inch deep in peat pots. Transplant seedlings in their peat pots to the garden after the soil has warmed and all danger of frost is past, spacing them 18 to 24 inches apart. For firm, tart fruits, harvest when the husks turn from green to tan. For sweet, ripe fruits, wait until the fruits drop off the plant. Tomatilloes keep well in the refrigerator.

TOMATOES

'Better Boy'

Hardiness: *warm-season annual*

Planting method: *transplants; direct sowing*

Plant spacing: *3 to 4 feet*

Light: *full sun*

Juicy, meaty, red, yellow, pink, purple, or white fruits ranging from bite-sized miniatures to 2-pounders. Depending on the variety, all tomato varieties belong to one of two groups, based on the type of vine they have. The indeterminate tomatoes have tall, lanky vines and bear fruit over a long period, while the determinate tomatoes tend to be compact and bushy and to produce the season's crop all at once. Varieties mature at markedly different times. Early tomatoes set fruit in about 55 to 65 days from the time seedlings started indoors are set out in the garden, or a total of 85 to 90 days from seed; midseason tomatoes set fruit in about 65 to 75 days from the transplanting date, or 95 to 105 days from seed; and late-season tomatoes begin fruiting in 80 to 100 days after the transplanting date, or 110 to 130 days from seed.

The largest fruits are the enormous beefsteak varieties, which have a high proportion of seeds and juice to flesh. Large and medium-sized slicing tomatoes also have a high proportion of juice to pulp. Slice or chop them fresh for use in salads, sandwiches, and garnishes; stuff them, or bake, simmer, or sauté them for main or side dishes. The paste tomatoes are smaller and have a higher proportion of flesh to seeds and juice.

Ideal for cooked relishes, salsa, and sauces, they can be dried for long-term storage. Small-fruited tomato varieties have grapelike clusters of tiny sweet fruits that are good raw or cooked.

Selected varieties: Large-fruited varieties include: 'Ace 55'—broad, smooth fruits in 75 days on disease-resistant determinate vines. 'Beefmaster'—extremely large, somewhat flattened fruits in midseason on vigorous, disease-resistant indeterminate vines in 80 days. 'Beefsteak', also called 'Red Ponderosa' or 'Crimson Cushion'—meaty, thick-ribbed tomatoes weighing 2 pounds or more on indeterminate vines in 90 days. 'Better Boy'—round fruits weighing up to a pound on strong, disease-resistant indeterminate

'Early Girl'

vines in 72 days. 'Big Boy'—firm, thick-walled, aromatic fruits weighing a pound or more on indeterminate vines in 78 days. 'Big Early'—½- to 1-pound fruits with thick walls on indeterminate vines in 62 days. 'Big Girl'—large, crack-resistant fruit weighing a pound or more on disease-resistant indeterminate vines in 78 days. 'Burpee's VF'—thick-walled, crack-resistant medium-sized fruits on indeterminate vines in 72 days. 'Celebrity'—crack-resistant ½-pound fruits on compact, disease-resistant determinate vines in 75 days. 'Delicious'—record-setting fruits weighing up to 3 pounds or more each with excellent flavor on indeterminate vines in 77 days. 'Early Cascade'—large clusters of early-ripening 1½ to 2-inch heart-shaped tomatoes on disease-resistant indeterminate vines in 55 days. 'Early Girl'—clusters of early-ripening small, meaty, deep red fruits summer on indeterminate vines in 54

days. 'Fantastic'—smooth 3- to 5-inch tomatoes in 70 days on indeterminate vines. 'First Lady'—flavorful, early-ripening 4- to 6-ounce fruits on compact, indeterminate vines in 60 days. 'Heatwave'—medium-sized fruits on compact, disease-resistant determinate vines that

'Quick Pic'

will set fruit at temperatures above 90° F in 68 days. 'Heinz 1350'—crack-resistant 6-ounce fruits ideal for canning on determinate vines in 75 days. 'Heinz 1439'—meaty 6-ounce fruits good for sauces and canning on compact determinate vines in 72 days. 'Jubilee'—mild-flavored medium-sized yellow fruits on disease-resistant indeterminate vines in 80 days. 'Lady Luck'—large meaty fruits weighing up to a pound on adaptable, disease-resistant indeterminate vines in 78 days. 'Long-Keeper'—light red-orange fruits on indeterminate vines in 78 days; stores well for up to 12 weeks or more at 60° to 70° F. 'Marglobe Improved'—fruits ideal for canning on determinate vines in 75 days. 'Mountain Delight'—medium-sized fruits in clusters of three or four on disease-resistant determinate vines in 75 days. 'Northern Exposure'—half-pound flavorful fruits on compact semideterminate vines bred for cool seasons in 67 days. 'Oregon Spring'—early 4-inch tomatoes on disease-resistant, somewhat cold-tolerant determinate vines in 58 days. 'Patio'—medium to large firm, flavorful fruits on compact dwarf determinate vines suited for container growing in 60 days. 'Pilgrim'—small clusters of 7-ounce fruits on determinate vines in 65 days. 'President'—large, smooth red fruits on disease-resistant determinate vines in 68 days. 'Quick Pic'—early variety with medium-sized fruits on indeterminate vines starting in 68 days. 'Spring Giant'—large fruits with thick walls and small cores on determinate vines adaptable to many climate conditions in 65 days. 'Super Bush'—meaty fruits starting in 85 days and continuing over a long season on bushy determinate plants 38 inches tall and wide that require no pruning, staking, or caging so are ideal for containers and small gardens. 'Wonder Boy'—meaty 8-ounce fruits on vigorous indeterminate vines in 80 days.

Small-fruited varieties include: 'Florida Basket'—1- to 2-inch fruits in 70 days on very short determinate vines about 6 inches long, ideal for hanging baskets. 'Gardener's Delight', also called 'Sugar Lump'—clusters of up to a dozen bite-size, very sweet bright red fruits ripening

'Gardener's Delight'

early on indeterminate vines in 65 days. 'Red Cherry Large'—clusters of sweet deep red 1½-inch round fruits ripening in midseason on vigorously branching indeterminate vines good for hanging baskets in 75 days. 'Sun Gold'—early apricot-colored fruits in grapelike clusters of up to 20 fruits on vigorous, disease-resistant indeterminate vines in 60 days. 'Sweet Million'—very sweet, crack-resistant 1- to 1¼-inch fruits in clusters on highly disease resistant vines starting in 60 days and continuing for a long period. 'Sweet 100'—large elongated clusters of cherry-sized sweet fruits throughout the summer on indeterminate vines in 60 days. 'Tiny Tim'—very early variety with bite-sized tomatoes on compact 15-inch determinate vines in 45 days. 'Toy Boy'—early crop of 1½-inch fruits on 14-inch determinate vines in 58 days.

Paste tomato varieties include: 'Italian Gold'—firm, thick-walled golden-orange fruits on determinate vines in 82 days. 'La Roma'—very large crop of meaty 3- to 4-ounce fruits ideal for canning on determinate vines in 62 days. 'La Rossa'—pear-shaped 3½-inch fruits with thick flesh and thin skins in 75 days ideal for

'Sweet Million'

fresh use as well as for cooking. 'Mama Mia'—heavy crop of small pear-shaped fruits on determinate disease-resistant vines in 62 days. 'Roma VF'—heavy crop of meaty medium-sized pear-shaped fruits on disease-resistant determinate vines in 75 days. 'San Marzano'—large crop of elongated, pear-shaped 3½-inch tomatoes in 80 days on indeterminate vines. 'Viva Italia'—sweet, meaty 3-ounce fruits that can be stored for 2 to 3 weeks on vigorous, disease-resistant, heat-tolerant vines in 80 days.

Yellow tomato varieties include: 'Golden Boy'—large, mildly flavored golden yellow fruits on indeterminate vines in 80 days. 'Husky Gold'—half-pound deep yellow fruits on compact 4½-foot disease-resistant indeterminate vines that require no pinching or pruning in 70 days. 'Lemon Boy'—lemon yellow, low-acid 6- to 7-ounce fruits on disease-resistant indeterminate vines in 72 days. 'Yellow Canary'—clusters of bite-sized golden fruits on compact branching determinate vines only 6 inches long ideal for containers and hanging baskets in 63 days. 'Yellow Pear'—long clusters of tiny pear-shaped yellow fruits 2 inches long and an inch across ideal for salads and relishes on bushy, indeterminate vines good for container culture in 112 days.

White tomato varieties include: 'White

Wonder'—medium-sized 6-to-8-ounce, very low acid fruits with creamy white flesh and skin on indeterminate vines in 115 days.

Growing conditions: Tomatoes can be directly sown when the soil temperature reaches 50° F or more, but they do best when started indoors 4 to 6 weeks before the last frost and transplanted into compost-enriched garden loam about a week after the last frost, when soil has warmed. Set transplants deeply, burying the lower portion of the stem to stimulate it to form new roots. Cover with hot caps or cloches if frost threatens. Toma-

'Sweet 100'

toes set fruit best when nighttime temperatures are 76° F or higher and daytime temperatures are below 90° F. If nighttime temperatures drop below 50° F or daytime temperatures rise above 90° F, vines will not set fruit.

Plant bushy determinate varieties 24 inches apart. Plant indeterminate varieties that will be allowed to sprawl on the ground 4 feet apart. Allow 18 inches between plants that will be staked and 2½ to 3 feet between plants that will be supported with cages. Indeterminate vines that sprawl tend to produce more but smaller fruits, while those that are supported produce larger but fewer fruits.

Fertilize tomato plants when they are set out and again when the fruits begin to set with a balanced 5-10-10 organic fertilizer or manure tea. Foliar sprays of fish emulsion increase yields. Periods of wetness or dryness can stunt growth and cause blossom end rot. Mulch to maintain constant moisture levels, to suppress weeds, and to help keep the fruits of sprawling vines clean and free of decay.

If you grow indeterminate tomatoes in cages or tied to stakes, you may want to pinch off the suckers that grow at the junction of stems and side branches. Removing the suckers hastens fruiting, encourages sturdier vines, and forces more uniform ripening of larger fruits.

'Lemon Boy'

Use floating row covers to protect young plants from flea beetles. Use Bt to ward off tomato hornworms. Rotate tomato planting sites every 3 years to avoid nematode damage; when planning crop rotation, group tomatoes with eggplant, peppers, and potatoes, and follow them with a legume such as peas or beans. To prevent disease problems, choose disease-resistant varieties, prune lower branches to increase air circulation, and remove and destroy all garden debris at the end of the season.

Harvest tomatoes when they are fully ripe if the temperature is under 90° F. When the temperature is higher, pick tomatoes just before they reach full ripeness and finish the ripening process indoors at temperatures of 70° F or more. Allow tomatoes to ripen fully before refrigerating for short-term storage. Dry or can tomatoes or cook and freeze them for long-term storage; because of their high water content, tomatoes become mushy if frozen fresh. Save the seed of open-pollinated varieties for planting the following season. Hybrid varieties generally do not breed true.

TURNIP

'Purple-Top White Globe'

Hardiness: *cool-season annual*

Planting method: *direct sowing*

Plant spacing: *3 to 5 inches*

Light: *full sun*

Rumpled leaves and globe-shaped roots with a mild, sweet flavor in spring and fall. Enjoy turnip roots raw, cooked in side dishes, or cubed in stews. Cook the greens as you would spinach or collards.

Selected varieties: 'Purple-Top White Globe'—3- to 4-inch white globes with purple shoulders, fine-textured flesh, and dark green leaves in 55 days. 'Royal Crown'—early variety with deep purple shoulders and deep green tops in 52 days. 'Tokyo Cross'—disease-resistant variety with white 2- to 6-inch roots and glossy green tops in 40 days.

Growing conditions: For a late spring crop, sow seed ¼ to ½ inch deep in spring as soon as the ground can be worked. Sow again in late summer for a fall crop. Frost increases sweetness. Keep turnips constantly moist but not soggy. Use floating row covers or introduce parasitic wasps to prevent damage from flea beetles, cabbage loopers, and other insect pests that attack members of the cabbage family. To minimize soil-borne diseases, do not plant turnips where other brassicas have grown for at least 3 years. For tender turnip greens, pick when they are small, no more than 12 inches in height. Roots can be harvested when they are an inch or more in diameter. A 10-foot row of turnips yields 30 to 40 pounds.

Acknowledgments and Picture Credits

The editors wish to thank the following for their valuable assistance in the preparation of this volume:

Walter Chandoha, Annandale, New Jersey; Rosalind Creasy, Los Altos, California; Thomas E. Eltzroth, San Luis Obispo, California; Warren Empey, Meadowbrook, Pennsylvania; Mr. and Mrs. John C. Pritzlaff, Santa Barbara, California; Vivian Purdy, Wolf and Associates, Salem, Virginia; Robert W. Ritchie, Wrightstown, Pennsylvania; Bill Wolf, Wolf and Associates, Salem, Virginia.

The sources for the illustrations in this book are listed below. Credits from left to right are separated by semicolons, from top to bottom by dashes.

Cover: © Walter Chandoha. Back cover insets: Thomas E. Eltzroth—art by Fred Holz—Jerry Pavia. End papers: John Marshall. 2, 3: John Marshall. 4: Courtesy Shepherd Ogden. 6, 7: Stephen Swinburne/designed by Shepherd Ogden, The Cook's Garden. 8, 9: © Tony Casper; © Walter Chandoha. 10: Rosalind Creasy/designed by Rosalind Creasy. 11-14: Art by Fred Holz. 15: Dency Kane, courtesy Robert Jakob/David White, East Hampton, N.Y. 16: Art by Sanford Kossin—art by Fred Holz. 17, 18: Art by Fred Holz. 19: Jerry Pavia. 20: Art by Fred Holz. 22, 23: © Lynn Karlin/designed by Eliot Coleman and Barbara Damrosch. 24: Thomas E. Eltzroth. 25: © Walter Chandoha. 26: Art by Fred Holz. 27: © Walter Chandoha. 28: John Marshall. 29: Thomas E. Eltzroth. 30-32: © Walter Chandoha. 33: Art by Fred Holz. 34, 35: © Walter Chandoha. 36: Art by Fred Holz. 37: Thomas E. Eltzroth. 38: Art by Fred Holz. 39: Art by Fred Holz—Thomas E. Eltzroth. 40, 41: © Walter Chandoha—Thomas E. Eltzroth (2). 42, 43: Rosalind Creasy/designed by Rosalind Creasy. 44: © Walter Chandoha. 45: Rosalind Creasy. 46, 47: Joanne Pavia/designed by J. Liddon Pennock Jr., Meadowbrook Farm. 48, 49: Pamela Zilly/designed by Barbara Lynch; Dency Kane/designed by Marla Gagnum, English Landscape Design. 50, 51: Robert Walch/designed by Jack Staub. 52, 53: Bernard Fallon/designed by Janie Malloy, Home Grown Edible Landscaping; Jerry Pavia/designed by R. J. McArnarney. 54, 55: Rosalind Creasy/designed by Rosalind Creasy. 56: Joanne Pavia/designed by J. Liddon Pennock Jr., Meadowbrook Farm (2)—Pamela Zilly/designed by Barbara Lynch (2). 57: Dency Kane/designed by Marla Gagnum, English Landscape Design (2)—Robert Walch/designed by Jack Staub (2). 58: Bernard Fallon/designed by Janie Malloy, Home Grown Edible Landscaping (2)—Jerry Pavia/designed by R. J. McArnarney (2). 59: Rosalind Creasy/designed by Rosalind Creasy (2). 60, 61: Roger Foley/designed by Michelle Henkin Bader. 62: © Dwight R. Kuhn. 63: Art by Fred Holz. 64: Thomas E. Eltzroth. 66, 67: Leonard G. Phillips—© Dwight R. Kuhn. 68, 69: © Dwight R. Kuhn; © Walter Chandoha—Rosalind Creasy/designed by Rosalind Creasy. 70: © Stanley Schoenberger/Grant Heilman Photography, Lititz, Pa. 72, 73: Art by Fred Holz; © Walter Chandoha. 76, 77: © Walter Chandoha. 78, 79: © Walter Chandoha; art by Fred Holz. 80-89: © Walter Chandoha. 94: Art by Davis Meltzer and Rebecca Merrilees (2)—art by Robert E. Hynes. 95: Art by Robert E. Hynes (2)—art by Davis Meltzer and Rebecca Merrilees—art by Robert E. Hynes. 96: Art by Fred Holz and Robert E. Hynes—art by Robert E. Hynes (2). 97: Art by Robert E. Hynes (2)—art by Fred Holz—art by Robert E. Hynes. 98, 99: Art by Robert E. Hynes. 104, 105: Maps by John Drummond, Time-Life Books. 106: Jerry Pavia. 107: Thomas E. Eltzroth; © Walter Chandoha (2). 108: Joanne Pavia; Thomas E. Eltzroth; © Dwight R. Kuhn. 109: © Dwight R. Kuhn; Thomas E. Eltzroth; © Dwight R. Kuhn. 110: Thomas E. Eltzroth; © Dwight R. Kuhn; Thomas E. Eltzroth. 111: Thomas E. Eltzroth; © Walter Chandoha; Thomas E. Eltzroth. 112: Thomas E. Eltzroth; © Walter Chandoha; Thomas E. Eltzroth. 113: Thomas E. Eltzroth (2); Joanne Pavia. 114: © Walter Chandoha; Thomas E. Eltzroth (2). 115: Thomas E. Eltzroth; © Walter Chandoha; Thomas E. Eltzroth. 116: Thomas E. Eltzroth. 117: Thomas E. Eltzroth; Jerry Pavia (2). 118: © Walter Chandoha; Thomas E. Eltzroth; John Marshall. 119: Thomas E. Eltzroth (2); Joanne Pavia. 120: Jerry Pavia; Joanne Pavia; Thomas E. Eltzroth. 121: Thomas E. Eltzroth. 122: © Walter Chandoha. 123: © Dwight R. Kuhn; Thomas E. Eltzroth (2). 124: © Walter Chandoha; Thomas E. Eltzroth; © Dwight R. Kuhn. 125: Thomas E. Eltzroth. 126: Thomas E. Eltzroth (2); Jerry Pavia. 127: Jerry Pavia; © Walter Chandoha; Thomas E. Eltzroth. 128: Thomas E. Eltzroth; Jerry Pavia; Thomas E. Eltzroth. 129: Thomas E. Eltzroth. 130: Jerry Pavia; Thomas E. Eltzroth (2). 131: Joanne Pavia; Jerry Pavia; Joanne Pavia. 132: Thomas E. Eltzroth. 133: Thomas E. Eltzroth; Jerry Pavia; Thomas E. Eltzroth. 134: Thomas E. Eltzroth (2); Jerry Pavia. 135: Thomas E. Eltzroth; © David Cavagnaro; Jerry Pavia. 136: Jerry Pavia; Thomas E. Eltzroth (2). 137: © Walter Chandoha; Joanne Pavia; Thomas E. Eltzroth. 138: © David Cavagnaro; Jerry Pavia (2). 139: Thomas E. Eltzroth (2); © Walter Chandoha. 140: Thomas E. Eltzroth (2); Joanne Pavia. 141: Thomas E. Eltzroth; Joanne Pavia; Thomas E. Eltzroth. 142: Thomas E. Eltzroth; © Walter Chandoha (2). 143: Thomas E. Eltzroth. 144: Thomas E. Eltzroth (2); Jerry Pavia. 145: Thomas E. Eltzroth; Jerry Pavia; Thomas E. Eltzroth. 146: Thomas E. Eltzroth; Joanne Pavia; Thomas E. Eltzroth. 147: Thomas E. Eltzroth. 148: © Walter Chandoha; © Dwight R. Kuhn; Thomas E. Eltzroth. 149: Thomas E. Eltzroth. 150: Thomas E. Eltzroth (2); Jerry Pavia. 151: Thomas E. Eltzroth (2); Leonard Phillips. 152: Thomas E. Eltzroth.

Bibliography

BOOKS:

All about Vegetables. San Ramon, Calif.: Ortho Books, 1990.

The American Horticultural Society Encyclopedia of Gardening. New York: Dorling Kindersley, 1994.

The American Horticultural Society Illustrated Encyclopedia of Gardening: Vegetables. Mount Vernon, Va.: American Horticultural Society, 1980.

Bales, Suzanne Frutig. *Vegetables* (Burpee American Gardening series). New York: Prentice Hall Press, 1991.

Ball, Jeff. *Rodale's Garden Problem Solver: Vegetables, Fruits, and Herbs.* Emmaus, Pa.: Rodale Press, 1988.

Biggs, Tony. *Step-by-Step Encyclopedia of Practical Gardening: Vegetables.* New York: Simon & Schuster, 1980.

Bradley, Fern Marshall, and Barbara W. Ellis. *Rodale's All-New Encyclopedia of Organic Gardening.* Emmaus, Pa.: Rodale Press, 1992.

Brady, Nyle C. *The Nature and Properties of Soils* (10th ed.). New York: Macmillan, 1990.

Bubel, Nancy Wilkes:
The Country Journal Book of Vegetable Gardening. Brattleboro, Vt.: Country Journal Publishing, 1983.
Vegetables Money Can't Buy but You Can Grow. Boston: David R. Godine, 1977.

Bubel, Nancy Wilkes, and Mike Bubel. *Root Cellaring.* Emmaus, Pa.: Rodale Press, 1979.

Carr, Anna, et al. *Rodale's Chemical-Free Yard and Garden.* Emmaus, Pa.: Rodale Press, 1991.

Coleman, Eliot:
The New Organic Grower. Chelsea, Vt.: Chelsea Green, 1989.
The New Organic Grower's Four-Season Harvest. Post Mills, Vt.: Chelsea Green, 1992.

Cox, Jeff, and the Editors of Rodale's *Organic Gardening®* Magazine. *How to Grow Vegetables Organically.* Emmaus, Pa.: Rodale Press, 1988.

Creasy, Rosalind:
The Complete Book of Edible Landscaping. San Francisco: Sierra Club Books, 1982.
Organic Gardener's Edible Plants. Portland, Ore.: Van Patten Publishing, 1993.

Damrosch, Barbara. *Garden Primer.* New York: Workman Publishing, 1988.

Denckla, Tanya. *The Organic Gardener's Home Reference* (Garden Way Publishing). Pownal, Vt.: Storey Communications, 1994.

De Saulles, Denys. *Home Grown.* Boston: Houghton Mifflin, 1988.

Doscher, Paul, Timothy Fisher, and Kathleen Kolb. *Efficient Vegetable Gardening.* Old Saybrook, Conn.: Globe Pequot Press, 1993.

Doty, Walter L., and A. Cort Sinnes. *All about Tomatoes.* San Francisco: Ortho Books, 1981.

Easy Composting. San Ramon, Calif.: Ortho Books, 1992.

Ellis, Barbara W., and Fern Marshall Bradley (Eds.). *The Organic Gardener's Handbook of Natural Insect and Disease Control.* Emmaus, Pa.: Rodale Press, 1992.

Facciola, Stephen. *Cornucopia: A Source Book of Edible Plants.* Vista, Calif.: Kampong Publications, 1990.

Fell, Derek. *Vegetables.* Tucson, Ariz.: HP Books, 1982.

Gilbertie, Sal, with Larry Sheehan. *Home Gardening at Its Best.* New York: Antheneum/ SMI, 1977.

Goldman, M. C., and William H. Hylton (Eds.). *The Basic Book of Organically Grown Foods.* Emmaus, Pa.: Rodale Press, 1972.

Harrington, Geri. *Grow Your Own Chinese Vegetables* (Garden Way Publishing). Pownal, Vt.: Storey Communications, 1984.

Hill, Lewis. *Fruits and Berries for the Home Garden* (Garden Way Publishing). Pownal, Vt.: Storey Communications, 1986.

Hills, Lawrence D. *Fertility without Fertilizers.* New York: Universe Books, 1977.

Hirshberg, Gary, and Tracy Calvan (Eds.). *Gardening for All Seasons.* Andover, Mass.: Brick House Publishing, 1983.

How to Select, Use, and Maintain Garden Equipment. San Francisco: Ortho Books, 1981.

Hunt, Marjorie B., and Brenda Bortz. *High-Yield Gardening.* Emmaus, Pa.: Rodale Press, 1986.

Huxley, Anthony. *An Illustrated History of Gardening.* New York: Paddington Press, 1978.

Hynes, Erin. *Improving the Soil* (Rodale's Successful Organic Gardening® series). Emmaus, Pa.: Rodale Press, 1994.

An Illustrated Guide to Organic Gardening. Menlo Park, Calif.: Sunset Publishing, 1991.

Improving Your Garden Soil. San Ramon, Calif.: Ortho Books, 1992.

Jabs, Carolyn. *The Heirloom Gardener.* San Francisco: Sierra Club Books, 1984.

Jeavons, John. *How to Grow More Vegetables on Less Land than You Can Imagine.* Berkeley, Calif.: Ten Speed Press, 1991.

Leslie, Anne R. (Ed.). *Handbook of Integrated Pest Management for Turf and Ornamentals* (rev. ed.). Boca Raton, Fla.: Lewis Publishers, 1994.

McClure, Susan. *The Harvest Gardener* (Garden Way Publishing). Pownal, Vt.: Storey Communications, 1993.

McCord, Nancy. *Please Don't Eat My Garden!* New York: Sterling Publishing, 1992.

Michalak, Patricia, and Cass Peterson. *Vegetables* (Rodale's Successful Organic Gardening® series). Emmaus, Pa.: Rodale Press, 1993.

Newcomb, Duane. *Small Space, Big Harvest.* Rocklin, Calif.: Prima Publishing, 1993.

Nick, Jean M. A., and Fern Marshall Bradley (Eds.). *Growing Fruits and Vegetables Organically.* Emmaus, Pa.: Rodale Press, 1994.

Ogden, Shepherd. *Step by Step Organic Vegetable Gardening.* New York: HarperCollins, 1992.

Ogden, Shepherd, and Ellen Ogden. *The Cook's Garden.* New York: Wings Books, 1989.

Olds, Jerome (Comp.). *The Encyclopedia of Organic Gardening.* Emmaus, Pa.: Rodale Press, 1977.

Olkowski, William, Sheila Daar, and Helga Olkowski. *Common-Sense Pest Control.* Newtown, Conn.: Taunton Press, 1991.

The Organic Gardener's Complete Guide to Vegetables and Fruits. Emmaus, Pa.: Rodale Press, 1982.

Patent, Dorothy Hinshaw, and Diane E. Bilderback. *The Harrowsmith Country Life Book of Garden Secrets.* Charlotte, Vt.: Camden House Publishing, 1991.

Phillips, Roger, and Martyn Rix. *The Random House Book of Vegetables* (Random House Garden series). New York: Random House, 1993.

Protecting Your Garden from Animal Damage. San Ramon, Calif.: Ortho Books, 1994.

Raymond, Dick, and Jan Raymond. *Home Gardening Wisdom.* Charlotte, Vt.: Garden Way Publishing, 1982.

Riotte, Louise. *Successful Small Food Gardens.* Pownal, Vt.: Garden Way Publishing, 1993.

Roscoe, George Boggs. *Here's the Dirt.* Annandale, Va.: Sense Publications (Charles Baptie Studios), 1984.

Roth, Susan A. *The Weekend Garden Guide.* Emmaus, Pa.: Rodale Press, 1991.

Stokes, Donald W., and Lillian Q. Stokes. *A Guide to Animal Tracking and Behavior.* Boston: Little, Brown, 1986.

Thomson, Bob, with James Tabor. *The New Victory Garden.* Boston: Little, Brown, 1987.

Van Patten, George F. *Organic Garden Vegetables.* Portland, Ore.: Van Patten Publishing, 1991.

Vegetable Gardening (Sunset). Menlo Park, Calif.: Lane Publishing, 1988.

Welsh, Pat. *Pat Welsh's Southern California Gardening.* San Francisco: Chronicle Books, 1992.

PERIODICALS:

Beaubaire, Nancy. "A Buyer's Guide to Fertilizers." *Fine Gardening,* January/February 1992.

Blum, Jan. "A Good Packet." *Fine Gardening,* September/October 1988.

Bubel, Nancy. "A Well Stocked Cellar." *Horticulture,* October 1993.

"Critter Control." *Avant Gardener,* July 1995.

Frei, Jonathan. "Clover as Cover and Compost." *Fine Gardening,* November/ December 1990.

Kane, Mark:
"Composting." *Fine Gardening,* November/December 1990.
"Soil Amendments." *Fine Gardening,* July/August 1991.

Langsren, Louise. "Cover Crops." *Fine Gardening,* November/December 1990.

Sanchez, Janet H. "Soil Solarization." *Horticulture,* May 1992.

Starr, Jean. "Constructing and Keeping a Garden Journal." *American Horticulturist,* February 1992.

OTHER SOURCES:

"Cover Crop Gardening." Storey Publishing Bulletin A-5. Pownal, Vt.: Storey Communications, 1977.

Donohue, Stephen (Ed.). "Soils and Fertility." In *Virginia Master Gardener Handbook.* Blacksburg: Virginia Cooperative Extension Service, 1994.

Erler, Catriona Tudor. "Irrigation Can Reduce Water Use." *San Diego Union,* July 22, 1990.

Flint, Mary Louise. "Pests of the Garden and Small Farm." Publication 3332. Oakland: Division of Agriculture and Natural Resources, University of California, 1990.

Natural Insect Control. Handbook no. 139. Brooklyn, N.Y.: Brooklyn Botanic Garden, Summer 1994.

Index

Numerals in italics indicate an illustration of the subject mentioned.

A

Achillea: 6-7. See also Yarrow
Air circulation: 93, *chart* 94, *charts* 98-99
All-America Selections: 31
Allium: 6-7, 19
Alternanthera: 56
Alyssum: *29. See also* Sweet alyssum
Animal pests: 10, 61, *62, 63,* 65, 67, 69, *chart* 74-75, 91, 93
Annuals: 10, *50-51, 52-53,* 57, *58, 59*
Anthracnose: 25, 64, *chart* 65, *chart* 74-75, 115
Aphids: 62, 65, *chart* 65, 70, 71, *chart* 94, *chart* 98, 115; controls for, *chart* 68, *chart* 74-75, 117, 119
Apple: *6-7*
Armyworms: *chart* 68, *chart* 74-75, *chart* 94
Artichoke: 29, *chart* 100, *106,* 120
Arugula: 29, 57, *58, chart* 66, *85, chart* 100, *107*

Asparagus: *chart* 25, 26, *31,* 78, 87, *charts* 96-97, *chart* 100, *107*
Asparagus beans: *112*
Asparagus beetles: *chart* 74-75, 107

B

Bacillus thuringiensis: See Bt
Bacterial wilt: *chart* 65, *chart* 95, *chart* 99
Barbarea: 124
Barberry: 56
Barriers: for animal pest control, *60-61,* 65, 67, 69; for insect pest control, *38,* 65-67, *69,* 71, 93, *charts* 95-97, 115, 117, 119
Basil: *9, 29,* 32, 57, *chart* 100, *108*
Bean beetles: 115
Beans: *chart* 66, 91, 116; diseases of, 64, *charts* 98-99; growing, *chart* 28, *30,* 36, 37, 66, 82; harvesting of, 78, 79, 80; insect pests of, *charts* 95-97; yields of, *chart* 25. *See also* Dry beans; Fava beans; Filet beans; Green beans; Lima beans; Pole beans; Pur-
ple beans; Runner beans; Yardlong beans; Yellow beans
Bean weevil: 109, 111
Beds: creating, *16-17;* design of, *6-7, 46-47, 50-51, 54-55,* 57, *59;* layout of, 20, *26-27;* preparing for winter, 87, 87-89; raised, *9,* 10, *17,* 20, *26-27, 30,* 52, *58,* 87, *88,* 90; spacing of plants in, 37, *charts* 100-103
Beebalm: *66-67*
Bees: *chart* 74-75
Beet family: *chart* 66
Beetles: 62, *chart* 68, 72, *chart* 74-75
Beets: *58, 59, chart* 66, 76-77, *chart* 100, *113;* growing, 28, *chart* 28, 29, 34, 45, 93, *chart* 95, *chart* 100, *113;* storage of, 81, *chart* 82; yields of, *chart* 25
Belgian endive: 126
Beneficial insects: 61, 65, 67, *chart* 68, 71, *chart* 74-75, 92, *charts* 94-98, 107, 115, 117, 119, 152
Beneficials: 64, 65, *66-67, chart* 68, 69, 93
Berries: 67, 69, 88
Birds: 64, 65, *chart* 68, 69, *chart* 74-75
Blackberries: *chart* 74-75, *chart* 96, *chart* 100, *114*
Black-eyed peas: *chart* 96, *chart* 100, *115*
Black vine weevil: *chart* 68
Blights: *chart* 74-75, *chart* 98, 115
Bok choy: 29, *135*
Borers: *chart* 74-75
Boxwood: 56
Boysenberries: *114*
Broad beans: *109*
Broccoli: 10, *26-27, 50-51, 54-55,* 57, *58, 59, chart* 66, 76-77, 85, *chart* 100, *115;* growing, *chart* 28, 29, 32, 86, 93, *chart* 100, 107, *115;* harvesting, 79, 80; yields of, *chart* 25
Broccoli rabe: *chart* 100, *116*
Brussels sprouts: *chart* 66, 85, *chart* 100, *116;* growing, *chart* 28, 29, 30, 32, 86, *chart* 100, *116*
Bt: 71-72, *chart* 74-75, *chart* 94, 117, 119
BtK: *chart* 95
Bush snap beans: *chart* 25, 28, 34. *See also* Green beans
Butterflies: 62, *chart* 68, *chart* 94

C

Cabbage: *26-27, chart 66, 69, 76-77, 85, 88-89, charts 100-101, 116-117;* growing, 28, *chart* 28, 29, *30,* 32, 45, *chart* 65, 86, *chart* 96, *charts* 100-101, *116-117;* harvesting of, 79, 80; storage of, 81, *chart* 82; yields of, *chart* 25

Cabbage family: 93, 116; disease prevention for, 27, 115, 116, 117, 119, 122, 129, 143; insect pests of, 66, *charts* 94-95, *chart* 97

Cabbage loopers: *chart* 65, *chart* 68, 72, *chart* 74-75, *chart* 94, 115, 117, 119, 152

Cabbage maggots: 66, *chart* 97

Cabbage root flies: 71, *chart* 74-75

Cabbage root maggots: *chart* 68

Cabbageworms: *chart* 68, *chart* 74-75, 115, 117, 119. *See also* Imported cabbageworms

Calendula: 22-23

Canada: frost dates, *map* 104, *chart* 105

Cantaloupes: *chart* 25, 31. *See also* Melons

Cardoon: *chart* 66, *chart* 101, *118*

Carrot family: *chart* 66, *chart* 97

Carrot rust flies: 71, *chart* 97

Carrots: *22-23, 26-27, 58, 59, chart* 66, *78-79,* 85, 92, *chart* 101, *118-119;* growing, 28, *chart* 28, 29, *30,* 34, 36, 37, 45, *chart* 65, 86, *chart* 101, *118-119;* harvesting of, 78, 80, 88; storage of, 81, *chart* 82; yields of, *chart* 25

Casaba melons: *See* Melons

Caterpillars: 62, 65, *chart* 68, 70, 72, *chart* 74-75, *chart* 94

Cauliflower: *26-27, chart* 28, 29, 30, 32, *chart* 66, 85, 86, *chart* 101, *119*

Celeriac: *6-7,* 32, *chart* 66, 86, *chart* 101, *120*

Celery: *chart* 28, 32, *chart* 66, *chart* 95, *chart* 101, *120*

Celery cabbage: *117*

Celery root: *120*

Celtuce: *chart* 66, *chart* 101, *120*

Chafers: *chart* 68

Chard: *chart* 25, 29, *chart* 66, 86, *chart* 101, *121*

Chayote: *chart* 66, *chart* 101, *121*

Chicory: 29, *chart* 66, *chart* 101, *122,* 126, 141

Chinese cabbage: 37, *chart* 65, *chart* 66, *117*

Chives: *6-7, 19, chart* 66

Chrysanthemum: 59, 76-77

Cilantro: *59*

Cleome: 60-61

Click beetles: *chart* 98

Cloches: 34, *35,* 83-84

Clubroot: 35, 117, 119, 129

Codling moths: *chart* 68

Cold frames: 34, 82, 83, *84,* 85-86, 87

Collards: 34, *chart* 66, 76-77, *chart* 101, *122*

Colorado potato beetles: 65, *chart* 68, 70, *chart* 74-75, *chart* 94

Companion planting: 91

Composite family: *chart* 66

Compost: 13, 15, 18, *chart* 21, 33, 88, 91, *charts* 98-99

Compost bins: *13, 14*

Composting: 70, 90, 91

Compost tea: 45

Consolida: 22-23

Containers: 10, 29, 30, *32,* 80, 82; gardening in, *10, 29,* 30-31, 44

Corn: *25,* 26, *52-53, 58, 62,* 67, 69, 89, *chart* 101, *122-123;* growing, 28, *chart* 28, 29, 34, 37, 38, 44, 45, *chart* 65, 82, *chart* 101, *122-123;* harvesting of, 78, 80; insect pests of, *charts* 95-96, *chart* 98; yields of, *chart* 25

Corn borers: *chart* 68, *chart* 74-75. *See also* European corn borers

Corn earworms: 64, *chart* 68, *chart* 74-75, *chart* 95

Corn poppy: *60-61*

Corn rootworm: *chart* 68

Corn salad: 85, *chart* 101, *124*

Cosmos: *58*

Cover crops: *26-27,* 38, 41, 44, 64, *chart* 68, 87, *88-89, chart* 89, *chart* 99

Cowpeas: *115*

Crenshaw melons: *See* Melons

Cress: *chart* 66, *chart* 101, *124*

Crop rotation: 24, 26, 27-28, *chart* 66; of cabbage family, 27, 115, 116, 117, 119, 122, 129, 143; for disease control, 27-28, 64, *charts* 98-99, 113, 126, 138, 152; for insect pest control, 28, 64, *chart* 94, *chart* 97

Crown rot: 107

Cucumber beetles: *chart* 68, 71, *chart* 74-75, *chart* 95, *chart* 99

Cucumber family: *chart* 95

Cucumber mosaic: 25, *chart* 65, *chart* 95

Cucumbers: 25, *26-27, 40,* 57, *chart* 66, 70, *chart* 101, *125;* diseases and, 25, *chart* 65, *charts* 98-99; growing, *chart* 28, 29, 30, 31, 34, *36,* 38, 39, 82, 83, *chart* 101, *125;* harvesting of, 79, 80; insect pests of, *chart* 95, *chart* 97; and sulfur, *chart* 74-75; yields of, *chart* 25

Currants: 91

Cutworms: 38, 64, 66, *chart* 68, *chart* 74-75, 93, *chart* 95, 115, 117, 119

D

Daffodil: *6-7*

Damping-off: *chart* 98

Daylily: *30*

Design: and container plants, *10, 29;* of edible landscape, *9, 10,* 47, *52-53, 54-55, 58, 59;* of intensive gardens, *30;* of kitchen gardens, *6-7, 46-47, 48-49, 50-51, 52,* 56, 57, *58, 76-77;* of rock gardens, *52-53, 58*

Diamondback moths: *chart* 74-75, *chart* 94

Dill: 65, *chart* 68, 92

Diseases: 25, 35, 39, 41, 61, 63, 64, 65, 72, 80, 90, *chart* 95, *charts* 97-99, 107, 113, 115, 117, 119, 126, 129; fungicides for, 72-73, *chart* 74-75, 93, *chart* 98-99; insects as vectors of, 62, 63, 65, *chart* 97-98. *See also* Crop rotation; Plant destruction; Plant selection; Sanitation

Disinfectant solution: 70, 87

Dittany of Crete: *58*

Downy mildew: 25, 64, *chart* 65, *chart* 74-75

Drainage: 10, 11-12, 17, 20, *chart* 94, *chart* 98

Drought: *chart* 98

Dry beans: 78, *chart* 100, *108-109*

E

Earthworms: *chart* 74-75

Earwigs: *chart* 68, 90

Edgings: *6-7, 9, 30, 46-47, 52,* 90

Edible landscaping: *9, 10,* 47, *52-53, 54-55, 58, 59*

Eggplant: *26-27,* 35, *57, chart* 101, *126;* crop rotation and, *chart* 66, 138, 152; diseases of, *charts* 98-99, 138, 152; growing, *chart* 28, 29, 32, 44, 91, *chart* 101, 107, *126;* harvesting of, 78, 80; insect pests of, *charts* 94-95, *chart* 97

Endive: *chart* 28, 29, 34, 57, *chart* 66, 85, *chart* 101, *126-127*

Environmental disorders: 63, *chart* 94, 119

Eryops (Eryops daisy): *59*

Erysimum: 59

Escarole: 29, *chart* 66, *126-127*

European corn borers: 72, *chart* 74-75, *chart* 95. *See also* Corn borers

F

Fava beans: *chart* 100, *109*

Fences: for animal pest control, *60-61,* 67, 69; and kitchen gardens, *6-7, 8-9, 48-49, 50-51, 57, 76-77*

Fennel: *6-7,* 27, *58, chart* 66, 76-77, 92, *chart* 101, *127*

Fertilizer: 15, *16,* 20, 30, 34, 40, 44-45, 81, 86, 88; and disease control, *charts* 98-99; and insect pest control, *chart* 94, *chart* 97, *chart* 99; organic, 13, 15, *chart* 21, 92

Filet beans: *52-53,* 57, *58, 60-61, chart* 100, *109*

Finochio: *127*

Fish: *chart* 74-75

Flea beetles: 71, *chart* 74-75, 93, *chart* 95, 115, 117, 119, 152

Flies: *chart* 68

Florence fennel: *127*

Foeniculum: 127

Frost-tolerant crops: 27, 85, 86

Fungicides: 72-73, *chart* 74-75, 93, *charts* 98-99

Fungus gnat: *chart* 68

Fusarium wilt: 64, *chart* 65, *chart* 99, 107

G

Garden journal: 22, 45, 62, 89

Garlic: 29, *58, chart* 66, *81,* 86, 88, 93, *chart* 101, *127-128*

Geranium: *57*

Germination: *chart* 28, 33-34, 37, 38
Goldenrod: *chart* 68
Grape hyacinth: *6-7*
Grapes: *76-77*
Grasshoppers: 67, *chart* 68, *chart* 74-75
Green beans: 26, *50-51*, 57, *chart* 65, 78, *chart* 96, *chart* 100, 107, *110*
Greenhouses: *34-35*
Green manure: 44, 89
Greens: *26-27*, *31*, 78, 79, 80, *83*, *84*

H

Handpicking: 70, *charts* 94-97, 107, 117, 119
Hardening off: 34, 36
Harvest: 40, 86; and chemical applications, *chart* 74-75; and storage, 79-80, 81; techniques for, 78-80, 79, 81; in winter, 86, 88-89; yields, *chart* 25, 25-26
Hedges: 8-9, 44, *46-47*, 56
Helianthus: 57, *60-61*
Hen-and-chickens: 56
Herbs: *50-51*, 56, 57, 58, 59, 88, 127
Honeydew: 62, *chart* 97
Honeydew melons: *See* Melons
Hornworms: *chart* 68, 71, 72
Horseradish: *chart* 101, *128*
Hot caps: 83

I

Imported cabbageworms: *chart* 65, 71, *chart* 94. *See also* Cabbageworms
Insect pests: 35, 40, 62, 65, 71, 89, 90, 91, *chart* 94-98; crop rotation for control of, 28, 64, *chart* 94, *chart* 97; as disease vectors, 62, 63, 65, *charts* 97-98; weeding for control of, 43, 64, *charts* 96-97. *See also* Barriers; Beneficial insects; Beneficials; Bt; Handpicking; Pesticides; Plant selection; Row covers; Sanitation; Traps; Water sprays
Intensive gardening: 10, 18, *30*
Interplanting: *24*, *25*, 26, 29-30, 40
Iris: *59*
Ivy: *56*

J

Japanese beetles: 67, *chart* 68, 70, *chart* 74-75, *chart* 96
Japanese painted fern: *56*
Jerusalem artichoke: *chart* 66, 87, *chart* 101, *128*
Jicama: *chart* 101, *129*
Johnny-jump-up: *6-7*, *58*
Joseph's-coat: *56*

K

Kale: *chart* 25, *26-27*, *28*, *52-53*, *58*, *chart* 66, 85, *chart* 101, *129*; growing, 28, *chart* 28, 29, 34, 35, *chart* 101, *129*
Kohlrabi: 27, 29, 34, *chart* 66, *76-77*, *chart* 101, *130*

L

Labeling: 38
Ladybeetles (ladybugs): *chart* 68, *chart* 94, *charts* 96-98, 107
Lamb's ears: 57
Lamb's lettuce: *124*
Lamb's quarters: 93
Larkspur: *22-23*
Laurus: 56
Lavender: 57, *58*
Layout: 10, 20, 24, *26-27*, 26-30, 90
Leaf blight: 72
Leafhoppers: 62, 65, *chart* 68, 70, *chart* 74-75, *chart* 98, 115
Leaf miners: 65, *chart* 74-75, 93
Leaf spot: 25, 72, *chart* 74-75
Leeks: *chart* 28, 29, 30, 32, *chart* 66, 81, 85, 86, 88, *chart* 101, *130*
Legumes: 27, *chart* 66, 89
Lemon balm: 57
Lepidium: 124
Lettuce: *8-9*, *10*, *19*, *24*, *26-27*, *34-35*, *36*, *46-47*, 48, *52-53*, 56, 57, 58, *59*, 66, *chart* 66, *69*, *76-77*, 85, 86, *chart* 102, *130-131*; growing, 28, *chart* 28, 29, *30*, 32, 37, *chart* 65, *84*, 86, *charts* 97-98, *chart* 102, 127, *130-131*; harvesting of, 78, 80; yields of, *chart* 25
Light: 8, *32*, 34, 37, *chart* 98, *charts* 100-103
Lima beans: *chart* 25, *chart* 96, *chart* 100, *110-111*
Lobelia: *29*, *58*
Lobularia: 59. *See also* Sweet alyssum

Loganberries: *114*
Loopers: *chart* 74-75
Lovage: *57*

M

Mache: 85, *124*
Maggots: *chart* 68
Maintenance: *40-41*, 40-45, *42*, *43*, 62. *See also* Fertilizer; Mulch; Watering; Weeds
Malabar spinach: *chart* 103, *145*
Manure tea: 45, 92
Marguerite: *59*
Marigolds: *9*, *22-23*, 29, *32*, *58*, *72-73*, *76-77*, *chart* 99
Marjoram: 57
Mealybugs: *chart* 68, *chart* 74-75
Melon family: 27
Melons: *40-41*, *chart* 66, *chart* 102, *132-133*; growing, *chart* 28, 29, 30, 32, 38, 39, 82, *chart* 99, *chart* 102, *132-133*; insect pests of, *chart* 95, *chart* 97; and sulfur, *chart* 74-75
Mexican bean beetles: *chart* 74-75, *chart* 96
Mexican ground cherry: *149*
Mites: *chart* 68, 70, *chart* 74-75, *chart* 97, 115
Mizuna: *31*
Mole cricket: *chart* 68
Mosaic viruses: *chart* 98
Mosquitoes: *chart* 68
Moths: 62, *chart* 68, *chart* 94
Mountaingrass: *124*
Mountain spinach: *135*
Mulch: 37, *40-41*, 87, *88-89*, 92; for insect pest control, *charts* 94-95; in paths, *17*, *19*, *22-23*; for weed control, *22-23*, 41, 43, 65; in winter garden, 78, 86, 88-89. *See also* Plastic mulch
Muscari: 6-7
Muskmelons: *See* Melons
Mustard: 27, 29, 34, *chart* 66, *chart* 68, 93, *chart* 102, *133*

N

Narcissus: 6-7
Nasturtium (cress): *124*
Nasturtium *(Tropaeolum)*: 29, *50-51*, 57, *58*, *chart* 102, *133*
Nematodes: *chart* 65, *chart* 68, 72, *chart* 99, 115; beneficial, *chart* 68, *chart* 74-75, *charts*

95-98
New Zealand spinach: *chart* 103, *145*
Nightshade family: 93
Nitrogen: 12, 13, 15, *chart* 21, 41, 44-45; crop requirements for, 27, *chart* 28, 45; and damping-off, *chart* 98; and insect pest control, *chart* 94; plants providing, 27, 29; and sheet composting, 90
Northern corn leaf blight: *chart* 65
Nutrients: 11, 12, 27, 41, 44-45, *chart* 98; for container-grown plants, 44; cover crops and, 64, 87, 89; crop requirements for, 27, *chart* 28, 45; fertilizer and, 13, 15, 88; and soil amendments, *chart* 21. *See also* Fertilizer; Nitrogen; Phosphorus; Potassium

O

Ocimum: 57
Okra: *chart* 25, 37, 80, *chart* 96, *chart* 102, *134*
Onion family: 27, *chart* 66, *chart* 97
Onion maggots: *chart* 68, *chart* 97
Onions: 6-7, *9*, *24*, *26-27*, *58*, *chart* 66, 66-67, 78-79, 85, 91, *chart* 102, 130, *134-135*; growing, 28, *chart* 28, 29, 32, *chart* 65, 86, *chart* 102, *134-135*; harvesting of, 78, 80, 81, 86; yields of, *chart* 25
Onion smudge: *chart* 65
Orach: *chart* 66, *chart* 102, *135*
Organic matter: 11, 12, 18, *chart* 21
Origanum: 58
Overwintering: 78, 85, 86, 87, *88*
Oyster plant: *143*

P

Paeonia: 6-7
Pak-choi: *59*, *chart* 102, *135*
Paludosum daisy: *54-55*, *59*
Pansy: *54-55*, *59*
Papaver: 60-61
Parasitic wasps: 65, *charts* 94-97, 107, 115, 117, 119, 152
Parsley: *9*, *26-27*, *29*, *32*, 56, 57, *59*, *chart* 66, *chart* 68, *chart* 102, *136*

Parsley worms: *chart 94*

Parsnips: *6-7, 22-23, 26-27, 58*, *chart 66, chart 102, 136*; growing, *chart 28, 29, 34, 45, 88, chart 102, 136*; yields of, *chart 25*

Paths: cover crops in, *88-89, 89*; creating, *17*; in kitchen gardens, *6-7, 30, 46-47, 48-49, 50-51, 52, 54-55, 56, 57, 59, 76-77*; mulch in, *17, 19, 22-23*; and raised beds, 20, 90

Peanuts: *chart 66, chart 102, 136*

Peas: *22-23, 26-27, 48, 56, 58, 59, 62, chart 102, 137*; and crop rotation, *chart 66, 116*; growing, *chart 28, 30, 34, 36, 37, 39, 82, chart 95, chart 102, 107, 137*; harvesting of, 79, 80; yields of, *chart 25*

Peony: *6-7*

Peppergrass: *124*

Peppers: *10, 26-27, 35, 50-51, 57, 64, chart 102, 138*; crop rotation and, *chart 66, 126, 152*; diseases and, *64, chart 65, charts 98-99, 126, 152*; growing, *chart 28, 29, 32, 44, 91, charts 94-95, chart 102, 138*; harvesting of, 78, 80, 83; yields of, *chart 25*

Perennials: 10, *50-51, 57, 59*

Perennial vegetables: 26, 27, 87, 88

Periwinkle: *29*

Persian buttercup: *59*

Pesticides: 61; commercial, 71-72, 73, *chart 74-75*, 92, 93, *charts 94-97*, 117, 119; and harvest, *chart 74-75*; homemade, 72, 73, *chart 74-75*, 93; safety of, 73, *chart 74-75*; spraying techniques for, *72*. *See also* Repellents

Petunia: *58*

pH: 12, 15, *chart 21*, 91, *chart 94*

Phlox: *50-51, 57*

Phosphorus: 12, 13, 15, *chart 21, chart 28*

Pill bugs: *chart 74-75*, 90

Pincushion flower: *57*

Pink root: *chart 65*

Pinks: *58*

Planning: 24-30, *chart 25, 26, chart 28*; for container gardening, 30-31; for crop rotation, 24, 26, 27-28; of garden layout, 24, *26-27, 26-30*; for

interplanting, *24, 25*, 26, 29-30, 40; plant selection and, 24-25; site selection as part of, 8-10; for succession planting, 24, *26-27*, 28-29; for yield at harvest, *chart 25*, 25-26

Plantain lily: *56*

Plant bugs: *chart 68, chart 96*

Plant destruction: for disease control, 70, *charts 98-99*, 107, 125; for insect pest control, *chart 97*

Plant selection: 24-25, 26, 81, 85; for disease resistance, 25, 61, 64, 65, *chart 65, charts 98-99, 107, 125*; of healthy stock, 35, 63, 114, 142, 148, 149; for insect pest resistance, 25, 64, *chart 65, charts 94-96*

Plastic mulch: 37, *40-41*, 43, 65, 87, 89, 92

Pole beans: *8-9, 26-27, 60-61, chart 65, chart 100, 111*; growing, 29, 30, 31, 34, *chart 100, 111*; supports for, *36, 37*, 39; yields of, *chart 25*

Potassium: 12, 13, 15, *chart 21, chart 28*, 45

Potato beetles: *chart 74-75*. *See also* Colorado potato beetles

Potatoes: 24, *58, chart 102, 139-140*; and crop rotation, *chart 66, 152*; growing, *chart 28, 34, 44, chart 98, chart 102, 139-140*; harvesting of, 78, 80; insect pests of, 65, *charts 94-96, chart 98*; storage of, 81, *chart 82*; yields of, *chart 25*

Powdery mildew: 25, 64, *chart 65, 72, chart 74-75, chart 99*, 115

Pruning: *39, chart 94, charts 96-97*

Pumpkins: 25, 26, *chart 66, chart 102, 140*; growing, *chart 28, 36, 38, charts 95-96, chart 99, chart 102, 140*; harvesting of, *79-80*, 81; and sulfur, *chart 74-75*; yields of, *chart 25*

Purple beans: *chart 100, 112*

Q

Queen Anne's lace: *92*

R

Radicchio: *chart 66, 85, chart 102, 141*

Radishes: *26-27, 48, 56, chart 66, 85, 93, chart 102, 104, 113, 141*; growing, 28, *chart 28, 34, chart 102, 141*; yields of, *chart 25*

Raised beds: 9, 10, *17*, 20, *26-27, 30, 52, 58*, 87, 88, 90

Ranunculus: *54-55*

Rapini: *116*

Raspberries: *chart 74-75, chart 96, charts 102-103, 141-142*

Repellents: 67, 69, 73, *chart 74-75*, 93

Rhubarb: *chart 25*, 26, 29, 57, 87, *chart 96, chart 103, 142*

Rocket: *107*

Rock gardens: *52-53, 58*

Romaine: *9*. *See also* Lettuce

Root cellars: 81-82

Root maggots: *chart 74-75, chart 97*

Root rot: 107, 113

Root vegetables: 78, 79-80, 81, 82, *chart 82*, 86

Root weevils: *chart 68*

Rose: *50-51, 57*

Rosemary: *56*

Row covers: 65-66, *68-69, 83, 84-85*, 86, 93, *charts 94-97*, 152

Rudbeckia: *50-51, 57*

Runner beans: *48-49, 57, chart 100, 112*

Rust: *chart 65, chart 74-75*, 107

Rutabaga: *chart 66, chart 103, 143*

S

Sage: *10*, 57

Salsify: *6-7, chart 66*, 88, *chart 103, 143*

Salvia: *76-77*

Sanitation: and disease control, 64, 87, *chart 94, charts 98-99*, 152; and insect pest control, 64, 87, *chart 94, charts 96-97*, 107

Scab: 25, *chart 74-75*

Scale: *chart 68, chart 74-75*

Scallions: 78. *See also* Onions

Scalloped squash: 25-26. *See also* Summer squash

Scarlet sage: *76-77*

Scorzonera: *6-7*. *See also* Salsify

Season-extending devices: 25, 29, *34-35*, 66, 83, *83-86, 84*, 87

Seed corn maggot: *chart 68*

Seedlings: 69; caring for in-

doors, *32*, 33, 34-35, 36; diseases of, *chart 98*; insect pests of, *38*, 67, *chart 95*; mulching and, 40-41; purchasing healthy, 35; transplanting of, *33*, 34-35, 36-37. *See also* Cutworms

Seeds: presprouting, 36; saving, 82; soil for, 32-33, *chart 98*; soil temperatures and germination, *chart 28*, 33-34, 37, 38; sources of, 31; sowing indoors, *32, 32-34, 33*; sowing outdoors, 34, 36, 37-39; watering of, 38-39, 42, 86

Sempervivum: *56*

Shallots: *6-7*, 29, *58, chart 66*, 86, 88, *chart 103, 143*

Shelling beans: 78, *108-109*

Shrubs: 8-9, *50-51*, 56

Slugs: 65, 66-67, *chart 68*, 71, *chart 74-75*, 90, *chart 97*, 107

Snails: 66-67, *chart 68*, 70, 71, *chart 74-75, chart 97*, 107

Snakes: 64, 65, *66-67, chart 68*, 93

Snap beans: *110*

Snapdragon: *58*

Snow peas: *chart 102*. *See also* Peas

Soil: 8, *11*, 11-13, 15, *chart 94*; air in, 11, 12, 13, 18, 20; amendments for, 13, 15, *chart 21*; analyzing, 11-12; cover crops and, 87, 89; cultivation of, *16-17, 18*, 20, 44, 64, 88, *charts 94-98*; diseases and, 61; double digging, *18*; fertility of, 12, *chart 94*; fertilizer and, 13-15, 18, *chart 21*, 44-45; nutrients in, 12, 29, 41, 44-45; pH of, 12, 91; profile of, *11*; for seeds, 32-33, *chart 98*; solarization of, 71, 89, *chart 99*; temperatures for germination, *chart 28*, 33-34, 37, 38; tools for cultivating, *16-17, 18*, 20

Solarization: 71, 89, *chart 99*

Sooty mold: *chart 97*

Sorrel: 29, 57, *chart 103, 144*

Southern corn leaf blight: *chart 65*

Sowbugs: *chart 68, chart 74-75*

Sowing: *32, 32-34, 33*, 36, 37-39

Soybeans: 27, *chart 66, chart 96, chart 103, 144*

Spaghetti squash: 25-26. *See also* Winter squash

Spider flower: *60-61*

Spinach: *26-27*, 66, *chart 66, chart* 103, *144*; growing, 28, *chart 28*, 29, 34, 86, *chart* 103, *144*; yields of, *chart 25*
Springtails: *chart 68*
Squash: *60-61, chart 66*; growing, *chart 28*, 29, 32, *36*, 38, *44*, 82, *charts 98-99, chart* 103; insect pests and, *chart* 65, *charts 95-97*; and sulfur, *chart 74-75*; summer, *146. See also* Summer squash; Winter squash
Squash bugs: *chart 68, chart 74-75, chart 96*
Squash family: 27, *chart 66, charts 96-97*
Staking: *22-23, 38-39*
Stink bugs: *chart 74-75, chart 96*
Storage: 80-82, *chart 82*, 86; facilities for, 81-82, 85; harvesting and, 79-80; of root crops, 78, *81*, 82, *chart 82*, 86, 88
Strawberries: 29, 66-67, 93, *charts 96-97, chart 99, chart* 103, 126, *147-148*
Structural supports: *8-9, 36, 37, 38-39, 62*
Succession planting: 24, *26-27, 27*, 28-29, *31*, 86
Sugar snap peas: *chart 97, chart* 102. *See also* Peas
Summer squash: *chart 25, 26-27*, 39, 78, 80, *chart 103, 145-146*; growing, 29, 34, 79, *chart 103, 145-146*
Sunflowers: 29, *50-51*, 57, *60-61, chart 66*, 69, *chart 103, 148*
Swede turnip: *143*
Sweet alyssum: *29, 52-53, 58, 59*
Sweet anise: *127*
Sweet bay: *56*
Sweet fennel: 127
Sweet potatoes: *chart 25*, 91, *chart 103, 149*
Swiss chard: *22-23, 26-27, chart 28, 31*, 34, 57, 58, *121*

T

Tachinid flies: *chart 68*
Tagetes: *58*, 76-77
Tampala: *chart 103, 149*
Tansy: *chart 68*
Target leaf spot: *chart 65*
Tarnished plant bugs: 71, *chart 74-75, chart 96*
Temperature: under season-extending devices, 84, 85; of soil for germination, *chart 28*, 33-34, 37, 38; for storage, 81-82, *chart 82*
Thinning: 34, 40, 86
Three Sisters of the Cornfield: 29
Thrips: 65, *chart 68*, 71, *chart 74-75*
Thyme: *56*, 57
Tobacco: 93
Tobacco mosaic: 64, *chart 65*, 126
Tomatillo: 29, *chart 66, chart 103, 149*
Tomatoes: *10, 22-23*, 24, *26-27, 29*, 35, *39, 48-49*, 57, *60-61, chart* 103, *150*, 150-152, *151, 152*; and crop rotation, *chart 66*, 126, 138; and diseases of, *chart 65, charts 98-99*; growing, *chart 28, 29, 30*, 31, 32, *39*, 42, 44, 45, 82, 91, *chart 103*, 127, *150*, 150-152, *151, 152*; harvesting, 78, 80, 83; insect pests of, *38*, 66-67, 71, *charts 94-97*; supports for, *38-39*; yields of, *chart 25*
Tomato family: 27, *chart 66, chart 97*
Tomato fruitworms: *chart 94*
Tomato hornworms: *chart 68, chart 74-75, chart 94*, 152. *See also* Hornworms
Tools: 40, 73, 87; for harvesting, 78, 79, 80; for soil cultivation, *16-17, 18, 20*; for sowing, 32, 37; for transplanting, 34-35; for watering, 42-43; for weed control, 43-44

Transplanting: *33*, 34-35, 36-37, *38, chart 95*
Traps: 61, 67, *70-71*, 93, *charts 95-98*, 107
Trees: *8-9*
Troubleshooting: diseases, *charts 98-99*; insect pests, *charts 94-98*. *See also* Diseases; Insect pests
Turnip family: 116
Turnips: *26-27, 58, chart 66*, 81, 88, *chart 103, 152*; growing, *chart 28*, 29, 34, 45, *chart 98, chart 103, 152*

U

United States: frost dates, *map* 104, *chart 105*
Upland cress: *124*

V

Vegetable families: 27
Vegetable gardens: in containers, *10, 29*, 30-31, 44; design of, *6-7, 30, 46-47, 48-49, 50-51, 52, 56, 57, 58, 76-77*; interplanting in, *24, 25*, 26, 29-30, 40; layout of, 10, 20, 24, *26-27*, 26-30, 90; location of, 8-10; preparing for winter, 87, 87-89; size of, 9-10; starting, *16-17*; succession planting in, 24, *26-27*, 28-29
Vegetable pear: *121*
Verticillium wilt: 64, *chart 65, chart 99*, 126
Viola (violet): *6-7, 59*
Viruses: *chart 97*

W

Wallflower: *59*
Water: 10, 11-12, 13, 18, 20
Watercress: *124*
Watering: 40, 41-43, *42, 43*, 81; and black plastic mulch, 40, 43; of container-grown plants,

30, 34; and disease control, *chart 98, chart 99*; methods for, 41-43; of newly sown seeds, 38-39, 42, 86; of plants in cold frames, 85; and transplanting, 37
Watermelons: 24, *chart 25*, 78. *See also* Melons
Water sprays: 70, *chart 94, charts 96-97, chart 99*, 117, 119
Wax beans: *113*
Weeds: 24, 40, 43-44, 66, 87, 89, 90; cover crops and, 44, *88-89*; and insect pest control, 43, 64, *charts 96-97*; mulch as control for, *22-23*, 40-41, 43, 65, 89
Whiteflies: *chart 68*, 70, 71, *chart 74-75, chart 97*
White grubs: 67, *chart 68, chart 74-75*
Wilts: *chart 99*
Windbreaks: 8-9
Winter squash: *26-27, 41*, 78, *79-80*, 81, *chart 82, chart* 103, *146-147*; growing, 29, 34, 39, *chart 103, 146-147*
Wireworms: *chart 68, chart 74-75, chart 98*
Wisteria: *57*

Y

Yardlong beans: *chart 100, 112*
Yarrow: *6-7, 30*, 65, *chart 68*
Yellow beans: 57, *chart 65, chart 100, 113*
Yew: *9*
Yields: *chart 25*, 25-26
Youngberries: 114

Z

Zinnia: *22-23*
Zucchini: 30, 40, *50-51*, 57, 58, 145, *146*